It's a Jungle in There

It's a Jungle in There

How Competition and Cooperation in the Brain Shape the Mind

DAVID A. ROSENBAUM

OXFORD

UNIVERSITY PRESS

OXFORD
UNIVERSITY PRESS

Oxford University Press is a department of the University of Oxford.
It furthers the University's objective of excellence in research, scholarship,
and education by publishing worldwide.

Oxford   New York
Auckland   Cape Town   Dar es Salaam   Hong Kong   Karachi
Kuala Lumpur   Madrid   Melbourne   Mexico City   Nairobi
New Delhi   Shanghai   Taipei   Toronto

With offices in
Argentina   Austria   Brazil   Chile   Czech Republic   France   Greece
Guatemala   Hungary   Italy   Japan   Poland   Portugal   Singapore
South Korea   Switzerland   Thailand   Turkey   Ukraine   Vietnam

Oxford is a registered trademark of Oxford University Press
in the UK and certain other countries.

Published in the United States of America by
Oxford University Press
198 Madison Avenue, New York, NY 10016

© Oxford University Press 2014

First issued as an Oxford University Press paperback, 2015.

Library of Congress Cataloging-in-Publication Data
Rosenbaum, David A.
It's a jungle in there : how competition and cooperation in the brain
shape the mind / David A. Rosenbaum.
p. cm.
Includes bibliographical references and index.
ISBN 978-0-19-982977-4 (hardcover : alk. paper); 978-0-19-026316-4 (paperback : alk. paper)
1. Cognitive psychology.   2. Brain.   3. Neuropsychology.   I. Title.
BF201.R67 2014
153—dc23
2013028959

Contents

Preface

Most people wonder what makes them tick and what makes others tick, tock, or whatever else they do. We humans are naturally curious, and that curiosity extends to our desire to understand ourselves and others. That same curiosity led me to become a psychologist, specializing in the branch of psychology known as cognitive psychology—the science of mental function. Cognitive psychology is mainly concerned with basic processes of learning, thinking, perceiving, acting, and feeling. In recent years, cognitive psychology has formed tighter links with neuroscience than it had in the past. This is a healthy shift, reflecting an appreciation that the study of the mind is inseparable from the study of the brain. Increasingly, cognitive psychologists have seen that cognitive psychology, like psychology more broadly, should be viewed as a branch of biology.

This book takes that perspective to its logical conclusion. The argument offered here is that the overarching theory of biology, Darwin's theory, should be the overarching theory of cognitive psychology. The way I mean this is a bit different from the currently popular view that mental and behavioral phenomena can be explained in terms of our evolutionary past, a perspective known as evolutionary psychology. The approach offered by evolutionary psychologists is one I will discuss here, though only near the end of the book and only briefly because it is not central to my argument. What I'll focus on instead is the idea that Darwin's insights apply to the inner workings of individual brains. The mind, I will argue, reflects competition and cooperation within the brain. The internal dynamics of such neural competition and cooperation give rise to the mind as we experience it.

Others have said similar things before, though they have focused mainly on the nervous system or—at the other end of the reductionist continuum—consciousness. This book focuses on what's in between, on the kinds of basic mental phenomena that have been studied in the everyday world and, from there, in cognitive psychology labs. The mental phenomena discussed here are ones covered in cognitive psychology textbooks, of which there are many, and in cognitive psychology classes, of which there are still more. Yet such textbooks (and perhaps such classes) have lacked a theory within which, or around which, to organize and motivate the material. A theme might be offered every so often to summarize some aspect of the research, such as the maxim that the mind goes beyond the information given, a phrase used by Jerome Bruner in a 1973 book that helped launch cognitive psychology. But telling students that they're inquisitive doesn't tell them much they don't already know. Having a guiding theory is more satisfying, both pedagogically and scientifically.

My realization that Darwin's theory could be usefully applied to cognitive psychology came in a lecture I was giving while teaching Introduction to Cognitive Psychology at Penn State University, where I have been on the faculty since 1994. It occurred to me in the midst of the lecture that it would be useful to summarize the facts I was presenting with a single phrase: "It's a jungle in there."

After I said this, I felt silly, like I had just said something that would come across as so cute, so juvenile, that the students would scoff at it. Yet after the words spilled from my lips, the students I thought were sleeping betrayed grudging signs of amusement, the students I thought were concentrating on crossword puzzles put down their pencils and looked up at me expectantly, and the students who always looked at me imploringly—the ones in the front who laughed at all my jokes no matter how poor the punch lines—smiled more sincerely than usual.

Encouraged by the students' responses, I found myself saying the same thing over and over again. (We professors are subject to reinforcement by students as much as the reverse.) "It's a jungle in there," I repeated. The phrase became a mantra. I would describe a phenomenon and before I knew it, some student would raise his or her hand and say, "It's a jungle in there, right?" The fact that the quote applied so often and resonated so well with the students led me to think the "jungle principle" is a useful way to present cognitive psychology. I also came to feel that the principle deserved more than passing reference in one class taught at one university by one professor. It deserved to be disseminated more widely, not just to students who might find the concept useful as a portal to cognition, but also as a preface to a theory that my colleagues could contemplate.

To pursue the idea that the mind reflects Darwin's drama, you have to allow that there are inner entities doing things that unwittingly affect their chances of survival. The thesis of this book, accordingly, is that minds are inhabited by such entities. To liven up the discussion, I'll often refer to these entities as "demons," "elves," "imps," "gnomes," and other similar terms. Of course, I mean these only as metaphorical expressions. The cranial creatures to which I'll refer eke out their livings by exciting or inhibiting their neighbors, doing so with no notion of their role in the larger ecosystem of which they're a part. Different members of this neural tribe play special roles by virtue of where they happen to live in the neural neighborhood. Those on the "sensory shoreline" are specialized for sensing. Those on the "motor shoreline" are specialized for acting. Those in the interior are specialized for other functions, less directly tied to sensing or to acting but to functions in between. When I speak of neural gnomes, I never mean to ascribe to them intentions or awareness of what they are about. They are, simply, dumb mechanisms surviving or not depending on their fits to the environments they occupy.

Seeing the mind as an emergent product of a Darwinian ecosystem is a familiar gambit, echoing intellectual trends now popular in biology and cognitive science. Yet as far as I know, no one has used Darwin's idea to cover cognitive psychology, at least in the broad-brush way offered here. I have pursued this approach believing that this manner of covering cognition may be useful not just for communicating "cog-psych" to students and a general audience, but also for building a theory around which cognitive psychologists and cognitive scientists more broadly (neuroscientists, philosophers, linguists, computer scientists, and anthropologists) can rally.

A rallying point for the field is needed, I think. For too long, cognitive psychology has been pursued without concern for a general theory. There are some researchers who have sought one, but what the field has mainly had on the research side, and on the teaching side too, is a series of disconnected phenomena, a rag-tag collection of curiosities—what you might find at a psychologist's garage sale. I believe Darwin's theory or, more generally, a theory that adopts a selectionist (survival-of-the-fittest) perspective, provides a way to place all cognitive phenomena under one tree.

Because a major aim of this book is to make cognitive psychology as inviting as possible for both students and seasoned professionals, I have tried to make this book as fun and accessible as I can. It's saucy in spots (I'm not talking about food), it's irreverent in other places (devout theists, be warned, though I mean no disrespect), and it takes seriously the advice, "Write as you speak." My speaking style is chatty and, to the extent possible, humorous. If you want a deadly serious tome, this book is not for you. On the other hand, if you want a book that doesn't take itself too seriously despite its serious pedagogic and theoretical aims, this text may be more to your liking.

The argument offered here is meant as a scaffold, not a complete edifice. Someday the main idea sketched here may lead to a theory that makes specific, testable predictions. So far, it makes no pretense of doing so. Nor does it pretend to offer a comprehensive review of every topic. The subjects covered here are ones I find particularly interesting given my fascination with human perception and performance, a fascination that led to my being the editor of the *Journal of Experimental Psychology: Human Perception and Performance*, a publication of the American Psychological Association. (I edited the journal from 2000–2005.) Other topics that some might find essential aren't detailed here. Selectivity is part of mental function, however, as students of attention know. This book is the result of one person's mental functioning, such as it is.

As you go through this book and see the scheme of the argument, I hope you'll be tempted to apply it to phenomena of interest to you. I venture to say that every phenomenon of interest in cognitive psychology can be explained in terms of the perspective offered here, at least in general terms. Meanwhile, phenomena that are imaginable but have never been observed—kids doing calculus before they can add, people remembering everything that ever happened to them to the point where most experiences are déjà vu, people being unable to attach suffixes to verbs only on Tuesdays—should be precluded by the theory, and I think they are. A fun exercise would be to invent neuropsychological disorders that are extremely unlikely though logically possible and then to articulate why they are so improbable.

A caveat for those who see themselves as visual thinkers: This book doesn't have many pictures. The few that are here are ones that would take too many words to describe or that could never be fully conveyed with words alone. I chose to keep the number of pictures to a minimum because I believe in the image-making power of words and also because, nowadays, it is so easy to grab images from the Internet. I invite you to look up relevant images as you read this book. Where it's not obvious how to find the best images for the material at hand, I've pointed to search terms, hoping to help you find them.

Though this book reflects my own mental functioning, that mental functioning, like everyone's, occurred in a social milieu. Like neurons in the brain living in the niches they occupy, I've lived in a niche that made it possible for me to develop the ideas in this book. My work on this project has benefited from others, and I want to thank them here.

First, a student who took my cognitive psychology course surprised me with a gift after the course was over (and after grading was complete). The student, Shengan Chang, presented me with a metal sign modeled on a yield sign, so it was yellow and shaped like a diamond. The words inscribed on the sign were "It's A Jungle In There." I've kept her gift in my office, both as a reminder of her kindness and as a conversation starter for visitors not familiar with my course. Some useful insights have come out of the resulting discussions.

Several faculty and postdoctoral fellows helped with the book's intellectual development. Rich Carlson, Nancy Dennis, Paula Droege, Giuli Dussias, Danny Fitousi, Chip Gerfen, Cathy Hunt, Rick Gilmore, Ping Li, Bill Ray, Jonathan Vaughan, Dan Weiss, Michael Wenger, and Brad Wyble all helped in this way. One faculty colleague, who also happens to be my wife, Judith Kroll, deserves the most thanks.

Several graduate students and undergraduate students gave me useful comments. I express my thanks to Katie Chapman, Sangdi Chen, Chase Coelho, Jeff Eder, Lanyun Gong, Joe Santamaria, Amanda Thomas, and Ben Zinszer. Colleagues who kindly replied to my questions via email were Geoffrey Hinton, Daniel Rankin, Craig Speelman, and Anne Treisman.

The staff at Oxford University Press were helpful, not just in their openness to this project but also for their help in the book's realization. I thank Catharine Carlin and Martin Baum, who long ago, and more recently, conveyed their interest in my writing. I also express my gratitude to Melissa Lewis, Tracy O'Hara, Miles Osgood, and Emily Perry, who shepherded the work through to completion. Joan Bossert, my editor at Oxford University Press, deserves the most thanks for her support and effective prodding.

The reviewers who read the manuscript at the behest of OUP provided very useful comments. For their enlightening goads and encouraging words I thank Sue Barry, Raymond Klein, and Robert Proctor. Any mistakes or other shortcomings in the final work are my fault, not theirs, nor the fault of anyone else mentioned here.

I also want to thank the foundations and grant agencies that have supported my research over the years. My research has focused on just one of the topics covered in this book—motor control or, more broadly, perception and action—but the support I got afforded me the luxury of stepping back to ask how questions and answers arising from my own investigations might reflect larger truths. The sources of support have included the National Institutes of Health; the National Science Foundation (NSF); the Dutch and German equivalents of NSF; Penn State's Children, Youth, and Families Consortium; Penn State's Social Science Research Institute; and the John Simon Guggenheim Memorial Foundation.

Just as my work on this project benefited from others' input in the past, I hope to continue to benefit from others' thoughts in the future. Regardless of whether you are a professor, a student, or some other interested party, I invite you to get in touch with me. Please feel free to offer questions you may have, corrections you think I should consider, or challenges you think I should take up. My email address is DAR12@PSU.EDU.

Authors have a habit of dedicating their books to others. Because the jungle principle arose from my teaching of cognitive psychology, I am happy to dedicate this book to the many students I have had the privilege of teaching and from whom I have learned so much.

I

Welcome to the Jungle

Everyone has heard the expression "It's a jungle out there." The saying refers to a competitive environment in which you'd better hone your skills if you hope to survive. You'd better talk the talk and walk the walk if you hope to make it in this dog-eat-dog world. And you'd better do what you can to keep a roof over your head, food in your belly, a leaf on your loins, and a mate who'll help pass on your genes to the next generation of Jungle Jims and Janes.

It turns out that it's not just a jungle *out* there. It's also a jungle *in* there. What I mean is that your brain's a competitive arena. Competition within your brain does as much to shape who you are as does the competition—physical and figurative—you face externally.

It may be disconcerting to read that your brain's a war zone. How nice it would be if it were otherwise! How gratifying it would be if your mental interior were a haven where you could retreat after a hectic day. But it's not that way. If your brain purred all day like a contented cat, you wouldn't be the man, woman, or child you are. You are, for better or worse, the host of an inner battlefield.

As evidence of this disconcerting fact, think about the trouble you may sometimes have falling asleep. Inner conflicts keep you awake at night. If this happens, it shows that your mind can be a place of upheaval. You may lie there thinking about things you wish you wouldn't be considering: Should you have turned down that job offer? Is that dog of yours really worth all the trouble he's been causing lately? Is it true that your supposed friend will be out of town when you decided to throw a party? Ideas like these turn over in your mind even though you tell yourself to stop thinking about them. Memories come and go no matter how hard you urge yourself to settle down. How odd that *you* can't quiet *your* own mind!

Sleepless on the Savannah

Saying your brain's a jungle goes deeper than saying your mind's less tranquil than you'd like. Imagine that you're not trying to sleep in your own bed but instead are lying in a sleeping bag in a meadow. You've bedded down far from the fray of your daily life, hoping for a peaceful night's sleep on a summer holiday.

Now that you're here in this pastoral setting, ready to close your eyes and drift off, you're jolted by all sorts of sounds—whistles and hoots, fluttering wings, high-pitched buzzes, low-pitched booms. The night seethes with noisy creatures beckoning their mates, issuing their warnings, settling their arguments. You came here to get away from it all, but you've come from one sleepless spot to another.

Why are these creatures yelping and yowling? Why can't they get a good night's sleep themselves? They, like you and the mental "creatures" in your head, are doing whatever they do that affects their chances of survival. The sounds they're making are the sounds of living. "Hook up with me," the throaty-voice frog bellows to froggy fräuleins. "I'm outta here!" shrieks an opossum running from a chasing fox. "Look out for that approaching bat!" shouts a mosquito darting through the air. None of these animals is actually speaking, of course. What they're doing is engaging in acts that, one way or another, affect the chances they'll survive and, in the long run, that they will have offspring who will survive.

The noises in your head are much the same. They may not arise from stand-alone creatures in your noggin, but they may be usefully likened to such creatures. Like organisms in the external world, "elves" in your head need to find useful functions if they're going to live on. Elves for seeing will be kept busy if your eyes get a healthy input of patterned light. Elves for hearing will be employed if your ears get a nice sound-soaking on a regular basis. Elves for touch will be in constant demand if you rub up against fleece or stubble. Likewise for elves with other functions.

Elves, Imps, and Demons

It may sound odd to speak of mental elves. Let me be clear that I use the term only as a metaphor. The term "elves" conjures up thoughts of little helpers for Santa Claus, or obsequious attendants to Snow White. When I say your mind's made of up elves, imps, demons, or whatever else they might be called, this is just for the sake of offering the present theory in the most engaging way possible.

Neural and cognitive scientists agree that the last thing we should do in explaining mental phenomena is to posit little beings in the head who know things. Doing so begs the question to be answered. If you say you know things because your mind is made up of little beings who know things, then you face an infinite regress, as seen in the following exchange.

Q: How do you know what you know?
A: Because I have little creatures in my head who know things.

Q: And how do those little creatures know what they know?
A: Because they have little creatures in *their* heads who know things.

Q: And how do *those* little creatures know what *they* know?
A: Because they have little creatures in *their* heads who know things.

This dialogue could go on forever. Realizing this, no respectable cognitive or neural scientist would abide such a story. It's not helpful to say that mental processes are due to little beings in the head who know things.

So if it's a bad idea to speak of cognizant beings inside larger cognizant beings, why do I speak of mental elves, imps, or demons? (When I speak of demons, I don't mean personal worries!) Most emphatically, it is *not* to suggest that there are little animals in your brain with their own agendas. Nowhere in the brain do such beings exist, except perhaps for bacteria, which infest every nook and cranny of your brain and the rest of your body. Bacteria aside, the reason I speak fancifully of little creatures in the brain is that relying on this metaphor provides a fun, friendly way to think about thinking itself.[1]

Pandemonium

I first discovered the usefulness of this way of contemplating cognition in the mid-1970s, when I was making the transition from graduate school to my first job as a research psychologist. At the time, I read a textbook featuring charming pictures of functional demons (Figure 1).[2] These little beings fawned over their favorite inputs. One loved vertical lines. Another obsessed over oblique angles. Another coveted curves. These creatures, or the functional mechanisms to which they referred, were hypothesized to underlie visual pattern recognition. They shouted loudly when inputs conformed to their preferences. They were quieter when inputs did not pertain to their penchants.

According to the model, demons favoring the features of the capital letter A—horizontal lines, right-facing oblique lines, and left-facing oblique lines—yelled when those features were presented. Higher-level demons were subsequently emboldened by news that their favorite configuration had appeared. As a result, a letter was recognized—the capital letter A—and not some other letter or object.

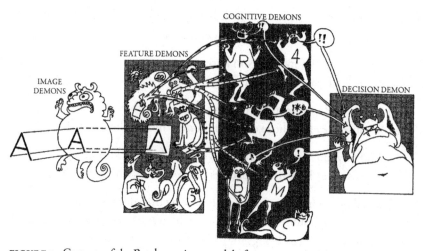

FIGURE 1. Cartoon of the Pandemonium model of pattern recognition.

From LINDSAY. *Human Information Processing*, 2E. © 1977 South-Western, a part of Cengage Learning, Inc. Reproduced by permission. www.cengage.com/permissions

The model instantiated by these little fellows was called *Pandemonium*.[3] I found the model and its depiction charming. The model helped me think about cognitive processes more clearly than I had before, and to the extent that I still found science a little scary at that point in my career, I found it reassuring that some scientists believed, as I did then and still do now, that science can be pursued in a way that is fun rather than fearsome.

Pandemonium is, by definition, anarchic. Even so, such a seemingly disorganized system can afford surprisingly coherent, rational decisions. This is a reason why I use the jungle metaphor throughout this book.[4] If I thought anarchy afforded nothing in the way of cognitive control, I wouldn't offer it as a useful model of the brain. On the other hand, seeing that seeming disorganization (or minimal organization) can lead to coherent, rational choices makes this an attractive option for understanding cognition. If intelligence can be explained without invoking intelligent design, that can be very satisfying.

It turns out, ironically, that the Pandemonium model as introduced by its developer was not quite as anarchic as it could have been. In the model, communication among components goes only one way—from bottom to top. We now know that among the levels of the brain, there is communication every which way—from bottom to top, from top to bottom, and so on. Across all the levels of the brain, neural ensembles communicate with each other directly or indirectly. Out of this seeming disorder come thought, perception, action, and emotion. The brain's unruliness is not an inconvenient truth to be rued. Rather, it's what gives rise to the mind as we experience it.

Mental Functions

If you allow for an unruly ruckus in your head, you don't have to be undisciplined in your theorizing about what goes on there. You can speak of elves, imps, and demons for the fun of invoking these metaphorical beings, but all the while you can, and indeed must, appreciate that these entities are just functional mechanisms.

Functional mechanisms are required in a theory of the brain because mechanisms, in general, are needed to explain how things work. Also, and less trivially, brain mechanisms map onto the mental and behavioral functions they afford. Experience has aspects. Smelling is different from seeing, hearing is different from feeling, and so on. This basic fact of phenomenology (experience) suggests that the mind has distinct mechanisms corresponding to distinct qualities of experience.

A second reason to sanction the idea of distinct functional brain mechanisms (to which this book's demons, elves, and gnomes correspond) is because the way we learn is, in general, gradual. No one learns to play a major piano concerto from day 1 at the piano. Piano students learn the elements of keyboarding first, gradually building up to more complex works. Even then, they study any given concerto one part at a time. Likewise for learning layouts of buildings or figuring out what it takes to satisfy your boss or your new *beau* or *bella*. If you agree that memories have different features, you need a way of explaining how those features are remembered. A useful way of doing so is to say that features are retained if their retention happens to heighten the chance for survival.

A third reason for assuming different functional mechanisms in the brain is that damage to the brain can result in selective deficits. A bop on the back of your head can make you blind. A blockage of blood to your left temporal lobe can make you aphasic (unable to use language). An injury to the front of your brain can leave you less feisty than you were before. Such selective deficits suggest that the brain has specific functional mechanisms.[5]

From the last statement, it's important to stave off a possible misunderstanding. While it's convenient to say that if there are mechanisms for *hearing*, for example, it's important not to assume that those mechanisms reside only on "Eardrum Avenue." Similarly, if there are mechanisms for *seeing*, it's just as important to say that those mechanisms don't live only on "Retina

Road." Some aspects of experience may be traceable to particular regions of the brain—what I meant by Eardrum Avenue and Retina Road (fanciful names, in case you're unsure)—but many aspects of experience are not. Understanding the meaning of a word, for example, is not traceable to just one place in the brain, at least as far as we know. Even if some place in the brain may appear to code a concept such as a famous actress, it can do so only by virtue of where it is physically situated in the brain and to which other parts of the brain it connects.[6] Similarly, appreciating the beauty of a painting or feeling blue doesn't have a single cranial locale, as far as we know. Many aspects of experience, or possibly *all* aspects of experience, reflect the goings-on of multiple brain regions acting as a population.

This remark is important apropos the appeal to little beings in the head. When I speak of those little beings, referring to them always metaphorically and never literally, I don't mean to suggest that there is a one-to-one mapping between them and particular brain sites. The equation I am drawing instead is to functional mechanisms, which can be either widely distributed or locally represented in the brain.

I said above that many aspects of experience, or possibly all aspects of experience, reflect the goings-on of multiple brain regions acting as a *population*. I want to underscore that last word—*population*—because it is important for the thesis of this book.

When evolutionary biologists consider how species fare in the environment, they usually pursue population-level analyses. In fact, one of the most influential evolutionary biologists of the twentieth century, Ernst Mayr, made his most noteworthy contribution by exhorting evolutionary biologists to engage in "population thinking." He argued that it makes more sense to think in terms of *groups* of organisms comprising a species than to think in terms of one individual at a time.[7] By his reckoning, one raccoon might be worth considering in connection with that animal's going through your garbage, say, but to understand the place of any given raccoon in the larger ecosystem, it makes more sense to think about raccoons *en masse*, as a *population*. Population thinking, as Mayr called it, lets scientists make use of powerful quantitative tools like those employed in statistics to analyze the group as a whole. The population approach is useful not just in studies of evolutionary biology but also in studies of neural ensembles.[8]

Competition, Cooperation, and Levels of Control

If it makes sense to speak of populations, why speak about individual mental fellows—those demons and elves to which I've referred? The reason is didactic (for teaching). As I've already mentioned, this way of speaking about the brain can make the material fun and engaging, which is not to diminish the profundity of the questions to be addressed about the brain, nor to sidestep the often sad consequences of brain damage. In addition, and just to emphasize what I've already said, I don't mean to ascribe full-bodied ambitions, hopes, or desires to the cranial creatures I'll credit with undergirding cognition. On the contrary, I want to emphasize that every mental elf is totally dumb, doing just what it does with no awareness of how it fits into the larger scheme of things. No mental gnome has any more idea of the neural ecosystem of which it's a part than does an amoeba in a lake or a fungus on a tree. But like conglomerates of amoebas or fungi, populations of neural demons have emergent properties, and that is where things get interesting.

How can those emergent properties arise from the collective actions of individual neural elves that, on their own, are clueless to their places in the neural ecosystem? Though the elves are ignorant of where or how they fit in, they're not clueless about who their "friends" and who their "foes" are. With their friends they cooperate; with their foes they compete. The way they express cooperation, mechanistically, is through excitation, and the way they express competition, mechanistically, is through inhibition. If a neuron is friends with another neuron, it excites that other neuron. If a neuron is enemies with another neuron, it inhibits that other neuron. These two simple mechanisms—excitation and inhibition—allow for amity and animus, respectively, in the neural jungle.

One way that cooperation and competition are manifested is in levels of control. Much as there are dominance hierarchies in nature—pecking orders among poultry, for example—there are dominance hierarchies in the brain. The idea that neural ensembles dominate other neural ensembles is widespread in neuroscience. Oddly, though, there has been little discussion of how the levels of control come into being or why they exist. Thinking about these questions helps clarify the brain's (and so the mind's) dynamics.

Consider what it means to have dominant and less dominant mechanisms in the brain—to have "big guns" and "little pistols," if you will. The bigger the guns, the fewer of them there can be. This may help explain why attention is limited, and why it exists at all. The defining feature of attention—a topic covered in Chapter 4—is selectivity, and the ultimate result of selectivity is being able to think of only one thing at once.[9] Your mind may flit back and forth from one idea to the next, but it's impossible to have more than one thought at a time. If you're thinking hard about this paragraph, for example, you can't think equally intensively about what you'll do on Saturday night. You might momentarily jump to that topic now that I've just mentioned it, but for you to think as carefully about the topic of this paragraph as you did before, you have to return to it, leaving Saturday night to another time.

The fact that only one idea can be kept in mind suggests that some mental function is taken over by that idea. Whatever that mental function is, it's the top spot in the mental milieu, the spot where competition is most intense.

Why should there be a top spot? To survive, mental creatures need helpful inputs. One way they can get helpful inputs is by affecting the output system that directs inputs back to them. If you're a creature that survives by getting auditory input from the voice of the person you inhabit, then for you to survive it's essential that that voice be heard. So if there is something you can do to increase the odds of that event, so much the better. Likewise, if you're a creature that lives by the wafting of julep molecules into your owner's nose, your chance of survival is better if he or she sniffs julep every so often. If something you do has the effect of getting your owner to sample that minty smell, your chances of survival can increase. You, being a dumb neural element, have no idea that what you're doing may trigger julep sniffing, but if it does, you will be more likely to survive than if it doesn't.[10]

With many mental demons facing the constraint of needing input, there's intense competition for access to the system that affects that input. The system that does this is, ultimately, the motor system, the system that moves muscles. To sniff you have to make movements that achieve sniffing, to speak (in order for you to hear your own voice) you need to move your mouth, and so on. There are only so many actions you can perform at once. You can't move your hand forward and backward at the same time. You can't speak and eat at the same time. Because you can do only a few things simultaneously, there is competition for the system controlling those actions. And those actions, in turn, affect what comes back into the nervous system, thereby affecting the survival chances of the creatures relying on those special inputs.

Turning to the headier realm of thought, I venture to say that if you can think of only one thing at a time, it's because you can *do* only one thing at a time. Think of cars entering the Lincoln or Holland Tunnel on their way to Manhattan from New Jersey. The cars making their way to the toll collector funnel down. The closer the cars get to the entryway, the smaller the number of cars there can be.

Just as few cars can get very close to the toll collector or E-ZPass, very few thoughts can get close to consciousness at any one time—somewhere between 4 and 9 of them for most people.[11] The smallness of the number of items that can be maintained reflects competition among cognitive candidates. To the extent that few actions can be carried out at once, competition for access to the launch pad for action is likely to be intense.[12]

Competition isn't the whole story, however. Just as vehicles need to make way for other cars, trucks, and buses at portals to tunnels and bridges, neural systems must make way for other neural systems. There must be *cooperation* in the brain as well as *competition*. The cooperation needn't be deliberate or explicit, as in signing a treaty or holding a door open for a follower.[13] Instead, it can be more implicit and may simply take the form of sending signals that tend to excite rather than inhibit other neurons or muscles. If exciting a neuron or muscle that tends to excite you tends to increase your chance of surviving, then, over time, it's likely you'll excite that neural system. You needn't realize you are doing so and certainly don't need an explicit plan to do so, but if the effect of your signaling other parts of the nervous system is, indirectly, to excite yourself, then that action is one you will perform repeatedly.

No Chief Executive

It is critical for the account developed here not to require that somewhere in the brain there is some single, most powerful, mental creature. There must be no chief executive officer, no awe-inspiring pooh-bah.[14] Why not?

Suppose you're perched on the edge of a cliff and there, on the other side of the ravine, is another cliff you have to leap to in order to continue your journey. You feel yourself hesitating. "Should I really jump across that chasm?" "No," you or some other part of you replies. Then you hear another voice in your head saying, "Go for it," and then some other voice chimes in: "No, don't!"

To whom do these voices belong? To you, of course, yet they seem to come from different individuals within you—a brave you, a cautious you, a you who triumphs, a you who trembles. It's hard to tell which you is the real one. The chorus of voices makes you feel like you're not one person but many. The truth is, you are many. You are a *population*.

Abandoning the idea that you're a single self may be disconcerting. Can you decide anything if you're not one person? The answer is that you can, because populations do so all the time. In elections, populations decide who will be mayor, governor, or president. In the market, populations decide things too. At the time of this writing, it was stylish for female students at my university to wear shorts that had the word "Pink" brandished in large letters across their behinds (not that I noticed, of course). A while ago, Penn State students proudly carried the word "Aeropostale" across their sweaters. Earlier, Tommy Hilfiger was the *nom de style*. Fashions are decided through collective decision making. Neither Tommy Hilfiger, Amy Aeropostale (a name I made up), nor Paula Pink (another name I made up) issued edicts decreeing that everyone should wear their brands. The students decided collectively that those were the styles they'd favor.[15]

You, too, as an individual perched on a precipice or on some less scary site, make decisions that reflect your collective activity. That this is so can become clear to you introspectively. In midair, having decided to leap, you may feel strangely like a witness to your own resolve. "I'm flying across the ravine," you may say to yourself in a kind of out-of-body experience. "If I'm aloft, I must have decided to jump." In this brief avian moment, you may even be reminded of René Descartes' famous declaration, "I think, therefore I am." In your case, given where you are at the moment—in midair, flying from one cliff to another—you may say, "I jumped, therefore I decided."

This is a strange way to make up your mind, of course, but for better or worse it's how you do so. If you go one way or the other, over the cliff or back from whence you came, you made up your mind. There's no escaping that conclusion. Still, if you remain undecided in the midst of the action itself, then it feels like what you did was heed the outcome of a referendum rather than enact some clear-headed decision you made like the decisive captain of a ship.

These considerations suggest that it may be illusory to say you're one coherent being. You're not. You're *many* beings. Your mental interior is inhabited by mental gnomes all living in your neural ecosystem. The motto of the United States, *E pluribus unum* (*Out of many one*), applies to you, just as it does to the USA.[16] You're a plurality. When you think, you engage in group-think. When you act, you act on behalf of untold numbers of beings within you who function in ways that may or may not happen to ensure their own survival.

This view of yourself as a population made up of beings, none as intelligent as you but collectively comprising you with no one in charge, is the view of cognition I wish to advance in this book. I hope you, all of you, will find the perspective useful.

2

Darwin and the Boss

Declaring that your mind doesn't have a head honcho can be scary. It violates your sense of self, your sense that you're an individual. Seeing yourself as a conglomerate of self-interested imps rather than a clear-headed captain of your own fate can leave you feeling disoriented. Where's your compass? How do you know which way to go?[1]

If you think it's scary to fire your own mental guy or gal in charge, think what it must have been like for Charles Darwin, the hero of the story to come, who suggested that no chief executive is needed to explain the formation of species, including the species to which we humans belong, *homo sapiens*, otherwise known as "knowing man."

You probably know the core of Darwin's theory, but I'll review it here to set the stage for what's to come. I won't go into details about evolutionary biology. My aim will simply be to lay out Darwin's theory as a general model for the kind of cognitive theory I wish to propose for mental function.

Darwin and the Deity

Charles Darwin was born in 1809 into an affluent British family. His grandfather was Erasmus Darwin, a well-known thinker and physician in his day.[2]

Charles didn't have to work for a living. Blessed as he was with the freedom to contemplate nature without having to sweep chimneys or swab floors, he could ponder at leisure the diverse forms of life he observed as he ambled through the countryside and wandered on the shore. His most famous ambling occurred on the Galapagos Islands, off the coast of Ecuador, which he visited on a voyage around the world aboard a boat called, aptly enough, the *Beagle.*[3]

As a child, Darwin learned that God created the heavens and the earth. Darwin learned as well that soon after God created the heavens and the earth, God created all of the earth's plants and animals. Finally, young Darwin learned that God created Adam and, from Adam's rib, God created Eve. God did all this in just a few days, after which God took a one-day sabbatical and then returned to work, doing God-knows-what ever since.[4]

Darwin would later question the authenticity of the Bible's Creation story. Doing so took courage, for God is all-mighty. Among God's abilities are making the sun and stars, parting the seas, forming mountains, and knowing everything that can possibly be known, even while giving people the freedom to think for themselves.

Charles Darwin was raised in a politically progressive Christian (Unitarian) family. The book in which he proposed his radical idea is one of the most famous books in the history of science, *On the Origin of Species by Means of Natural Selection*.[5]

Darwin was vilified for his radical proposal. For example, in a cartoon that appeared in his lifetime, his head was drawn atop a chimpanzee's body. But as so often happens when an author's work stirs debate, the arguments about *Origins* drew a great deal of attention to the work being criticized and helped make the book a bestseller.

Darwin's fame lived after him. He was buried in Westminster Abbey, a place where monarchs, great poets, and other famous scientists were interred. Darwin was buried there because, despite the controversy around his work, he was recognized as a truly important thinker, one whose idea could hardly be ignored. Over time, Darwin came to be hailed as one of the most important thinkers in the history of Western civilization—along with such luminaries as Newton (a fellow interree at Westminster Abbey), Karl Marx, Albert Einstein, and Sigmund Freud (none of whom lies there). The book you're now reading is just one of many that have applied Darwin's thinking to a domain beyond which Darwin originally intended. High tribute, indeed, to his idea!

Darwin's Idea

What was Darwin's idea? It was that the species of the earth can be traced to a single, original species and that all the species that have ever been here got here, stayed here, or died off through a process called natural selection.

Natural selection is a simple process. The way it works can be summarized in one sentence: *Species that produce offspring tend to survive*. It doesn't hurt to state that principle another way as well: *Species that don't produce offspring tend not to survive*.

"Wait a minute!" you might exclaim. "That can't be the whole story! I could have thought of that myself!" Perhaps, but the idea has so suffused our culture that it's hard to imagine not knowing it, at least if you're the kind of person who reads books like this one. Being ignorant of Darwin's idea of natural selection is nearly as unimaginable as not knowing that the earth is round. Because of hindsight bias—the difficulty of recreating what it's like to not know something you once didn't know but do now—you may find it incredible that there was ever a time when you or others didn't have command of Darwin's concept.[6,7]

The elegance of Darwin's idea is the way the story plays out, coupled with the fact that it relies on a small set of functional mechanisms and assumptions. Those functional mechanisms are three in number. They can be rattled off easily: *replication*, *variation*, and *selection*. The assumptions that go along with the mechanisms are *sex*, *death*, and *finite resources*.

Before I describe how these functional mechanisms and assumptions play out to yield the panoply of species, I should explain why I have begun this chapter by intoning God and why, for that matter, this chapter has the title it does: *Darwin and the Boss*. The main reason is that there is an analogy behind what I have written here and what I plan to write about later: Natural selection is to God what the jungle principle is to the mental executive. Let me explain.

The functional mechanisms and background assumptions that Darwin offered are sufficient to explain the origin of species. Saying this another way, you don't need to invoke a divine guiding figure who designs, creates, and kills off species to explain how species originate within the Darwinian system. By the same token, you don't need a central executive to explain how thoughts arise or die, how behaviors are chosen or suppressed, or how motives arise and subside. What I mean is that Darwin's suggestion for the origin of species applies to the origin of mental events and the behaviors they allow. Darwin's attempt to supplant a theistic account of the origin of the species with a self-organizing account inspires the attempt to supplant an executive-laden theory of mental phenomena with an account that eschews a mental overseer. This is not to deny that some mental processes can be called "executive processes." That term is used by cognitive psychologists today to refer to volition. But saying that the mind as a whole acts as if someone inside directs traffic needn't imply that there really is such an inner director.

To understand this more fully, consider the following question: How do the mechanisms and assumptions of Darwin's theory of natural selection lead to the diversity of life forms we see? In particular, how can the observed diversity of life forms be explained without appealing to a divine being who runs the show?

A way to answer this question is to consider an imaginary world that has just one animal and just one plant. Fortunately for the plant, the animal exhales carbon dioxide. Fortunately for the animal, the plant exhales oxygen. Also, luckily for the plant, the animal poops near the plant, so the plant, through its roots, ingests essential nutrients. And happily for the animal, the plant has lots of yummy leaves that the animal likes to eat.

At first, this looks like a happy scenario. The plant and animal could go on like this for a long time—forever, perhaps, in a happily-ever-after scenario. But as in fairy tales, where the characters are supposed to live on forever but you know that's impossible, the happily-ever-after ending for the cohabiting plant and animal is also unlikely to last long. If a strong wind comes along and blows the plant's leaves off its branches, that's it for the plant and for the animal too. If the animal gets stuck under a rock or freezes or drowns, that's curtains for the animal and its leafy friend. The story ends all too suddenly. Life ceases to exist if either of these two living things perishes.

To keep things going, what's needed is multiplicity. Many plants and animals must be on the scene. That way, nature avoids putting all her eggs in one basket. With many animals, if one of them happens to get pinned beneath a rock or happens to freeze or drown, some other animal may be able to take its place. If there are many plants and one gets plundered by flood or gets blown away by a strong gust of wind, some other plant that's still rooted in the soil can carry on. Having many plants and animals boosts the chances that life continues. This is *replication*, one of the three functional mechanisms in Darwin's theory.

Another functional mechanism in Darwin's scheme is *variation*, otherwise known as diversity. Diversity allows species to be prepared, in effect, for what may happen. If all the members of a species are the same, with exactly the same capacity for lifting themselves out from under fallen rocks, for withstanding cold temperatures, or for escaping floods, then all the members of the species will be equally susceptible to those mishaps. However, if the members of the species happen to differ in their physical or behavioral features, then some of them will be more likely to survive than others.

The term used in Darwin's theory to refer to survival is *selection*. That's the third functional mechanism in his model. Selection is vital in natural selection because it provides the means of choosing members of a species that have what it takes over those that don't. The choosing isn't divine. There's no Zeus hurling lightning bolts at creatures whose time, he has decided, has come.

Rather, the process is random. Organisms that happen to have features that enable them to survive tend to generate more offspring than organisms that don't. The surviving organisms are selected-for. The others, the ones that don't make it, are "selected out."

Even well-adapted organisms don't live forever. Darwin appreciated that it would be bad for organisms to live interminably. Elephants surviving endlessly would pile up. Impalas enjoying immortality would run out of running room. This is because resources are scarce. There are only so many goods to go around—only so many leaves for lunching, so many holes for hiding, and so on. Surviving requires competition for food and shelter, not to mention mates.

Sex

Mentioning mates brings up the matter of sex, which is another key part of Darwin's theory. Why should sex exist? What's the point of it? The question, I realize, may sound ridiculous. "It feels good!" you may exclaim, not quite sure what planet I live on. Before you focus too much on my hedonics—no worries there, I assure you ☺—it's more pertinent to recall the pragmatic, less hedonistic, side of sex: Sex produces offspring. Without sex, there would be no babies, no puppies, no kittens, no cubs.

The feeling-good part of sex is, strictly speaking, not critical to its practice. Still, the hedonic (pleasure) part of sex promotes its continuation in generations to come. People don't watch X-rated movies because they want to fantasize about wheeling baby strollers. They don't ogle sex gods or goddesses because they're contemplating the tax deductions they'll enjoy by claiming more dependents. Sex, or at least the kind that comes with pleasurable moans and groans, is all about the here-and-now. When you watch Nature TV and see animals copulating, you know they're not planning for their children's educations. Instead, they are reveling in the buildup to *oh-that-feels-good*. That feeling, or the drive toward it, impels animals (including humans) to do all the strutting, prancing, dancing, and displaying that constitute courtship.

The fact that sex feels good motivates organisms to do what they do to complete sex acts, thereby generating next generations. Sex also spreads genes. If a guy has one set of genes and a gal has another, their offspring get a mélange of ma and pa chromosomes. The genes the kids pick up may be good ones from dad and bad ones from mom, or vice versa. It's impossible to tell in advance all the genes that will have positive or negative effects.

"Good" and "bad" are relative terms, defined *a posterior* rather than *a priori*. Beth may have married Bud despite his dandruff, but the genes that caused Bud's flakes may later, when expressed in Bud's and Beth's baby, bestow on that kid immunity to some disease. Bud may have married Beth because of her freckles, but the genes for those winsome flecks may later predispose Beth's and Bud's kid to get some illness no one would wish on a friend. The good or bad consequences of a gene, then, are a matter of chance. Accordingly, sex, in Darwin's theory, has the statistical consequence of quickening chance effects. Were there no sex (or were there sex with only oneself) the opportunity for genetic diversity would be low.

Sex or, more specifically, competition for mating provides a forum to show off features that, as far as the participants can tell, bode well for survival.[8] In humans, clear skin may signal resistance to infection, a firm butt may signal strength, and a capacity for cool dance moves may signal agility. It's rare for physical or behavioral features that prospective mates find appealing to be obviously *bad* for survival. They may not be especially *good* for survival once history runs its course except insofar as they are useful for attracting mates. Peacock plumes are the paradigmatic example of sexual attractants with an advantage other than attracting mates. Basso voices in human males may be another.[9] Breasts in human females may also serve that function, for lactation in other mammals comes without swollen mammaries.[10]

Some More from Evolutionary Biology

The Darwinian drama of individuals finding themselves more or less able to spawn offspring is a drama whose future direction no one knows or needs to know. The reason is that it can run its course without a prior plan. Indeed, there may be no plan at all.

This last point is of inestimable importance for the theory of cognition to come, especially because cognition is so much about predicting and planning.[11] Later in this book I will suggest that what we take to be plans are just activities of neural populations shaped in basically the same way as other biological populations. Believing that we have plans need not imply that plans *per se* exist in our minds. Plans could be internal responses to situations (stimuli) we encounter that in turn trigger behaviors we call voluntary, intentional, or, indeed, planned.

Returning to evolutionary biology, scholars in that area of study have said much more about natural selection than I have here. My aim has just been to give the flavor of the Darwinian process in simple and, at times, fanciful terms.

Speaking fancifully is not meant to diminish the sophistication of the tools used by evolutionary biologists and their colleagues to explore the dynamics of natural selection. Those tools include studying fossils, counting organisms with different features in different environmental niches, and developing mathematical models of real and artificial life forms. With such methods, it has been possible to confirm Darwin's theory or, saying this another way, to show that Darwin's theory can withstand efforts to disconfirm it.[12] Darwin's theory has gained so much credibility that it is possible to say it is no more speculative than Newton's theory of gravitation.[13]

Evolutionary biologists have also uncovered some phenomena of special interest for what's to come in this book. I will discuss three of them here: (1) the founder effect, (2) punctuated equilibrium, and (3) niche opportunities.

The Founder Effect

The *founder effect* is the tendency of initial, successful occupants of a niche to have an exceptionally strong effect on succeeding generations. The effect holds when the rate of interbreeding among first settlers and their seed exceeds the rate of breeding with newcomers.[14]

One illustration of the founder effect concerns the Amish, who live in Central Pennsylvania, where I happen to reside. The Amish live in insular communities. They mainly keep to themselves and mainly marry in-county. As a result, they enjoy less genetic variation than other, more open communities. As a further result, they have unusual traits. Due to a recessive allele shared by two members of the founders of this colony in the mid-1700s, a disproportionately large number of Amish have Ellis-van Creveld syndrome.[15] Individuals with this syndrome are shorter than usual, have unusually broad hands and faces, and have malformed wrists and an extra finger—a syndrome known as *polydactyly*. Ellis-van Creveld syndrome is traceable to two of the small number of individuals who first settled in the area that the Amish now inhabit.

The founder effect has psychological analogues. One is imprinting. Here, in the case of ducklings, the sight of a figure that may plausibly pass for Mama Duck is latched onto by recent hatchlings. They follow this figure even if she, he, or it is not their parent, provided it's the first reasonable facsimile of a parental figure they encounter. This phenomenon was made famous by the Austrian ethologist Konrad Lorenz, who, it happens, worked with grey-lag geese rather than ducklings, though the phenomenon works with either species.[16] Imprinting is analogous to the founder effect in that primary experience has extraordinary impact.

Two other psychological analogues of the founder effect can be mentioned. One is the tendency of words that are learned first to be read aloud at exceptionally high speeds—much higher than would be expected based solely on how often they are repeated. This has been shown both in tasks that require reading of printed words and in tasks that require naming of pictured objects.[17]

The other psychological analogue of the founder effect is speaking a language with an accent reflecting the dialect spoken where you were raised. In my case, I was raised in Philadelphia, so I speak with a Philly accent. When I say "noodle," I can't help but say "neeodle." When I say "legal," I can't help but say "liggle." I can try very hard to say these words without my Philly twang, but it's nearly impossible for me to do so. The same phenomenon occurs for people who speak English with a Russian accent, for people who speak Hebrew with a German accent, and so on. The fact that accents are so hard to shed—extensive voice coaching is usually required—attests to the founder effect for speech.[18]

Punctuated Equilibrium

Besides the founder effect, another phenomenon of special interest from evolutionary biology is punctuated equilibrium. This is a relatively sudden change in the rate of evolutionary change. The term *punctuated equilibrium* refers to the fact that fossil records have shown that, in evolution, there have been periods of relative stasis or equilibrium punctuated by periods of very rapid change.[19]

Punctuated equilibrium is important here because in mental development there are similar surges. One occurs around the age of 18 months, when in healthy human toddlers there is an explosion of language. From 18 months to 24 months, toddlers roughly double their vocabularies, from about 1,000 words to about 2,000 words.[20]

On a faster time scale, mental states also tend to change quickly after periods of seeming quiescence. You don't *gradually* see a shape, and you don't *gradually* learn a fact. As is true of evolutionary states, mental states are punctuated. Minds jump from state to state, from not understanding to understanding, from not seeing a solution to seeing one. If there is a stream of consciousness, as William James suggested, the stream doesn't flow continuously.[21] Rather, what you think of from moment to moment is a series of discrete realizations.

Niche Opportunities

The third phenomenon of evolutionary biology of interest here is the existence of *niche opportunities*. When niche opportunities arise, a species occupies a new habitat and survives within it with a low population density for a long time. Then, if conditions become more hospitable, the species proliferates.[22]

I mention niche opportunities because an analogous phenomenon may be recognized in individual experience. If you once learned to ride a bicycle, you will always be able to do so, provided you suffer no disabling physical change. Being away from a bike for years doesn't prevent you from knowing what to do once you recycle. The knowledge you have for bike riding is there all along and can be reawakened. Likewise for other skills.[23]

The ability to re-engage skills that have lain dormant for years seems at first to be inconsistent with a prediction that might be made by applying the theory of natural selection to individual brains. That prediction is captured by the familiar phrase "use it or lose it." If mental representations are untapped for long periods, the Darwinian account would seem to suggest that they should die. The phenomenon of niche opportunities shows, however, that, in the wild, species may "bide their time" if conditions for their survival are not too unfavorable. So too may neural ensembles that support long unpracticed skills, like long-ago biking or erstwhile skiing. As long as the neural ensembles supporting such skills are not crowded out by other competing elements, they can remain viable.

No Stone Goes Unturned

A last point about evolutionary theory that's central for what's to come can be called the "no-stone-goes-unturned" principle. This is not a phrase used by evolutionary biologists to capture a core principle in their field, as far as I know, but it's one that, for me, captures the essential idea that nature is virtually perfectly efficient and that, by implication given the analogy I'm pursuing here, what's good for the global goose (species) is good for the individual gander (the individual mind).

What I mean is that no potentially habitable niche goes unoccupied. Wherever living things can possibly live, they do so—under stones, under eaves, atop mountains, in the hottest deserts, in the coldest coves. Even in places where you'd least expect life to flourish, life can be found. The most salient example I know of are hydrothermal vents unfathomably deep in the sea, where there is scarcely a photon from the sun. Hydrothermal vent worms live there, comprising a life form no one knew about until its recent discovery by a deep-diving sub. So hardy are the life forms on Earth that pains are taken by NASA to ensure that no bacterium goes along for the ride to other worlds, lest extraterrestrial neighborhoods get infected by terrestrial bugs.

There's a tie-in between the no-stone-goes-unturned principle and brain use. A claim in the popular press is that we use only 1/8 of our brains, or some such fraction. Admittedly, some people act like they use less brain power than they should. But that's different from saying parts of their brains lie idle. Wherever neuroscientists have looked, they've found brain regions that are busy. As long as healthy neurons are present in an area of the brain, neurons studied there have been shown to be active. Finding a healthy region of the brain that's completely dormant is as likely as looking under a stone and not finding a weevil, worm, or wily bacterium. The trillions of living things on Earth find places to live in every nook and cranny. If a "Vacancy" sign appears anywhere in the outer jungle, it doesn't stay up for long. Vacancies are filled in the blink of an eye. The brain, too, provides a welcome environment for opportunistic bands of neural gnomes to flourish, as long as the living conditions aren't too difficult. Given the hospitable environment of the brain, a wondrous diversity of neural, and then mental, life can spring up.

3

Fighting Neurons, Friendly Neurons

If it's a jungle in there and you're curious how the jungle works, you'd better screw up your courage, put on our hiking boots, and grab your walking stick. Brace yourself for the scenes to come. You might see mice munched by minks, goats gulped by gators, doves downed by dogs. If your nerves jangle at such sights, the jungle might not be the place for you.

Of course, I'm speaking only metaphorically here, stretching the jungle metaphor to the point of silliness. But if you come along with me in pursuit of the metaphor, you'll recall that jungles aren't the only kind of ecosystem. Others are deserts, tundra, swamps, forests, cliffs, and plains. All these niches afford different perils and potentials. A bluff is a good place for beasts that fly. A cove is a good place for beasts that swim. Species that thrive in different niches are well adapted for them. Those that aren't tend to die.

Recognizing that different places afford different adaptations can help you approach the functioning of the brain with positive expectations. You can expect the internal environment of the brain to have different ecosystems, with different cranial creatures thriving within it. In the brain, as in the outer world, different functions flourish depending on the niches they occupy.

This chapter is about the brain. A wonderful aphorism about the brain by a cognitive neuroscientist at the University of Toronto captures a profound truth about how the brain is organized. According to this cognitive neuroscientist, Geoffrey Hinton, "The brain is locally global and globally local." What did he mean?[1]

The first part of the sentence, "The brain is locally global," means that on a local scale, the components of the brain are alike. If you look at the brain with a microscope, figuratively or literally, you can see the elements all doing the same thing more or less: sucking up nutrients, expending energy, and so on. The second part of the sentence, "The brain is…globally local," means that on a larger scale, the components of the brain do *different* things; they have their own special *local* features. Different regions act differently. One area leans toward language, another veers toward vision, another heads toward hearing, and so on. In general, the farther apart two areas of the brain happen to be, the less similar their functions. This isn't because some brain supervisor declares that there should be a language zone, a vision zone, and a hearing zone. Rather, different regions tend to have different functional properties because of where they happen to reside or, more importantly, with whom they happen to interact most closely. The structuring of mental function follows this fellowship.

A Little about Neurons

To pursue this idea, it will help to say more about the elements of the nervous system. The nervous system, as you probably already know, is a complex web made of the central nervous system (including the brain, retina, and spinal cord) and peripheral nervous system (sensory receptors and muscle-activating fibers).

The main building blocks of the nervous system are *neurons*. These come in a variety of shapes and sizes depending on where they're situated. Neurons specialized for detecting mechanical pressure occupy the skin, neurons specialized for detecting airborne chemicals occupy the nose, and so on. Within the brain, there are also different kinds of neurons.[2]

Despite structural differences among neurons, prototypical neurons have three main sections. *Dendrites* receive incoming signals. The *cell body* integrates incoming signals and metabolically sustains the cell as a whole. *Axons* serve as transoms for the release of signals to other neurons or muscles.

Prototypical neurons integrate incoming signals over space and time. The space over which the integration occurs covers the dendritic inputs to the neurons. The time over which the integration occurs is the period over which the inputs sum.

If the integrated inputs to a prototypical neuron exceed a threshold, the neuron can generate a burst of activity called an *action potential*. An action potential races down the axon at a speed that is higher if the axon is coated with myelin (a fatty material) than if it is not.

Myelin takes time to form over the course of development. Not until adolescence is its formation complete in human beings, but by the time of adolescence, myelination isn't the only neural process that gets completed. Unnecessary connections between neurons are pruned away. Pruning begins in infancy and is completed in the teen years. Pruning can be seen as straightforward example of natural selection.[3]

Synapses

Until the late 1800s, it was not known whether the nervous system is a kind of diffuse cotton ball or a honeycomb of distinct cells with gaps between them. Thanks to the work of the late nineteenth- and early-twentieth-century Spanish physiologist, Santiago Ramón y Cajal, we now know that neurons are separated by tiny spaces called *synapses*, a term coined by a British physiologist, Charles Sherrington, who, like Ramón y Cajal, won a Nobel Prize for his work on neurophysiology.[4]

Synapses are important because of what goes on in and around them. At synaptic junctions, chemicals are emitted by presynaptic neurons and are picked up by postsynaptic neurons or muscles. The chemicals that are released into the synapse—*neurotransmitters*—are molecules that can affect the postsynaptic membranes. Postsynaptic neurons that have suitable receptors for a neurotransmitter may become more or less excited when they take in the neurotransmitter coming to them. Muscles may likewise contract if they are in a state of readiness to do so and if the neurotransmitter knocking on their doors is one the muscles accept.

Neurons that take up neurotransmitters can respond in either of two ways—by becoming *more* likely to fire or *less* likely to fire. If the neuron is *more* likely to fire upon receipt of a neurotransmitter, the neurotransmitter is said to have an *excitatory* effect on the neuron. If the neuron is *less* likely to fire upon receipt of a neurotransmitter, the neurotransmitter is said to have an *inhibitory* effect on the neuron.[5]

Neurotransmitters produced by any given neuron have different effects depending on the neurons to which they project. Which neurons produce which neurotransmitters, which neurons accept which neurotransmitters, and whether a neuron gets more or less excited when it takes in a neurotransmitter are matters are of no concern here. More relevant are the effects of neurons being activated or deactivated.

Active neurons suck up more oxygen and glucose than do less active neurons. Active neurons are also more likely than less active neurons to form liaisons with other neurons. The more often two nearby neurons fire in close temporal proximity, the tighter the link between them. Neuroscientists express this principle with a catchy phrase: "Neurons that fire together wire together."[6]

How to Survive If You're a Neuron

Because neurons that fire together wire together, it's good for neurons to team up with other neurons. Teaming up is important because the neural ecosystem has a limited supply of oxygen, glucose, and other needed materials. Individual neurons benefit from joining up with other "like-minded" neurons—that is, neurons tuned to similar functional events—just as we humans tend to do better if we join with others than if we go it alone.[7]

I have just emphasized cooperation among neurons. In response, you might say, "Now wait a minute. If it's a jungle in there, shouldn't neurons just *inhibit* their neighbors as much as possible? Shouldn't neurons be as aggressive as possible all the time, suppressing their neural neighbors as fiercely as they can? Why excite your neural neighbors if it's a dog-eat-dog world in there?"

Neurons need to be on good terms with other neurons with whom they have connections. If you're a neuron, you need input to get activated. It won't serve you well over the long run to deflate all the neurons with whom you have ties because, through their activity, they might promote your own future functioning. Biting the neural hand that feeds you won't help you over the long run.

Suppose you're a neuron that happens to be activated whenever the person in whom you live sees a hamburger. You'd be foolish to inhibit a fellow neuron that plays a role in seeing such a meal. You needn't know that this other neuron helps in this regard. You needn't know that that neuron is a "vision neuron," that there is such a thing as an eye, or anything of the sort. You, as a neuron, are simply doing your thing. You needn't know that you're a nerve cell, that you're in a nervous system (whatever that is), that you occupy a person (whatever *that* is), that your survival depends on the sight of hamburgers, and so on. All you need to know or, more precisely, all you need to *do* is excite cells that happen to result in your own activation and inhibit cells that happen to result in your own deactivation. If you do this reliably, and if the other neurons in your network act similarly, your chances of surviving will be good.

The Bell-Magendie Law

The examples I've just given for justifying interneuronal excitation and inhibition are rooted in a feature of neural functioning that is so fundamental to the way scientists view the nervous system that it's hard to imagine there was ever a time when they didn't know it. The feature I'm referring to is the distinction between sensing and acting, between perceiving and moving. It turns out that this distinction is built into the structural organization of the nervous system itself. This was shown in the mid-1800s by an English physiologist named Charles Bell and a French physiologist named François Magendie. They discovered a feature of neural organization that proved to be pivotal for neuroscience. According to their Bell-Magendie Law, fibers on the dorsal side of the spinal cord serve sensory functions, while fibers on the ventral side of the spinal cord serve motor functions.[8] It will help to unpack these terms to show how the Bell-Magendie Law demarcates the neural landscape, and that, in turn, will set the stage for the application of Darwin's principle to neural organization.[9]

As just stated, one claim of the Bell-Magendie Law is that dorsal fibers serve sensory functions. You've encountered the word "dorsal" in connection with fish. The dorsal fin of a fish is the fin jutting up from its torso. Sharks trawling the ocean surface betray their presence to us landlubbers by their dorsal fins. Snorkelers beneath the surface also need to be wary of sharks' *ventral* fins, the fins on the sharks' bellies.

Bell and Magendie's great discovery was that stimulation of *dorsal* nerve fibers elicits feelings of the skin being touched, of the muscles being stretched, of the joints being flexed or extended, and so on. Stimulation of *ventral* nerve fibers, on the other hand, causes muscles to contract.

These distinct functions of dorsal and ventral fibers become all too familiar when there is neural damage. If dorsal nerve fibers are hurt, sensory loss can follow. If ventral nerve fibers are hurt, motor loss can result. Paralysis or paresis (partial paralysis) can ensue.

The discovery that sensory and motor functions can be separated, at least for spinal dorsal nerve fibers and for spinal ventral nerve fibers, shows that there are two basic neural niches—one that deals with stimuli and one that deals with responses. Neuroscientists have developed terms for these two sorts of nerve fibers: *afferent* fibers, which carry signals with sensory consequences, and *efferent* fibers, which carry signals with motor consequences.[10]

My reason for focusing on these two kinds of fibers is that they help constrain the Darwinian drama that can unfold in the nervous system. To see what these constraints are, ask yourself what kind of neuron you'd like to be. If your main priority is survival, you'd want to be a neuron that fires often. You'd want excitement that occurs fairly regularly but not nonstop, for that could exhaust you. And you would not want to be endlessly isolated or interminably inhibited, for then your draw on metabolic resources could get dangerously low.

Being a sensory neuron or a motor neuron would give you a good chance of being called on regularly. Your neighbors would want to be in contact with you because sensing and moving are primary tasks. Afferent and efferent fibers are like essential personnel. They serve critical functions. Everyone relies on them.

Other neurons, so-called interneurons—the neurons lying between the afferent and efferent neurons—are important too because they allow for communication between the fibers that directly contact sensory receptors and muscle effectors. Interneurons that are removed from direct contact with afferent and efferent fibers tend to support functions that are less directly tied to specific afferent or efferent functions. What they do is more abstract or intellectual. The farther interneurons are from the sensory and motor edges of the nervous system (measured in number of synapses), the more abstract or intellectual their functions tend to be.

Macroscopic Features of Brain Organization

Just as neural fibers entering the back of the spinal cord serve sensory functions, whereas neural fibers exiting the front of the spinal cord serve motor functions, fibers in the back of the brain (opposite the face) also tend to support perception. Brain fibers in the front of the brain (toward the face) tend to support action. This generalization helps make sense of the quote from Geoffrey Hinton, "The brain is locally global and globally local." Globally speaking, action-related functions are represented toward the front of the brain while perception-related functions are represented toward the back. Between these two poles, the functions are more graded, shading roughly from less to more action-based the farther frontward you go.

The second generalization concerns side-to-side organization. Considering the left versus the right side of the brain, a different division emerges. The left cerebral hemisphere of the human brain is thought be specialized for language, at least in most people. Meanwhile, the right side of the brain is thought to be specialized for spatial processing and artistic or intuitive thinking, again in most people.

These differences were made famous by Michael Gazzaniga and Roger Sperry in the 1960s. Gazzaniga and Sperry studied neurological patients who underwent split-brain surgery to alleviate severe epilepsy. Cutting the major neural tract separating the left and right cerebral hemispheres—the *corpus callosum*—created a kind of "fire lane" that stopped the spread of the neural storm producing epileptic symptoms.

Separating the two cerebral hemispheres led to a surprising result. Visual stimuli shown briefly to the visual field that projected to the *left* cerebral hemisphere could be named by the split-brain patients, but visual stimuli shown briefly to the visual field that projected to the *right* cerebral hemisphere could not. This outcome suggested that the left cerebral hemisphere had access to language while the right cerebral hemisphere did not.

It was not that the right cerebral hemisphere was simply dumb, however, as shown in another test where the same visual stimuli were shown to the left or right cerebral hemispheres of the same patients. This time, the patients were instructed to reach out and grasp the visually pictured object. The reaching was done without visual feedback. When the visual stimulus was projected to the *right* cerebral hemisphere, the correct object could be identified through touch, but it could not be named. When the visual stimulus was projected to the *left* cerebral hemisphere, the correct object could be named but could not be identified through touch. Thus, the right hemisphere could display haptic recognition of the seen object, but the left hemisphere could not. Meanwhile, the left hemisphere could display verbal recognition of the seen object, but the right hemisphere could not.

These results and others led Gazzaniga and Sperry to propose that different "mega-functions" are served by the left and right cerebral hemispheres. The left cerebral hemisphere supports verbal-analytic thinking, while the right cerebral hemisphere supports nonverbal-holistic thinking. In terms of the broader message of this chapter, just as macroscopic differences can be found between ecosystems in the outer world, macroscopic functional differences can be found between neural systems in the brain.

Methods for Identifying Brain Specialization

At this point, I could ask you to join me on a more detailed tour of the brain, considering what the many parts of the brain do—what functions, in other words, those brain regions seem to carry out with regard to cognition, perception, action, and emotion. We could move from place to place, noting the apparent specialization of each locale. The review would show that things change gradually as we move from one neural neighborhood to the next.

I will refrain from providing such a tour, however, because we could lose sight of the larger principle I want to emphasize. It suffices to say, in my opinion, that there are three aspects of brain specialization that bear on the jungle principle. These pertain to the methods used to infer the specialization, the claim that brain functions are localized, and the issue of whether the brain is hard- or soft-wired.[11] I'll take up each of these issues in this and the next two sections.

Regarding method, it pays to consider how the functional properties of different brain regions are discerned. One method—perhaps the most straightforward—is to ask what happens when a part of the brain is damaged. The logic is straightforward. If damage to some brain region disrupts some activity, then that region can be said to play some role in that activity.

Sometimes people go beyond this modest inference and say that if damage to a part of the brain impairs an activity, then that part of the brain *controls* that activity or is *necessary* for that activity. Such a conclusion is premature, however, and here's an anecdote that shows why.

Suppose you're a songwriter and, like many aspiring tune-and-lyric creators, you write songs at home. One day, something annoying happens. The sewer line running from your house backs up and your basement starts to fill with the most foul-smelling ooze. I think of this disgusting example because this happened at my house one day while I was writing this book. I couldn't get the experience out of my mind and thought of it as I started to write this section.

If your sewer line backs up while you're trying to compose music, your writing suffers. In fact, your composing comes to a screeching halt, not because your sewer line is strictly necessary for your music generation, but because the unexpected plumbing problem interferes with your ability to concentrate on your art. This homely example shows how careful one must be about drawing causal conclusions from neural damage. If neural damage disrupts an activity, it doesn't follow that the activity depends in a direct way on the region that's impaired.

Now consider another possible outcome—that damage to some area of the brain does *not* impair or affect a function. What can you conclude from that outcome? You have to be careful here as well. You'd be incorrect to say that the lack of an effect following damage to that brain area implies that the brain area plays no role in the function. The brain area *might* play a role, but there might also be a backup system that takes over if the area takes a hit.

These cautions aside, it's unquestionable that a vast amount has been learned about the brain and nervous system by studying the effects of damage to its components. Such damage can result from accidents such as bullet wounds, interruptions to blood flow, or physiological mayhem wrought by cancer or infection. Interruptions of brain activity can also come about by deactivating parts of the brain through temporary (reversible) freezing, a technique used in many laboratories.[12]

Other methods also exist for inferring the role of brain systems in psychological functions. These fall into two broad classes: *stimulation* and *recording*. Neurophysiologists stimulate the brain and other parts of the nervous system with electrodes and then observe the consequences of the stimulation. When stimulation of a brain site gives rise to some effect, it's possible to infer that the brain region plays some role in the observed function. Saying that the region is *necessary* for the function is too large a leap, however, as already indicated.

It's also possible to *record* from the brain. Doing so can be achieved with tiny electrodes that pick up the electrical activity of individual neurons or small sets of neurons. Alternatively, it's possible to record from the brain as a whole or section by section, picking up larger swaths of activity. Within this class of recording methods, there are technologically advanced techniques known by an alphabet-soup's worth of acronyms: EEG, MEG, ERP, PET, CAT, MRI, fMRI, DOI. I won't review the methods here; doing so would take us far afield.[13] Suffice it to say that the methods have supported the view that different parts of the brain serve different functions, a principle known as localization.

Localization

One of the most famous sources of evidence for localization of function in the brain is the discovery of feature detectors in the visual cortex. These neurons were found by David Hubel and Torsten Wiesel in the early 1960s.[14] While recording from cells in this region of the cat's brain, Hubel and Wiesel noticed that when particular visual stimuli were shown, particular cells fired. For example, a given cell emitted a burst of action potentials when a dark bar was shown. The cell fired most when the bar was oriented at 90 degrees, but the more the bar's orientation shifted from 90 (or 270) degrees, the less vigorously the cell fired. Another cell fired the most when the same dark bar was oriented at 45 (or 135) degrees. Again, the more the bar's orientation departed from that angle, the less vigorously the cell fired. Similar distinctions applied to other cells. The stimuli that had these effects were of various kinds. They could be bars moving along paths with particular orientations, blobs in different parts of space, and so on.

Hubel and Wiesel referred to these neurons as *feature detectors*. The two scientists also distinguished between detectors that differed with respect to the complexity of the stimuli to which the detectors responded. "Simple" cells responded to elementary feature combinations. "Complex" cells responded to more complicated feature combinations. "Hyper-complex" cells responded to still more complicated feature combinations.

Analogous cells for other sensory modalities were found as well. Other researchers found neurons that respond preferentially to sounds of different frequencies, to odors of different chemical compositions, to touches on different parts of the body, to an animal's being in different spatial locations (so-called "place cells"), and so on.[15]

Do these results imply that psychological functions are localized in the brain? The answer is no, and the reason is that detecting an aspect of a stimulus isn't the same as experiencing it in all its aspects. In addition and no less importantly, none of the neurons lives alone. Each does what it does by virtue of where it lives—that is, by virtue of the other neurons with which it communicates most directly. Finally, there are limits on how far one can go with the feature detector concept. If you have detectors for faces, for example, you may or may not have a detector for your grandmother's face.

The search for "grandmother" cells has so far failed, presumably because grandmothers' faces appear in infinitely many poses. Even if a grandmother cell were found, you'd be left wondering whether there would be a specialized cell for the sight of grandma sitting at the piano with a red tulip in the green vase atop the keyboard, a different specialized cell for the sight of grandma sitting at the piano with a *blue* tulip in the green vase atop the keyboard, and so on.

The problem with high-level detectors is that they can't keep up with the endless combinations of experience. For any assortment of features, some other assortment can be imagined. It's hard to believe that every possible scene can be recognized only through activation of some particular specialized cell whose *raison d'être* is recognition of just that environment. All possible stimuli can't be anticipated, so all possible detectors can't be pre-formed. By having relatively low-level features that can combine in novel ways, however, you have the basis for perceiving endlessly varied inputs. Low-level feature detectors have a good chance of surviving because they're called on regularly. High-level features—or ensembles of features that correspond to more complex, varied arrangements—can survive as well but take longer to form and may have a more tenuous future.

Neural Plasticity

Another aspect of neurophysiology that points to the plausibility of the inner jungle principle is *neural plasticity*. To understand the idea of neural plasticity, it's useful to think of a convenient but now outdated fiction about the brain. The fiction is that every region of the brain serves a fixed, hard-wired function. According to this view, cells for feeling are faithful to touch all their lives, cells for seeing are loyal to looking from cradle to grave, and so on. At a more microscopic level, the particular sensory features that individual cells are tuned to—lines of some orientation for seeing, sounds of some frequency for hearing—remain the same forever. Like sailors whose girlfriends' names remain tattooed to their arms forever, neurons stay faithful to their first functional flames. That, anyway, was the belief associated with the hard-wired view.

It turns out that the functional properties of different brain regions are not engraved in stone but instead are malleable, or *plastic*. The term "plastic" conjures up images of squeeze bottles. More generally, though, plastic means reshapable. The brain is plastic in the sense that its functions are not hard-wired, but instead can be recast through experience.[16]

Brain plasticity is central to the theme of this book. In fact, it was when I was teaching about neural plasticity that I first uttered the phrase, "It's a jungle in there." Neural plasticity illustrates the jungle principle vividly—perhaps more vividly than any other phenomenon in neuroscience.

What exactly is neural plasticity and how was it discovered? I'll begin with the second question.

In the 1980s, a young neuroscientist named Michael Merzenich was puzzled by observations he made in his neurophysiological recordings of squirrel monkey brains.[17] From his training, Merzenich had a pretty good idea of the functions served by the brain structures he was studying. He knew that vision is served by one region, that hearing is served by another, that touch is served by still another, and so on.[18] He also knew that adjacent regions within each of these brain regions tend to have similar functions. Within the somatosensory cortex, for example, some neurons fire in response to touch on the left index finger, adjacent neurons fire in response to touch on the left middle finger, and so on.[19]

Another principle that Merzenich was aware of was that some neural enclaves are bigger than others. Neurons turned on by tongue touches are more plentiful than neurons turned on by foot feels, neurons activated by digit dabs are more numerous than neurons aroused by belly brushes, and so on. The thumb's representation in this part of the brain is especially large (Figure 2). What Merzenich expected was that the sizes of the brain regions from which he recorded would remain more or less the same in the brains of all the monkeys he studied.

To his surprise, Merzenich and his coworkers found that brains of different monkeys varied considerably in how much of their brains were devoted to the same functions. Though the animals were roughly the same age and size, the sizes of their brain regions devoted to any given function varied considerably.

What was going on here, Merzenich and his coworkers wondered? One possibility was that different animals were genetically disposed to have differently sized brain regions. According to this view, one animal, through inheritance, had lots of brain space for touch on its *index* finger; another animal, owing to *its* genetic constitution, had more neural real estate devoted to touches on its *middle* finger, and so on. According to this nature-rather-than-nurture view,

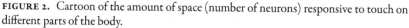

FIGURE 2. Cartoon of the amount of space (number of neurons) responsive to touch on different parts of the body.

what determined the amount of brain space for a function was genetic determination. According to another view, the nurture-as-well-as-nature view, the differences in the sizes of the brain zones reflected experience as well as genes.

To decide between these hypotheses, Merzenich and his colleagues performed experiments in which they altered the experiences of their experimental subjects. Their logic was straightforward: If the organization of the brain is fixed, experience shouldn't change it.

In one study, Merzenich et al. amputated the middle finger of a monkey to see how that would affect the monkey's somatosensory cortexes. This manipulation provided a particularly strong test of the experience hypothesis and so was deemed ethically acceptable.

Merzenich and his colleagues found that cells in the somatosensory cortex that had previously responded to touch on the middle finger but not to touch on the adjacent ring or index finger became responsive to touch on the still-present adjacent fingers after the middle finger was removed. In other words, the middle-finger region of the somatosensory cortex, which had been unresponsive to touch on the ring or index finger, became responsive to touch on the ring and index digits after the middle finger was removed.

How should you interpret this result? The best interpretation, I believe, is that it's a jungle in there. A neuron engaged in transmitting signals from the *index* finger to the brain, or a neuron engaged in transmitting signals from the *ring* finger to the brain, can be said to have always sought to make contact with the middle-finger region. That region was next to the place where those neurons mainly projected. But something kept those neurons from extending their tendrils to the middle-finger zone. Keeping them out were the neural tendrils from the middle finger. After surgical removal of the middle finger, afferents to the middle-finger region of the somatosensory cortex no longer delivered signals to that cortical zone, so index-finger inputs and ring-finger inputs had less competition for entry to the middle-finger area. Once they made that entry and could do so on repeated occasions, they could form reliable connections to it.

Do such changes occur only after unfortunate events like amputations? The answer, happily, is no. Enlargements of neural territories also accompany practice. Merzenich and his colleagues demonstrated practice effects in other, more benign experiments. In one, they gave monkeys practice on a task requiring fine tactile discrimination by the middle finger. After prolonged practice on this task, more brain tissue in the somatosensory cortex became responsive to touch on that finger. Other neighboring regions that were previously responsive to touch from the adjacent fingers *lost* neural space in the process as they became responsive to stimulation of the highly practiced middle finger. One zone's gain was, therefore, another zone's loss.[20]

Neural plasticity has also been found for modalities other than touch. People who go blind have been found to develop sound sensitivity in brain regions that would have otherwise been devoted to vision.[21] The neurons in the so-called visual cortex that have this crossover property lie next to the primary auditory cortex, consistent with the view that neural plasticity mainly reflects infiltration by neural neighbors.

Plasticity and Experience

Does neural plasticity have consequences for experience, or is it just something picked up by neurophysiologists in laboratories—a curious phenomenon, perhaps, but not of any practical value? Many findings indicate that the malleability of neural representations affects experience outside the lab. Some of these findings relate to the fact that when more brain area comes to be devoted to a function, better perception or performance results. For perception, this translates to better detection or discrimination. For performance, it translates to finer coordination or dexterity.

Consider the super-sized thumb of the sensory homunculus, shown in Figure 2. The thumb is a very sensitive area. When you try to determine whether someone is touching you with one toothpick or two, your discrimination threshold is small on your thumb. You're very sensitive there and can pick up a small difference. Only one other part of the body is more sensitive than the thumb when it's subjected to two-point discrimination tests: the tongue.

Sensitivity to touch as measured through two-point discrimination is related to how much brain tissue is devoted to that body part. The tongue has lots of brain representation and so does the thumb. But the abdomen, whose two-point discrimination threshold is much larger, is much less "brainy," with much less neural territory devoted to the abdomen on a per-square-centimeter basis than to the tongue or thumb. The thigh and calf are likewise scantily represented in the somatosensory cortex.[22] What this shows is that there is a relation between the amount of neural territory devoted to or associated with touch and the fineness of tactile discrimination that the associated patch of skin can support.

This relation is mediated by experience in humans. This was shown in studies of violin players. People who spend long periods practicing the violin develop enlarged receptive fields for the somatosensory cortex on the side of the brain receiving inputs from the left hand (the hand used for fingering on the violin).[23] Similarly, blind individuals who learn to read Braille develop greater tactile sensitivity as a result of this experience. This change is partly due to the growth of tactile sensitivity in *visual* areas. Visual areas—so named because they're typically tuned to visual inputs but not to other kinds of inputs—become touch sensitive in Braille readers.[24]

Strange Consequences of Neural Plasticity

Sometimes, when an area that was responsive to input of one kind is usurped by input of another kind, experience can change in strange ways. The researcher who has done the most to explain these strange effects is Vilayanur Ramachandran, a psychologist at the University of California, San Diego. He has shown that a couple of bizarre phenomena are attributable to neural plasticity.[25]

One strange phenomenon is that touch on one part of the body can elicit feelings in other, absent body parts. Ramachandran discovered this while interacting with a man whose arm had been amputated. Acting on reports from the man, Ramachandran asked him to indicate what he felt when Ramachandran touched him gently on his face. "As I've told you," the man said, "when my face is touched, I also feel my hand being touched." "Do you mean the hand that's no longer there?" Ramachandran asked. "Yes," the man replied.[26]

The explanation that Ramachandran gave for this strange effect was based on his knowledge that the face and hand regions of the somatosensory cortex are adjacent. Relying on the idea that neurons try to form connections, Ramachandran suspected that sensory inputs from the young man's face formed stronger-than-normal connections with the young man's somatosensory cortex. Ramachandran reasoned that if the hand sector no longer received afferent inputs from the hand, but if touch to the face activated the hand region, then higher centers would treat the inputs as hand-based. Touching the amputee's face would therefore cause the amputee to think his actually absent hand had been touched.

Ramachandran's second observation was even droller. It concerned a topic that might better be talked about behind closed doors. If you're prudish, skip the next three paragraphs.

Some people get their jollies by having their feet fondled. Fondling the soles of the feet or sucking and kissing the toes turn on these foot fetishists. Why such stimulation can lead to so much pleasure is a bit of a mystery, except if you follow the line of reasoning that Ramachandran pursued.

Imagine you're a neuron—in this case, an afferent neuron projecting from sensory receptors in the foot to the foot region of the somatosensory cortex. Being such a neuron, each time your owner's foot is touched, you send a signal to the foot zone of the somatosensory cortex. You have no idea, of course, being a neuron, that the signal you're sending concerns foot touches *per se*. Nor do you know that the region to which you're sending the signal is the region that gets more signals from the foot than from anywhere else. You're also unaware that the area next to the foot region happens to be the region that gets signals from the genitals.

Being a typical neuron, however, you try to form connections with neighboring zones. Happily, from your point of view, some of your foot axons get hooked up with the nearby area, the genital area. Because the genital area sends signals to parts of the brain that elicit pleasure, the outcome is the one of interest: Pleasure comes from foot feels because inputs from the foot also feed the part of the brain that gets inputs from the genitals. If you're someone in whom this cross-talk is especially strong, you may be especially fond of having your feet fondled.

Synesthesia and Summing Up

A third strange phenomenon related to neural plasticity is not one that Ramachandran happened to have studied extensively. This one is *synesthesia*. People who experience synesthesia have vivid associations between sights and sounds (to name just two sensory modalities). When they *see* something, they also *hear* something, though what they see is objectively silent. What they hear is also consistently associated with what they see.[27]

Synesthesia is due in part to neural plasticity. Sensory inputs get crossed and go where they normally wouldn't. A sight leads to an illusory sound because inputs that normally go to visual centers also penetrate auditory centers. Likewise for other cross-modal connections. Synesthesia arises, then, because the nervous system isn't a perfectly regimented place. Rather, it's a place where interactions can take on surprising twists and turns. This isn't to say that what goes on in the nervous system is utterly wild and unpredictable. Neural connectivity has considerable orderliness, as indicated in the opening sections of this chapter, but it's also subject to considerable variability, as indicated in the final sections, starting with the section on neural plasticity. These and the other functional properties of the brain reviewed here are consistent with the view that it's a jungle in there. Even in a jungle—neural or otherwise—there's considerable order, but there can also be staggering variety.

4

Pay Attention!

Earlier in this book you saw how important it is to resist the idea that your mind has a single head honcho, a top dog who decides things for you. The problem with postulating such a cognitive captain is that granting his or her existence begs the question of how that chief executive decides what to do. Who tells the CEO what commands to issue? You don't want to end up with a Russian-doll problem, with beings inside beings endlessly passing the ruble.

If you deny that an executive decides things for you, you're left with the question of how you make decisions. You can say your brain holds elections and, as it turns out, that account does a reasonably good job of explaining neural and behavioral data. But if you go with the election view, you're still left with questions: How are elections set? What issues are worth voting on? How is the collective attention of the electorate directed to one thing or another? How, if at all, is attention managed? What is attention anyway?

To set sail for explaining attention in Darwinian terms, it helps to think about the problems that are solved by invoking attention. One is filtering. Imagine you're on a train and you're trying to read. People in nearby seats are jabbering away, oblivious to your quest for quiet. The topic they're discussing doesn't interest you in the least. Who cares if their Aunt Helen smoked more than she should have? Why should it matter if their Uncle Ben knew less about pickles than he claimed? But their chitchat cuts through anyway, leaving you unable to concentrate on the reading you want to do. Try as you might to filter out those other speakers, you can't help overhearing them. Why can't you tune them out? At some point you may succeed in doing so, ignoring their chatter to the point you're no longer aware of doing so. But achieving this state is elusive, like falling asleep or falling in love. It comes unbidden.

The downside of filtering things out is missing what's important. You may become so engrossed in your reading that you miss the conductor's call for your station. Filtering needs to be done at the right level. Otherwise you could end up not where you want to go, but in *Nowheresville.*

The Cocktail Party Phenomenon

Some of the earliest research on attention posited that the gate to the mind, if there is one, is on the sensory side. A psychologist at Oxford University, Donald Broadbent, was led to this view by focusing on a task similar to the one described above. In that task, people were asked to listen to two messages at once.[1] One message was delivered to one ear. Another message was delivered to the other. When participants were instructed to focus on the message coming to one ear, they successfully recalled much of that message, but they recalled virtually nothing of the other. From that outcome, Broadbent drew a reasonable conclusion: People can attend to what reaches one ear but filter out what comes to the other.[2]

This conclusion makes sense if you try to read a book on a train and people to your right prattle incessantly. Closing your right ear, as it were, keeps your left ear open. That way, if the conductor calls your station and his or her voice comes to your "open" left ear, you can hear the call; the prattle to your right won't derail you. On the other hand, if the conductor's call happens to come to your right ear when he or she calls your station, you won't hear the call and you'll miss your stop.

Of course, in a railroad car with ambient noise going to both ears at once, you'd be unlikely to miss a call if you happened to be paying more attention to one side than the other, so I mean this example figuratively, not literally. Still, people do miss their train stops on occasion, often as a result of missing calls for their stations. Perhaps they do so for the reason Broadbent suggested.

There's a problem with Broadbent's filter theory, though, that's not about the prevalence of ambient noise in the environment. The problem is that the hypothesis is factually flawed, as shown by a couple of undergraduates who broadsided Broadbent's hypothesis with a simple experiment.[3]

The two students who disproved their teacher's hypothesis carried out a variation of the simultaneous listening task. They noted that the version of the task that Broadbent used had subjects listening to two messages that were equally sensible if recalled by either ear. The student experimenters asked what would happen if people listened instead to two messages that made more sense if the listeners *switched* attention from ear to ear. The messages they presented were similar to those appearing below. Each row represents a moment in time. Each column represents an input coming to the left ear (left column) or right ear (right column).

Dear	8
2	Aunt
Sally	5
7	How
Are	9
3	You

To read these words in a meaningful way, you can shunt your attention back and forth while going from top to bottom. The students who conducted this study reasoned that if their listening subjects did this, they would not behave as Broadbent predicted, which would be to say "Dear 2 Sally 7 are 3" or "8 Aunt 5 how 9 you." Instead, the students hypothesized, their subjects would say, "Dear Aunt Sally, how are you?" or "8 2 5 7 9 3." Many participants did just this, suggesting that they tracked what made *sense*, not what entered one ear or the other.[4]

If this result vitiates the claim of Broadbent, does it fit with *Darwin's* theory? Can the result be explained by appealing to an inner jungle?

If you attend to what makes sense rather than to what strikes one eardrum or the other, the signals coming through your ears must be analyzed sufficiently to let you know what the signals mean. This implies that cognitive demons for analyzing meaning aren't kept out by other demons blocking input to one of your ears.

Donald Broadbent was a professor at Oxford University (hardly a fly-by-night academy), so it's a bit disquieting to think that an Oxford don could be dinged by anyone, let alone a couple of undergrads.[5] Even Oxford profs can be wrong, however, though being wrong isn't quite so shameful as you might think. In science, being wrong but being enduringly stimulating is better than being right and quickly forgotten. One mark of the impact of a scientific theory is how long people dwell on it, even if only, in the end, to disprove it. Aristotle's theory of motion was accepted for centuries before Newton supplanted it with something better. Newton's theory of motion held for hundreds of years before it was overturned by Einstein. The fact that Aristotle was wrong and that Newton was also incorrect (at least beyond the range of everyday experience) doesn't mean Aristotle and Newton are now derided. They're both revered for the durability of their claims.

Should Broadbent's model be rejected just because data from a particular experiment went against it? Maybe that experiment created an unusual situation, one that tapped into some unusual ability. Consider the following scenario, however.

Imagine that you're at a crowded party, standing in the middle of a room, conversing with someone who strikes your fancy. What this person says captures your attention. You don't have to try hard to focus hard on what he or she is saying. The other sounds in the room—the conversations, the laughter, the loud music—dissolve as you speak with this new acquaintance.

Then an odd thing happens. Out of the background, you hear your name. It isn't yelled. It isn't amplified through a megaphone. No one grabs your arm, tugs on you, and exclaims, "Ernesto, I'm talking to *you*!" Your name grabs you even though it's mentioned quietly. Despite its low volume, it directs you to it. Though emanating from the background, the name attracts your attention the way a moth is drawn to a light in the darkness. The moth can't help being pulled there. Likewise for your attention when your name sounds.

If your name pops out this way, you couldn't have really shut out the auditory input containing it, could you? Instead, your name and, by implication, other sounds must have been subject to some sort of scrutiny. Cognitive imps in your head must have been listening all the time, and the cognitive imps linked to your name must have been pushier than others. When your name came in, those little demons must have jumped up and down feverishly, yelling "That's me! That's me! That's me!" (metaphorically, of course).

The tendency to respond to your name even when it's presented to an ostensibly unattended channel is called the *cocktail party* effect.[6] The term harks back to a time when people sipped cocktails at parties.

Is the cocktail party a reliable phenomenon, or does it only arise around martinis, whiskey sours, and Southern Comforts? It's very reliable, as I show in a classroom demonstration in which I invite a student volunteer to come to the front of the class. I stand to one side of the student, read out loud from a book, and ask the student to repeat each word I say. This task is called *auditory shadowing*. With just a bit of practice—a minute at most—the student can perform the auditory shadowing task very well, provided the words he or she hears are familiar and the rate is comparable to his or her natural speech rate.[7]

In the second part of the demonstration, I ask another student to stand on the shadower's other side and read from another book. The shadower is now asked to repeat what the student reader reads and to pay no attention to what I say—something I figure the student has experience with, having sat through my lectures. In a matter of seconds, the shadower can do this. He or she can repeat what the other student says and is able to tune out what I say, or at least that's what appears to happen. When I ask the shadower after the shadowing event what I read, he or she shrugs.

Then I demonstrate the cocktail party effect. In the midst of my reading, being careful not to raise my voice or do anything else to attract special attention, I utter the student's name. If the student's name is Ernesto, I say "Ernesto" as discretely as I can, as if the name were part of the text I'm reading.

When I say the student's name, a remarkable thing often happens. The student immediately turns and looks at me, and says, "What?" or something similar. The effect is so dramatic that when the demonstration works, it gets gales of laughter from the students in the audience.[8]

What does this demonstration reveal about the brain? It shows that it's a jungle in there. In a jungle, there are dominance hierarchies. Similarly, when it comes to auditory perception, some representations (the dominant ones) need very little input to get highly activated whereas other representations (the less dominant ones) need more. Other representations are less dominant because their inputs fail to seize attention so reliably.

Attention and Action Selection

The way you can tell your name has special status is that you do something special when your name comes along. If you're at a cocktail party, you stop listening to the person you've been listening to and look at the person who just mentioned you. If you're standing in front of a class engaged in a shadowy demonstration with your cognitive psychology professor, you stop in your tracks and look at him or her when s/he refers to you. The fact that you stop what you're doing and do something else suggests that attention permits action selection.

This view of attention as a vehicle for selecting actions was anticipated by the late-nineteenth-century philosopher and psychologist, William James, often called the dean of American psychology. In his encyclopedic work, *Principles of Psychology*, James wrote, "Everyone knows what attention is. It is the taking possession of the mind, in clear and vivid form, of one out of what seem several simultaneously possible objects or trains of thought. Focalization, concentration, of consciousness are of its essence. It implies withdrawal from some things in order to deal effectively with others."[9] This definition does not restrict the effects of attention to the overt performance of selected acts but points, instead, to a more subtle, inner selectivity. Can this more subtle view be explored scientifically? To the extent that it highlights internal rather than only external experience, does this vitiate an action-centered view?

FIGURE 3. The Rubin figure.

Consider an image that can be seen in one way or another, the so-called Rubin figure (Figure 3), named for the Danish psychologist, Edgar Rubin, who introduced it in 1915.[10] The Rubin figure can be seen either as a wine goblet or as two faces looking at each other. The most interesting feature of the figure is that you can see it in either of these ways, but not as both of them at once. The two perceptions flip back and forth. No matter how hard you try, you can't see both of them simultaneously.

When I show the Rubin figure to students in my class, I ask them to raise their hands when they see a goblet and to lower their hands when they see the faces. For the students who are willing to participate in this exercise, their hands go up or down once every few seconds.[11]

A similar outcome is obtained with another reversible figure, the Necker cube (Figure 4), named after Louis Albert Necker, a Swiss crystallographer who first published an image of his famous cube in 1832.[12] The Necker cube is a two-dimensional rendering of a 3D wire-frame box. Because the 2D depiction is visually impoverished, lacking cues about the figure's 3D orientation, it tends to be seen with one side close to the observer and the other side far from the observer. The two interpretations switch back and forth. The side that seems farther away suddenly jumps to the front, or vice versa. The flipping occurs again and again, as if of its own accord. Students who raise and lower their hands to show which side seems frontward change their hand positions at about the same rate as when they indicate their perceptual switches while viewing the Rubin figure.

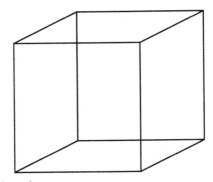

FIGURE 4. The Necker cube.

What accounts for this perceptual vacillation, and why am I speaking of it here in this discussion of attention? One reason is that perceptual instability suggests inner conflict. Two inner factions seem to duke it out. One wants one side of the Necker cube to be close; the other wants that side to be far. Each fights so hard for its point of view that your perception—your response to the image—gets jostled back and forth.

The other reason I'm speaking about the Necker cube is that the perceptual reversal of this stimulus also points to the importance of action selection. Seeing the Necker cube one way or the other is an action, albeit of an elementary kind. The action can take the form or lowering or raising your hand, or it can take the form of verbally reporting the position of a vertex of the cube: "Now it's in front. Now it's in back." A reason for the vacillation may be that attention is not just for deciding how to interpret things but also for deciding what to do physically in relation to them. In the case of the Necker cube, it may be that you can see only one side of the cube as the front and one side as the back because if you were you to reach out and grab the cube in 3D, you'd be unable to grab one side in a near place and in a far place simultaneously. If you put your fingers around the back edge, your hand would be in the back, not in the front, and if you were to put your fingers around the front edge, your hand would be in the front, not in the back. Which edge is in the front or in the back is perceptually ambiguous in the 2D image, but the need to commit to a front reading or a back reading is *required* for the perception to serve action.[13]

By this way of thinking, you don't have to see attention as something mysterious. Attention exists, according to the view suggested here, because there are factions in the nervous system whose fates ultimately depend on the actions carried out.

An implication of this view is that any attentional bottlenecks that might exist in the nervous system should exist at the action side. A cognitive psychologist at the University of California (San Diego), Harold Pashler, has argued for this position.[14] He has described experiments that fit with the action-selection (or response-selection) hypothesis. Instructions to subjects in his experiments go something like this.

1. If a light appears on the left, press a button with your left hand.
2. If a light appears on the right, press a button with your right hand.
3. If a tone sounds, press a foot pedal.
4. Carry out each action as quickly and as accurately as possible.

In the actual experiment, the tone (for the foot) is often presented very soon after one of the lights comes on (either for the left hand or right). In conditions of special interest, the tone may come on so soon after the light appears that it actually comes on before the hand response is made. The interesting result is that the second (foot) response is delayed by an especially long time in this circumstance, as if the second (foot) response cannot be selected until the first (hand) response has been.

There is no *a priori* reason why this should be. A foot and a hand can move together, as is obvious from watching a drummer pound a bass drum with her foot while she taps a cymbal with her hand. Her hands and feet can move at the same time.

According to Pashler, the reason for the delayed foot response in the light-then-tone experiment is that the foot response can't be selected until the hand response has been. If one response is selected first, the second selection must wait its turn.[15]

Looking Behavior

One way you can see attention playing out in action selection is in people's looking behavior. It's not uncommon to see heads turning synchronously when a bunch of oglers notices an attractive passerby. Outside of group settings, eye movements of individuals acting alone provide a window to attentional states. By recording where individuals look, researchers have studied what captures people's attention and, therefore, how attention works.

An effective way to show where people look is to place dots on the places they gazed at. Plunking dots where the observers' eyes came to rest on inspected stimuli shows where the fovea (the part of the retina used for object perception) settled to get sustained exposure to regions of interest. Between those visual fixations, the eyes jumped, or made *saccades*, the French word for "jolts" or "jerks."

Some of the earliest imposed-dot pictures came from a Russian physiologist named Alfred Yarbus, who used primitive but scientifically path-breaking equipment to learn how people look at pictures. He found that people inspect pictures in nonrandom ways.[16] When they were shown a picture of a girl, for instance, they tended to look at the girl's eyes and mouth. They looked much less at her chin, ears, or hair. Yarbus showed that where observers looked depended on what they were looking for. The same picture attracted different gaze patterns depending on what question observers were trying to answer.

If you look where you attend, does that mean you attend only where you look? Can you attend to other places as well? What internal processes cause you to have your attention drawn to a given location? Is attraction always drawn to *locations*? And what, if anything, does the jungle principle have to say about these matters?

Moving your eyes from place to place hardly seems like a series of victories, yet is it. For your eyes to jump to some location, internal processes must pull your eyes from where they are to some other spot. There are many contenders for where you look. The number of places to which you can direct your gaze is effectively infinite. An inner agent pulling for one of those places has much at stake for directing gaze to that site. Like a business that bellies up if it's unnoticed, a place that rarely gets a glance may lose its claim to neural real estate.

Vision scientists have conducted many studies of the factors that predict looking behavior. These findings are interesting not only for students of vision and the brain but also for people with practical concerns. Advertisers want people to look at their wares. Educators want students to look at their texts. Where people look can affect what they buy and what they study.

In vision laboratories, it has been found that bright, unexpected stimuli tend to attract attention. So pronounced is this effect that the tendency to look at such stimuli is considered a *reflex*—the so-called *orienting* reflex. The orienting reflex doesn't just include turning the *eyes* toward alerting stimuli. The head and entire body can point in that direction. As a result, if you're Ernesto and your name is mentioned at a cocktail party or in a classroom demonstration, you may turn your torso toward the person who names you.

A reflex is a response that is automatic and tightly coupled to its trigger stimulus. A bright spot of light coming on at an unexpected location draws visual attention to that location, not somewhere else. The ensuing response occurs very quickly, as if the neural gnomes governing the orienting reflex are kings and queens of the jungle. Their royal status, measured by the immediacy of the responses they trigger, is derived from their privileged access to the system responsible for generating saccades, which in turn carry out the precious function of exposing the brain to selected stimuli.[17]

Even saccade latencies can benefit from attention, as shown in experiments by Michael Posner and his colleagues at the University of Oregon.[18] Posner asked university students to perform a simple task. "When you see the second stimulus in each experimental trial," Posner said, "press a key as quickly as you can."[19] Posner knew the second stimulus would be a dot that would appear on the left or right on a computer screen. He also knew that the first stimulus could be an arrow pointing to the left or right, or a double-sided arrow, the kind that points two ways at once. Any of these three stimuli could appear in the center of the screen. The target dot that followed then appeared on the left or right.

The interesting feature of this experiment was that when Posner showed a *left*-pointing arrow, the next dot he usually showed was on the *left*, and when he showed a *right*-pointing arrow, the next dot he usually showed was on the *right*. However, on some occasions, after Posner showed an arrow pointing one way or the other, he (or his computer) showed a dot on the other side of the screen. The result was that detection latencies were longer in the invalid precue condition, intermediate in the neutral precue condition, and shortest in the valid precue condition. So participants were reliably fastest to press the "now-I-see-it" key when the arrow correctly informed them where the target dot would appear. They were reliably slowest when the arrow *incorrectly* informed them where the target dot would appear. And they were reliably in between when the precue was uninformative (when the precue was a two-sided arrow).

What accounts for this pattern of results? Posner argued that attention could be voluntarily shifted toward the cue location based on the precue. If the likelihood of the precue was high enough (80%), participants could direct their attention to the validly precued site, which led to short detection latencies. However, if the cue appeared on the *opposite* side of the screen, the detection time was much longer—longer even than in the control condition, when the precue was uninformative. Evidently, participants could take advantage of the precue and, as a result, abbreviate their detection times. This outcome is remarkable considering how short the detection times were to begin with—about a quarter of a second.

Was this effect just a result of eye movements? Did people in the experiment simply look to the right if the arrow pointed to the right, or look to the left if the arrow pointed to the left? Looking in the appropriate location would have made it easier to detect the stimulus that happened to appear there, but this might not tell you about attention *per se*—only that you can see something more easily (or report it more quickly) if you're looking at it, which is not very surprising.

Posner showed that the valid precue advantage wasn't just due to anticipatory eye movements. When he recorded his subjects' eye positions, he obtained shorter detection times for correctly precued stimuli even if the eyes pointed straight ahead after the precue arrow appeared. Similarly, he obtained longer detection times for incorrectly precued stimuli even if the eyes remained fixed in the middle of the screen. Thus, attention is dissociable from eye positions. Where you look may reflect where you attend, but where you attend can be divorced from where you direct your eyes. Basketball players know this. They try to fake out their opponents by looking one way before bounding off in the other direction.

There are at least two reasons why eye movements are dissociable from attention. One is that shifts of attention may help trigger eye movements. Unless you believe eyes dart from place to place on a totally random basis, you need to assume that some inner state—call it attention—impels the eyes to dart where they do. The other reason why eye movements are dissociable from attention is that eye movements can be inhibited. You probably know this from personal experience. If you're looking somewhere you shouldn't, you can force your eyes to go somewhere else in a hurry.

Are Posner's data explained, then, by the jungle principle? I think so. Detection times can be seen as times to complete two inner battles. The first battle is the one between detecting or not detecting a new stimulus. Recall that Posner's participants merely pressed a button when a stimulus appeared. His participants didn't have to press one button or another depending on which stimulus came on. All they had to do was detect the stimulus and show when they did this.

The second battle was deciding to make a response rather than withholding a response. Getting an informative prime in the Posner cuing paradigm presumably excited the neural systems associated with the relevant perceptual and response events. Presumably, too, getting an informative prime inhibited the neural systems associated with their antagonists. The combination of excitation and inhibition allowed for the speed-ups that occurred when stimulus onsets were accurately heralded. Excitation and inhibition probably also caused the slow-downs that occurred when the information given in advance was inaccurate.[20]

Why Inhibition As Well As Excitation?

With all this talk of inner inhibition and excitation, you might wonder whether I'm being too militaristic. "Must you speak of such a hostile interior?" you might ask. "I hate the idea that my mind's a jungle with feuding foes!" you might exclaim.

Let me rephrase. The claim that it's a jungle in there really boils to two overarching claims, neither of which needs to be controversial and both of which, when combined, are meant only to integrate what has been appreciated for a long time in cognitive psychology. One claim is that the nervous system relies on excitation and inhibition. The other is that it's imperative that a theory of mental function not fall into the trap of positing executives who know more than others in the neural arboretum. Regarding the second claim, believing that there's a Mr. or Ms. Know-It-All begs the question of how s/he knows all s/he does. Positing such an inner agent amounts to kicking the cognitive can down the road.

Granting these things, you may still ask whether both ingredients of the jungle principle—competition and cooperation—are needed to account for Posner's data, not to mention the other data obtained in attention laboratories. "Maybe excitation alone can tell the story," you might muse.[21]

One reason to posit inhibition is that if only excitation existed, the excitation could grow endlessly. Real physical and biological systems have limits. It's unrealistic to say that excitation builds up with no end in sight.

"Well, all right," you might reply, "but still, the excitation could subside over time." To this I'd say, "Yes, it's possible the excitation could die down passively. That would help solve the too-much-of-a-good-thing problem. But there's a difficulty with relying entirely on passive decay. Attentional dynamics would slow to a crawl. For speedy changes, the best mechanism is one that manages quick shifts of inhibition and excitation. The ups and downs, suitably dialed, can produce the rapid shifts of attention that all of us display."

The third reason to allow for inhibition as well as excitation is that the nervous system relies extensively on both forms of interaction. You don't have to look hard for inhibition in the nervous system; it's pervasive. The extensive reliance on inhibition, as found in neurophysiology (see Chapter 3), provides the third reason why inhibition should be invoked in accounts of attention. The nervous system relies on inhibition in all it does. There's no reason why it shouldn't rely on inhibition in attention or, for that matter, in any other cognitive domain.

Fourth and finally, there is direct evidence for inhibition in attention. Some of the most telling support comes from other work by Michael Posner.

Here, he noticed that when participants were shown stimuli at locations where the stimuli were recently presented, the participants took longer than usual to detect them. It was as if the participants were inhibited from returning to those locations. Posner called this phenomenon *inhibition of return*.[22] The term may remind you of the title of a famous novel by Thomas Wolfe, *You Can't Go Home Again*.[23] Posner, along with Asher Cohen, showed that you *can* go home again, at least in the modest world of looking back to a recent stimulus location. But if you do, it takes longer to get there than to go somewhere else.

Researchers who have studied inhibition of return have suggested that the phenomenon is explicable in terms of prediction and responsiveness. Being responsive to stimuli at *new* locations makes more sense than being responsive to stimuli at locations you've been to lately. If you're a hungry canine who's just wolfed down a field mouse, the odds are low that another mouse will emerge soon from that same silo. The rodent roommates at the wolfing site will get the message that they'd better lay low for a while. From the wolf's perspective, it makes more sense to look elsewhere than to keep monitoring the same spot. Such reasoning may underlie inhibition of return at the attentional level.

Another phenomenon suggests that it helps to be a downer when it comes to analyzing attention. Suppose you're in a situation where you need to ignore some distracting stimulus. Suppose, for example, that you're playing in a golf tournament and must work hard to ignore someone standing in the gallery whose physical assets are eye-catching. To fulfill your golfing duties, you need to focus on the tee rather than the tee shirt. After hitting the ball and watching where it lands, you might expect your eye to veer headlong to the taboo zone, getting there in record time. That's not what happens, however. Surprisingly, your eyes get to that site more slowly than usual.

If you first looked at the tee shirt, gazing where you shouldn't, the slow return look is an example of inhibition of return. Your tendency to look more slowly at a site you weren't supposed to illustrates *negative priming*.[24] In experiments where people have to ignore distracting stimuli (not encased in tee shirts), if those stimuli later become targets for visual searches, it takes longer to respond to the targets than if they weren't distracters before. The distracters become stigmatized, so to speak, or negatively primed. In the parlance of cognitive psychology, they become inhibited. The inhibition sticks, at least for a while.

Here's another example of the importance of inhibition in attention. Suppose you agree to participate in an experiment in which you're supposed to detect letters in the middle of a display. You're supposed to press one button as quickly as possible if you see the letter S and a different button if you see the letter T. The experiment has a devilish twist, however. You're not shown one letter—just the S or the T. Instead, you're shown the one target letter flanked by others. The flanker letters can complement or contradict the target. If the flankers complement the target and the target is S, you're shown two pairs of Ss on either side of the S in the middle, as seen in the first line below. On the other hand, if the flankers contradict the target and, again, S is the target, you may instead be shown two pairs of Ts on either side of the middle S, as seen in the middle line below. There's also a control condition where, as shown in the third line below, the middle S is flanked by pairs of neutral letters, like X, for which you don't have a specific associated response.[25]

SSSSS
TTSTT
XXSXX

What happens in this set of conditions? When the S is surrounded by Ss, reaction times are short, but when the S is surrounded by Ts, reaction times are long. Finally, when the S is flanked by Xs, reaction times are middling.

How can you explain this outcome? If the presence of non-S flankers (Ts or Xs) merely reduced the activation of the S response, you'd expect the reaction times to be no different when the S is surrounded by Ts or by Xs. But because S responses are longer when S is surrounded by Ts (to which another response is assigned) than when S is surrounded by Xs (to which *no* response is assigned), the T flankers lead to inner conflict. When an S appears, its inner agents are activated and they try to launch their associated response while also trying to inhibit the response of the "enemy" Ts. When the Ts appear, their inner agents are activated, and they try to generate their associated response while inhibiting the response associated with S. The correct response comes out only after the battle has been waged.

Positing an inner battle isn't just borne of a shoot-'em-up mentality. Direct evidence for such skirmishes in the flankers task has been obtained from studies of muscle activity.[26] Using electrodes that picked up muscle activity of participants performing the flankers task, Michael Coles and colleagues at the University of Illinois (in the same department where the flankers task was developed) showed that the muscles of the two hands become active when participants were shown competing stimuli. If the target stimulus called for a response with one hand and the flankers called for a response of the other hand, the muscles of *both* hands came on. Only gradually did the muscles of the wrong hand quiet down while the muscles of the correct hand contracted more intensely. Cognitive psychologists call this process *response competition*.

For response competition to be inferred, you don't have to see muscle co-activation in competing responses. Whenever decision times are elevated because mutually exclusive responses are called for, response competition is likely to play a role. Appealing to response competition is hardly controversial in studies of attention and performance. The concept is accepted in this field as widely as forces are accepted in physics. For response competition to be completed—for one response rather than another to be finally performed—the alternative response must be inhibited and the selected response must excited (or activated).

Is there is contradiction between saying, as I did earlier in this chapter, that the bottleneck for attention is in response selection and that response competition can be directly observed? If response selection is where the bottleneck exists, shouldn't you see perfectly quiet muscles for the hand that's supposed to stay still?

The answer depends on what you mean by a response. If you mean muscle movements or electromyographic activity, then it's incorrect to say that an attentional bottleneck exists for response selection. On the other hand, if by response competition you mean the instrumental outcome of physical movements, then there's no problem. Battles are waged when decisions must be reached about which outcome should prevail in the external environment. When cars jostle for positions as they approach toll booths, the outcomes they're vying for are getting through the toll booths before the next cars do. The desire for such victories accounts for the jostling in the approach lanes. Seeing the jostling doesn't mean there isn't a bottleneck. There's a bottleneck, to be sure, as every impatient driver and every impatient passenger knows.

By this way of thinking, studying jostling for position, whether on the approach to the George Washington Bridge or in the muscles of the two hands of people performing flankers tasks, lays bare the battles that go on prior to response selection. In Chapter 7, which will be concerned with motor control, I will provide more evidence for this jostling, manifested by the hands, eyes, and other effectors when movements are prepared or performed.

Automaticity

When people press one button for one stimulus or another button for another stimulus, they generally make their responses based on learning. Over the course of learning, stimulus-response connections become automatic. This has both an upside and a downside. The upside is that if the response that's called for by a stimulus is the response that's automatically activated by the stimulus, the response can occur very quickly, with little or no deliberation. The downside is that if the response that's needed is *not* the one that a stimulus calls for, things can get nasty.

In this connection, consider the Stroop task.[27] If you're a participant in a Stroop task, your responsibilities sound innocent enough. You're told, "When you see a word portrayed in green, yell 'Green'; when you see a word portrayed in red, yell 'Red'; and likewise for other colors. Just call out the color of the word's print."

"OK," you say. "Sounds simple enough. Let's go."

One word after another appears on the screen and you yell out the ink colors without much trouble. "Fox" appears in green and you yell out "green." "Chair" appears in red and you yell out "red." "Book" appears in blue and you shout out "blue." You beam at how quickly you respond, at how clever you are.

Then "Green" is shown in red. Your color-naming time skyrockets and, to make matters worse, you say something like, "Gree…red!" In another trial, "Blue" is shown in green and, again, not only do you slow down, but you say something screwy like "Bl…green."

What causes the problem? To say "red" when you see "Green" requires inhibition of your automatic response. To say "green" when you see "Blue" also takes inner censoring. You need to suppress the automatic response that you're on the verge of producing.[28]

For this effect to be shown—the Stroop effect, named for the person who invented this task—the participant must be a skilled reader. If the participant doesn't have the strong inclination to say "green" when seeing "Green" or the powerful urge to say "red" when seeing "Red," the effect washes out. From this it follows that susceptibility to the Stroop effect indexes reading skill.

Given the link between the Stroop effect and skill level, other cognitive psychologists have used Stroop or Stroop-like interference to investigate the development of automaticity. Such an approach was taken by Daniel Reisberg, Jonathan Baron, and Deborah Kemler, working together at the University of Pennsylvania.[29] They showed participants strings of digits and asked the participants (university students) to call out the number of digits in each display. Seeing "2 2 2" required "3," seeing "4 4" required "2," and so on. After a little practice, the participants quickly and accurately reported the number of numerals they saw rather than the names of the digits to which they were exposed.

Inviting people to report the number of digits they see provides a convenient medium for studying the development of automatic responding. Initially, when you're shown "2 2 2" you count the number of numbers. You might go so far as to say to yourself, "Let me count those digits: 1, 2, 3... OK, there are 3 digits, so I'll call out '3.'" Soon you don't need to count the digits. You just rely on a shortcut: "Whenever I see '2,' I'll call out '3.'" What began as a deliberate process turns into a prepackaged rule for relating a stimulus to a response—what cognitive psychologists call a *production*.[30]

A production is a condition-action instruction. Its canonical form is "If X, then Y," where X specifies a *condition*, such as "If the stimulus is 2...," and Y specifies an *action*, such as "...say 3." You can store many productions. The strengths of the productions can vary.

At first, when you participate in an experiment like the one run by Reisberg, Baron, and Kemler, you have a strong production at the ready: "If I see 2, then say '2.'" But after saying "3" over and over again in response to the sight of "2," a new production takes hold: "If I see 2, then say '3.'" Now you've got *two* productions that share conditions but dictate different actions. Because you can't say "2" and "3" at the same time, you have to make up your mind which response to produce. Deciding between the responses constitutes the moment of truth for the attention system, the moment when attention—whatever it is and whatever it does—gets you to do one thing rather than another. When multiple productions are activated, the sorting-out process gets difficult, but as a production is called for more often, it gets stronger than its competitors.

Such strengthening and weakening of productions provides a way of accounting for the data of Reisberg, Baron, and Kemler, who found that reaction times for correct completions of required productions decreased the more often the productions were called for. If subjects saw "2 2 2" several times with few intervening items—and, especially, with *no* intervening stimuli that had different numbers of 2s in them, such as "2" or "2 2" or "2 2 2 2"—the participants got faster and faster at saying "3" to the trio of deuces. But if the composition of the stimuli changed, so deuces were shown as singletons rather than as trios ("2"..."2"..."2") and so the necessary response was "1," the reaction times were long relative to what they had been earlier.

Such patterns of data are easily explained with the jungle principle. You simply need to appeal to the notion that just as the fortunes of creatures rise and fall depending on how well they fit their environments, so do the fortunes of productions within the brain.

More on Automaticity

When stimuli are responded to automatically, they're responded to with considerable speed, with little need for attention, and with little chance of slowing when potential distracters come along. These points were highlighted in one of the most famous demonstrations of the development of automaticity—a study by Walter Schneider and Richard Shiffrin, working together at Indiana University.[31] Schneider and Shiffrin asked people to look for targets among distracters. In each trial, the subjects were shown arrays of letters that either contained or did not contain a target letter. If participants found a target letter, they were supposed to press a button as quickly as they could.

Schneider and Shiffrin wanted to know how quickly subjects could detect a target depending on the subjects' learning histories. To address this question, the researchers varied two features of the participants' experience. One was the number of targets that could be presented over the series of experimental trials. The other was the role the targets could play as distracters.

If you look for a target, it can be the only target you're looking for or it can be one of several possible targets. Suppose the targets are siblings in a crowd. If you have just one sibling and you're trying to find him or her in a throng, the number of potential targets is 1. But if you have several siblings and all of them are in the gathering, the number of potential targets is more than 1. If you can automatically detect any of your siblings, it shouldn't matter how many of them there are in the crowd. You should be able to find any of them equally quickly no matter how many of your brothers and sisters are out there.

Schneider and Shiffrin pursued this idea with the more easily managed stimuli of letters in the alphabet. They sought to find out how quickly people could find a letter depending on the size of the target set. To vary the size of the target set, they varied the potential targets in successive blocks of trials. In a given block, their participants were given instructions such as, "The possible target in this block of trials is H," or "The possible targets in this block of trials are H or J."[32]

Behind Schneider and Shiffrin's interest in the size of the potential target set was the idea, already mentioned, that if detecting a target is automatic, it shouldn't matter how many potential targets there are. In other words, if you learn to automatically detect Bernie, Bill, and Buster (your three siblings) in a crowd, it shouldn't take you longer to search for any one of them when you know all three of them are possibly there than when you know that only two of them are possibly there or when you know that only one of them is possibly there. This predicted result should hold, however, only if the detection of targets is automatic. If the detection of targets is *not* automatic, the number of potential targets *should* impact the detection time: The more potential targets there are, the longer the detection time should be.

Schneider and Shiffrin found that as people looked for the same targets over and over again, the number of potential targets mattered less and less. With practice, the time to detect *H*, for example, depended to a decreasing degree on the possibility that other targets could appear. This outcome showed that participants developed the capacity to automatically detect the targets. In terms of the jungle principle, the demons responsible for finding *H* or *J* or *K* became sufficiently strong that they could yell equally loudly, or be heard equally well, no matter how many of their clique joined the claque.

What was the evidence that stimulus-response associations became automatic? The critical finding was that participants could detect targets automatically only when the targets were always associated with positive responses, and never or rarely when the targets were also associated with negative responses. If targets sometimes served as distracters, and so summoned negative responses, participants did not reach the level of automaticity they could if the same target was always a target. What was automatically triggered, therefore, were stimulus-response mappings, not stimuli alone or responses alone. Where automaticity took hold was at the point of response selection, where stimuli were used to determine which responses would be made. This is just what you'd expect if you thought attention aids action selection.

Attention and Inner Action

I've said that where the action is when it comes to attention is in action selection. My argument for this view echoes the ideas of Harold Pashler and his colleagues, as I said before. My position also accords with the so-called late-selection view of attention, a view that ascribes attention to a "late" process in stimulus-response translation—namely, at the response-selection side of the ledger, not at the stimulus processing side.[33] The antithesis to the late-selection view is the early-selection view, advocated most famously by Donald Broadbent in his sensory gate hypothesis (illustrated with "opening an ear" or "closing an ear"). I favor the late-selection view on the grounds that action selection is where, ultimately, decisions must be made.

Despite this perspective, I want to emphasize that it would be a mistake to say that attention cannot be directed to stimuli *per se* or to the features comprising stimuli. Clearly, you can listen for high-pitched tones rather than low-pitched tones, you can look for dark hues rather than light hues, and so on. There must be a way of accounting for the fact that low-level stimulus features can be objects of attention. Similarly, there must be a way of accounting for the fact that when people participate in studies where they attend to one type of stimulus, they invariably do worse at recalling or recognizing the stimuli to which they did not attend. For example, in dichotic listening experiments (experiments where two messages come to the two ears simultaneously), though participants may perk up when they hear their names, they cannot recall or recognize most other unattended stimuli.[34] This shows that there are objective grounds for saying that unattended stimuli receive less-favored status than do attended stimuli, which raises the question of whether the brain responds differently to stimuli depending on how much attention is directed to them. If it does but if no overt action is made, is this a problem for the view that attention is action-limiting?

With respect to the first question—does the brain actually respond differently to stimuli depending on how much attention is directed to them?—it turns out that neural activity in the auditory cortex is enhanced if sounds come in at or near the expected pitch.[35] Analogous effects are obtained for visual stimuli when recordings are made in the primary visual cortex.[36] In one particularly dramatic illustration of selective visual effects, researchers recorded from two regions of the brain known to respond to different aspects of visual inputs. One region, within the fusiform gyrus, is activated by seen *faces*. The other region, the parahippocampal place area, is activated by seen *places* (for example, seen *houses*). Using fMRI techniques, the scientists who did this study found that the face region of the brain became more activated when attention was directed to a seen face than to a seen house, but the house region of the brain became more activated when attention was directed to a seen house than to a seen face.[37] An especially striking feature of this demonstration was that the face and the house were overlaid. The fact that the two brain regions were activated to different degrees based on what the participants were attending to shows that different brain areas can be "goosed up" or "goosed down" depending on what information is sought. Another implication is that attention can be directed to *objects* as well as, or instead of, to *locations*.

Other studies have supported the hypothesis that attention can be object-based rather than location-based.[38] In all these cases, participants were more primed to direct their actions to the items being attended to than to the items not being attended to, thereby addressing the second question posed above: Is it problematic for the view that attention is action-limiting that participants don't have to make overt actions following the direction of attention? The answer is no. The actions can be inner actions or precursors of actions. Chapter 7 is all about what happens before actions are made.[39]

In the Spotlight

Can the phenomena I've summarized be accommodated with a single theory of attention? If so, is that theory of attention effectively embodied in the jungle principle? Toward answering that question, it's useful to say first what theory of attention *won't* work. Agreeing on what won't work can help narrow the field of what may.

One theory that won't work likens attention to a spotlight. Think of a prison escape movie. Imagine a scene where the convicts are trying to break out and find themselves in the prison yard at night. Periodically, a spotlight roves over the yard and the cons dash into the darkness to evade the roving beam. The guard guiding the spotlight is supposed to focus his or her attention on every place being illuminated. This, at least, is the guard's job description. If you think of the guard as the homunculus and the moving spotlight as the focus of the guard's attention, you have what amounts to the spotlight theory of attention.

I've already said that the spotlight theory of attention is wanting. What's wrong with it? One problem is that someone or something needs to move the spotlight. That someone or something is the homunculus, the irksome bloke we want to evict from our theory of the mind.

A second problem is that the enhancement allowed by the spotlight does...what exactly? The light makes it possible to see more and so, in theory, to attend to more detail than was possible otherwise. Attending more is a bit like casting a brighter light on an area of interest. But how do you cast a brighter light on a sound you're listening for, on a smell you're savoring, or on a feature of a mathematics problem you're trying to solve? The point is that casting more light is a nice metaphor that, ironically, may shed little light on the deeper problem to be solved.

A third difficulty is that spotlights can run in parallel. Theaters and circuses have multiple spotlights. Think of the proverbial three-ring circus. Nothing in the spotlight metaphor says there can be only one spotlight, but if there can be more than one, how many more can there be? 10^1? 10^2? 10^{12} (the number of neurons in the brain)? 10^{14} (the number of synapses in the brain)?

A fourth problem is that the spotlight idea is fuzzy in scope. How wide can a spotlight spread? If it does spread, does that mean everything under it can be attended to equally well? If what's in the center of the spotlight can be attended to more effectively than what's far from the center of the spotlight (but still within it), you've got spotlights within spotlights—not the sort of theory you want (Russian dolls within Russian dolls all over again).

Fifth, an important property of attention that you'd expect to hold if the spotlight metaphor were true turns out to be violated. Because a spotlight moves continuously between adjacent places of interest, any out-of-place object that's suddenly interposed at one of those places should disrupt processing. Yet adding such an object doesn't have this effect.[40] The implication is that if attention moves, it can move discontinuously, which is something a spotlight can't do unless it's granted so many *ad hoc* properties that its theoretical value dims.

Biased Competition

Considering all the things I've said in this chapter, is there a general theory of attention in reach? The theory I want to endorse is, of course, the one I've been endorsing all along, the jungle theory. Happily, a theory of attention that has achieved considerable notoriety has as its core claim one that aligns with the jungle perspective. The theory, advanced by Robert Desimone, now of MIT, and John Duncan, of the University of Cambridge,[41] was summarized as follows in a leading textbook on cognitive psychology: "...attention is seen as a form of competition among different inputs that can take place between different representations at all stages of processing."[42]

This *biased competition* theory, as it is known, departs from its predecessors in that it is remarkably unconstrained. It doesn't say attention works like a spotlight, with all the limitations that spotlights have. It doesn't say that attention works like a sensory gate, with the restrictions that sensory gates impose. It doesn't say that attention can operate only at the level of greatest meaning and personal significance, as you might suppose if you hark back to the cocktail party phenomenon. It doesn't even say that attention operates at the level of response selection, though I happen to believe that that's the case.

Desimone and Duncan didn't develop their theory in consultation with me or, apparently, in consultation with Harold Pashler, the advocate of the response selection model of attention (and a leading scholar in the field of attention). Desimone and Duncan based their conclusion on the basis of a wide range of considerations, including some data not reviewed here. All of these facts suggested to Desimone and Duncan that it's possible to see attentional bias effects virtually everywhere in the brain. For example, cells in one part of the brain concerned with vision (area V4 of the extra-striate visual cortex) that fire in response to either of two visual stimuli show greatly reduced firing to one of those stimuli if it's treated as a distracter.[43]

Saying that attention may be more important in some domains than others, as in saying that attention may be more important in response selection than in sensory intake, doesn't imply that attention must operate only in the supposedly most-important areas. Attention can operate anywhere, as Desimone and Duncan allowed. Their key idea, in fact, is that attention is, at heart, a competitive process that gets resolved by creating biases on the fly.[44] Those biases favor some outcomes over others wherever and whenever conflicts arise. Attention is also a cooperative process in that bias reflects preference. Giving preference to some events means granting cooperative relations between the relevant functions in the brain.

Because of this appeal to bias and competition, Desimone and Duncan called their theory the *biased competition* model, as I've already mentioned.[45] Their model is so similar in spirit to the jungle principle that I'd be less than candid if I didn't say that when I learned about their model I felt even more encouraged than I already was to embrace the jungle principle.[46]

5

Ready, Set, Go!

You've got to be quick to survive in a jungle, but speed alone isn't enough. You've also got to wait, and wait wisely. If you're a cat on the prowl who has spotted a munchy-looking mouse, you need to wait for the right moment to pounce on that unsuspecting prey. The mouse, meanwhile, has its own agenda. It wants to fulfill its feline-free fate for as long as possible, striving for a quick getaway no matter how pugnacious the puss.

The two characters in this little drama are in different states of preparedness. One is primed for pouncing. The other is braced for bolting. Each needs to act as quickly as possible. The situation they're in—having to respond as quickly as they can while maintaining preparedness in different ways—has been studied in detail by cognitive psychologists. Their favorite measure of preparedness is reaction time, or RT for short. In this chapter I'll consider how data from RT tasks bear on the jungle principle.

Simple and Choice Reaction Times

In the mid-1800s a Dutch scientist named Friedrich Donders asked a clever question.[1] What would happen, he wondered, if he measured the time to respond to stimuli when people were in different mental states? Suppose, for example, that in one condition participants were told to press a key as quickly as possible when a light came on. Simple enough, Donders thought, and he called this the "simple RT" task.

In another condition, Donders presented participants with *two* lights and *two* buttons. If one light turned on, the subject was supposed to press the button assigned to it. If the other light turned on, the subject was supposed to press the other button. A choice was required here, so Donders called this the "choice RT" task.

Donders thought the choice task might take longer than the simple task. When he recorded RTs, he found that this was the case. Simple RTs were about 200 milliseconds (200 ms, or .2 s). Choice RTs were about 500 ms, or .5 s.

Donders' approach was compelling because it was comparative. Simple RTs and choice RTs could be compared for the same stimuli and responses. Donders could look at the RT to make the very same response to the very same stimulus but in different contexts. This let him say something like the following: "The RT to respond with the left key to a left light is short if the left light is the only possible light and the left key is the only possible key. But the RT is longer if the left light is one of two possible lights and the left key is one of two possible keys."[2] Donders subtracted the simple RT from the choice RT and concluded that it takes about 300 ms (500 ms minus 200 ms) to make a choice.

Pursuing this line of reasoning leads to interesting predictions. If it takes 300 ms to make *one* choice, it might take 300 more milliseconds to make *two* choices, it might take an additional 300 ms to make *three* choices, and so on. It's easy enough to add choices to an RT task. If you're an experimenter, you can give your participants more stimulus-response (S-R) alternatives. For example, you can add more possible lights and keys.

When this experiment has been done, the data have not supported the prediction that choice RTs get longer by a constant amount with each additional S-R alternative. Instead, choice RTs increase by roughly the same amount with each *doubling* of the number of S-R choices. When the number of S-R alternatives climbs from 2 to 4, the RT increases by about 300 ms, when the number of S-R alternatives climbs from 4 to 8, the RT increases by another 300 ms, and so on. This relation was discovered in the early 1950s and is called the Hick-Hyman Law, in honor of the two researchers who discovered it, Edmund Hick and Ray Hyman.[3]

Information Theory

Why do choice RTs increase at a roughly constant rate with each doubling of the number of S-R alternatives? Is this outcome consistent with the jungle principle?

To begin with, consider a theory that was supposed to explain the result. The theory is one you've encountered in your daily life, though you may not know you have. It's called *information theory*.[4] You've encountered it when you thought about the size of your computer's hard drive. Does it hold 10 gigabytes? 100 gigabytes? A terabyte (1024 gigabytes)?

Bytes are strings of eight consecutive 1s and 0s. Each of those 1s and 0s is a "bit"—short for "binary digit" (either a 1 or a 0). For digital computers, all information is stored as strings of 1s and 0s. What makes computers "digital" is that they use just these two values, corresponding to two logic states: 1 for "true" and 0 for "false." Ultimately, the values map onto electrical switches that are either opened or closed when a computer's power is on.

According to information theory, knowledge can be usefully represented as sets of true-false values. If you're male, for example, you could be assigned a value of 1 for the proposition "You're male," or you could be assigned a value of 0 if you're not male. If you're over age 20, you could be assigned a value of 1 for the proposition "You're at least 20 years old" or 0 if you're not that old. Considering these two features—gender first and age second—you could be coded as 11, 10, 01, or 00.

For better or worse, this is how computers code everything. The digital era is all about representing information as strings of 1s and 0s. Representing information this way makes it possible to define information of any kind in digital form, whether it's text or sound or pictures. No matter how the information is formatted at the time of presentation—as words on a page, as sounds on a speaker, or as pictures on a screen—inside the computer, the information is just 1s and 0s (or their analogous switch settings).

How does information theory relate to choice RTs, and how do both topics relate to the jungle principle? Information theory predicts that choice RTs should increase by a constant amount with each doubling of the number of S-R alternatives. The reason is that information theory says that unique S-R alternatives are found by successively splitting the S-R set down the middle until just one S-R alternative remains. A person in an RT experiment trying to identify one of four people who are distinguished by gender and age might therefore ask, "Is the person male?" and then "Is the person at least 20 years old?" Those two questions are all that's needed to find the one person in four, provided there's just one person in each of the gender and age categories.

The scenario I've just described may remind you of the game "20 questions." Playing 20 questions is analogous to what might underlie the Hick-Hyman Law of choice RTs. If you're facing an array of eight lights laid out from left to right with a button beneath each one (a standard setup in cognitive psychology laboratories), the way you could identify the particular S-R alternative in a given trial is to "divide and conquer," as in 20 questions. In effect, you could ask the following three questions: (1) Is the illuminated light on the left? (2) Is the illuminated light on the left within the side selected in the first step? (3) Is the illuminated light on the left within the quadrant selected in the second step? By the time you've answered the third question, you've isolated the one required S-R alternative from the original set of eight, whereupon you can press the necessary key. You narrowed the options by splitting them successively down the middle.

As this example shows, it's possible to explain the relation between choice RT and number of S-R alternatives in terms of series of binary choices. If participants rule out half the S-R alternatives over and over again until they find the one required S-R alternative, choice RTs should increase by roughly a fixed amount with each doubling of the number of S-R pairs.[5]

This sounds lovely, doesn't it? So tidy, so mechanical! Indeed, when this theory was advanced in the early 1950s, psychologists were jubilant.[6] They had a way of measuring information, and they had evidence that the time to make decisions was lawfully related to the amount of information to be considered. Psychology was beginning to look more like a true science in that its data were orderly and it had a unit of measurement, the bit. Every self-respecting science needs well-defined units of measurement. Physics has its ergs, economics has its GDP (gross domestic product), and so on.

However jubilant psychologists were with information theory, something happened that dampened their enthusiasm for it. The theory proved to be less useful than psychologists first expected, at least when it came to predicting how much information people could remember. It turned out that the number of items people could recall after being exposed to material they were supposed to report immediately thereafter depended on how *meaningful* the items were, not on how many bits the items had. The relevant studies showed that people could remember just a few nonsense syllables such as "blig," "tuz," and "frip," but they could remember many more syllables if those syllables comprised meaningful sentences like this one: "The research I'm telling you about was introduced by a psychologist at Princeton University named George Miller, who showed that the number of meaningful elements, not the number of bits, predicted the amount people could remember." You could probably recall much of the foregoing sentence, though it has many more syllables than the number of syllables in the nonsense list given before.

George Miller presented this work in one of the most widely cited articles in the history of psychology, "The Magical Number Seven, Plus or Minus Two: Some Limits on Our Capacity for Processing Information." The number seven was the number of meaningful clusters of information, or "chunks," that people could hold in short-term memory. There was some variability in that number for different people, but for most people it was somewhere between 5 and 9.[7]

Miller showed that information theory fails when it comes to predicting immediate recall. What accounts for this apparent breakdown? Why does the number of chunks predict memory span, whereas the number of bits, as used in the Hick-Hyman Law and information theory more generally, seem to predict choice RTs?

A way to approach this question is to ask whether the 20-questions explanation of the Hick-Hyman Law is the best one. Do people in fact play 20 questions when they identify one S-R alternative from a set of possibilities? A psychologist at the University of Michigan, Sylvan Kornblum, realized that there was a confound in the experiments showing that choice RT depends on the number of S-R alternatives. Whenever the number of S-R alternatives grew, Kornblum realized, each S-R alternative was tested less often. Kornblum carefully analyzed data from choice RT experiments and found that the data were better predicted by the *history* of choices than by the sheer *number* of choices. The more often and the more recently an S-R alternative was tested, the shorter was its choice RT.[8]

It's possible to express this outcome in terms of the jungle principle: The stimulus-response pairs that were tested the most had the most aggressive representatives in the brain. When those S-R alternatives were called for, their internal representatives shouted more loudly than the representatives of the other S-R alternatives. Those other alternatives, in effect, became meeker the bleaker their chances of being tested. Kornblum showed that a mathematically expressed theory, for which the jungle account is just an informal metaphor, could explain the Hick-Hyman Law.[9]

Lexical Decision

How does the foregoing discussion relate to Miller's argument that chunks, and not just bits, determine memory span? Miller's chunks are meaningful elements, but figuring out what "meaningful" means is a daunting task.

Consider another choice RT task—one where people try to indicate as quickly and as accurately as possible whether a letter string shown on a computer screen is a real word. Is "blig" a real word? What about "tuz" or "frip"? This is a *lexical decision* task. People performing the task must check their mental lexicons (their mental "dictionaries") to see whether test items are represented there.

People can perform lexical decision tasks quite well. Considering how many words are known by typical participants in lexical decision tasks— 40,000 words or so among college students—it's remarkable how well they do. They manage to answer the is-this-a-word question in a second or less. How can they do this?

To address this question, it's useful to ask a simple question about the lexical decision task: What is a word, anyway?

A word is an often-encountered letter string (or sound pattern) that's marked by culture as a valid or "legal." If you've often encountered a non-word and have had to say it's a non-word, that can be difficult. College professors (of which I'm one) have many non-words in their heads—letter strings they know are non-words, given though they encounter the misspellings in their students' writing. When professors write their own prose, they have to suppress those lexical aliens. Suppression isn't unusual. All of us have to suppress words we know when we find ourselves in polite company and want to say things we know we shouldn't. Being able to suppress unwanted words, like being able to suppress unwanted actions, reflects inhibition.

Letter strings that are frequent enjoy relative freedom from suppression, as do legal letter strings. If you think of the number of chunks that can be retained in working memory as the number of alliances that can be strongly activated at a given time, you have the beginnings of an explanation of Miller's discovery. Strength may account for memorability and for choice RTs. (More will be said about lexical decisions later in this chapter.)

Memory Scanning

When you indicate whether a letter string is a word, you do so without regard to how long ago you first learned it. It would be useful to have a way of studying how well people can recognize items soon after they've learned them.

In 1966 a young scientist named Saul Sternberg published a brief but highly influential paper in which he described such a task.[10] He asked college students to memorize a small set of items, such as one to six letters. He used small set sizes of items because he wanted to see how quickly the items could be recognized, not *whether* they could be, as in traditional studies of memory.

Once Sternberg was satisfied that his participants knew the letters, he showed the letters one at a time and asked his participants to indicate as quickly as they could whether each letter was in the memorized list. If it was, the subject was supposed to press one of two keys. If it wasn't, the subject was supposed to press the other key.

The data from this task are presented in many textbooks in cognitive psychology because, besides being remarkably orderly, they distinguish among several hypotheses that Sternberg considered. Each hypothesis made a different prediction about the way the data could appear when RT was plotted as a function of the number of items in the memory set (Figure 5). It's instructive to consider these hypotheses because they bring to light several issues that argue for the jungle principle.

To convey the alternative hypotheses that Sternberg considered, let me tell you how I teach about them in my Intro-Cognitive class. First, I ask some

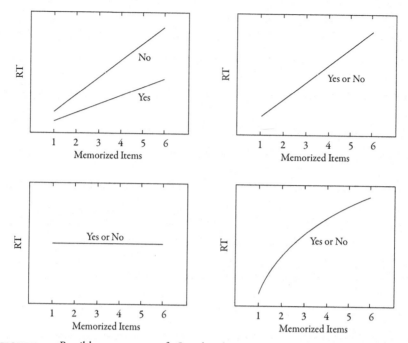

FIGURE 5. Possible outcomes of Sternberg's memory search experiment. **Top left:** Serial self-terminating search. **Top right:** Serial exhaustive search. **Bottom left:** Unlimited-capacity parallel search. **Bottom right:** Limited-capacity parallel search.

students to come to the front of the classroom to serve as representatives of the memory items. One student agrees to represent "W," another student agrees to represent "G," and so on. All the students stand in a line facing the class, and I ask another student to face this line of "memory elements." That student's job is to play the role of stimulus generator. On each trial, he or she calls out a letter that may or may not be in the memory set. I then illustrate how, according to different models, the test letter could be classified as belonging to the set or not.

In one scenario, after I hear the generator call out "W," for example, I run up to a student memory representative at one end of the line and ask him or her, "Are you W?" If the student answers "Yes," I turn around and yell "Yes." If the student answers "No," I run up to the next student and ask, "Are *you* W?" If that student says "Yes," I turn around and yell "Yes." I continue this one-on-one interrogation, stopping if a student responds affirmatively or continuing to the next student if not. At the very end, if the last student in the line does not say "Yes" in response to the question, "Are you W?" I shout out "No." This method is called *serial self-terminating* search. It's a memory search method that's *serial* because each item in the set is checked one at a time, and it's *self-terminating* because it stops on its own when a match is found. The serial self-terminating search method makes intuitive sense. If you look for something, you might as well stop when you've found it.

What prediction can be made from the serial self-terminating model? As shown in Figure 5, the model predicts that RTs for "Yes" responses should increase with the number of items in the memory set. It also predicts that RTs for "No" responses should likewise increase with the number of elements in the memory set, but with a slope about twice as steep as for "Yes" RTs. The reason is that "No" responses are given after all the items in the set have been checked. "Yes" responses, by contrast, are given, on average, after *half* the items have been checked.

Now consider another possible search model. It relies on serial *exhaustive* scanning. Here, each item is checked one at a time, and at the end of the series of checks, the "checker" determines whether a match was found. If a match was found, his or her response is "Yes," but if a match was not found, his or her response is "No." When I demonstrate this method to my students, I run up to one student after the other in the memory lineup and ask him or her, "Are you W?" (provided, of course, that "W" is the test stimulus). Each student answers "Yes" or "No." When I finish polling all the students in the line, I ask out loud, "Did I hear a Yes?" Then I answer my own question. If I answer "Yes," I yell out "Yes." If I answer "No," I yell out "No." My final, answer constitutes my response to the original query. When I play-act this model, the students laugh because the strategy seems ridiculous.

The model I just described is called serial exhaustive search because it involves a serial check (one item after another) and it's exhaustive; every item is checked. This model makes a different prediction about the relation between RT and memory set size than does the serial self-terminating model. As shown in Figure 5, the serial self-terminating model predicts that "No" RTs should increase with memory set size with a slope that is twice as large as the slope for "Yes" RTs. The serial exhaustive model predicts, by contrast, that "No" RTs and "Yes" RTs should increase at the *same* rate with the number of memory elements. The reason is that all the items in the memory set are always checked, regardless of whether the response ultimately turns out to be "Yes" or "No."

Before I show the students the data from Sternberg's experiment, I ask them to consider one more model. According to this other model, there's no little man or woman in the brain who checks each item one after the other. Instead, all the items are checked at the same time, in a so-called parallel search. I illustrate this method by asking the students in the lineup to shout "Yes" if they hear their letter name or to shout "No" if they don't hear their letter name. If a "Yes" is shouted by someone in the lineup, then that's the response. If only responses of "No" are shouted, then the response is "No." This model (without special assumptions) predicts that RTs should not depend on memory set size, at least if the number of shouters is unimportant. This is a different prediction than the ones made by the two previous models. Both of them predicted that RT would increase as the memory set increased.

Before I show the data that Sternberg actually obtained, I ask the students in the classroom which model they think was actually supported in Sternberg's experiment. About an equal number vote for the parallel model and the serial self-terminating model. Virtually no one votes for the serial exhaustive model.

Finally, I show the data. When I do, the students who have been paying attention gasp. Some of them drop their jaws in disbelief. "Are you sure you didn't make a mistake here, Professor?" one of the students sometimes asks.

The reason the students are so surprised is that the results conform to the least popular, least intuitive model, the serial exhaustive model. When I ask the students how this could be, either they shrug and wait for my explanation or they offer an interesting rationale. "When you take a multiple-choice test," they sometimes say, "it makes sense to check all your answers even if you find one that seems right at first."

This rationale provides one possible reason to take the serial exhaustive model seriously. Another comes from a consideration of the slope of the straight line fitted to the mean RTs plotted as a function of the number of items in the memory set. The slope of this straight line provides an estimate of the speed of memory scanning, the rate at which the elements of the memory set are supposedly interrogated, one after the other. The rate is impressive: around 40 ms per item. If there's a little man or woman running from one memory item to the next, he or she is a quick little devil! So impressive is the scanning rate that Sternberg titled his paper *High-Speed Scanning in Human Memory*.

My students are duly impressed with how quickly the little men or women in their brains run around. "Wow!" some of them exclaim. "That's really fast!"

"Yes it is," I reply. "But hang on a moment," I continue. "Before you get too excited by this estimate of memory search speed, let's do the following simple task. I'll ask you a question and then I'd like you to yell out your answer as quickly as you can. Ready?" I wait for their grudging affirmation and then ask them, with as much rah-rah as I can muster to spur their enthusiasm, "Is the following a word? . . . Blig!"

"No," the students reply a fraction of a second later. I pause a moment to see whether any of them get the point. I remind them that if each of them searched their memory at a rate of 40 ms per item, they wouldn't be able to say whether "blig" is a word so quickly. A typical college student knows about 40,000 words, I tell the students. How long, then, would it take to determine whether "blig" is a word if each item in memory were checked at a rate of 40 ms per item? The answer is 40,000 × 40 ms = 1,600,000 ms = 1,600 s, or 26.67 minutes!

What's wrong here? How can it take just a fraction of a second to indicate that "blig" is a non-word, though the rate of memory scanning (40 ms per item) predicts that it should take nearly half an hour to say it's not? One possibility is that serial exhaustive scanning applies only to very small memory sets. Logically, it's hard to eliminate this possibility, but it would be preferable to avoid special accounts for special circumstances. An explanation that applies to all circumstances would be simpler. It's better to pursue simpler explanations than complicated ones, a principle known as Occam's razor.[11]

Perhaps there's some other model that can account for data from the small-memory-set task of Sternberg versus the data from the lexical decision task: "Is *blig* a word?" Though I haven't described much more data from the lexical decision task—I'll say more about the task later in this chapter—I can share with you that I think there is such a model. As you can anticipate, I think it's one that accords with the jungle principle.

Suppose memory elements have neural representatives that clamor for activation. When some of those elements are identified as part of a memory set for a Sternberg experiment, they get excited. However, the degree to which they get excited is limited by the number of elements in the activated set, as shown in the bottom right panel of Figure 5.[12] As more elements occupy the set, the less loudly any of them can shout, or equivalently, the less clearly any of them can be heard by the response selector. This model can be expressed mathematically in a way that predicts that RTs will rise less and less as more items are activated. What's nice about the model is that it allows all the choice RTs to line up on one theoretical curve, a curve that contains the choice RTs for small memory sets like those studied by Sternberg, and choice RTs for immense memory sets like those probed in lexical decision experiments. No special account is needed for making choices in one part of the range or the other, so this is a simpler and therefore preferable model.[13]

Limited-Capacity Parallel Search

Cognitive psychologists have a name for the model I've just described. They (we) call it a *limited-capacity parallel search* model. You already know what a *parallel* search model is. It's one where all the elements are searched at once. The way I prefer to think of parallel search is that all the elements clamor for activation simultaneously, occupying an environment where it's up to them to get the activation they want. The way I think about parallel search as opposed to serial search is not just in terms of simultaneous versus sequential evaluation, but also in terms of the number of searchers. Just one searcher is involved in serial search, but many searchers are involved in parallel search. The many searchers in parallel search are all the cognitive creatures in the cranium, hoping, as it were, to be called upon. Some of those creatures are more eager than others. The ones who are especially eager are the ones encouraged by being selected for membership in the active memory set. Others not in that set are more remote or more retiring. By avoiding the need for one searcher, as required in the serial search, there is no need to establish a roadmap for where and when he, she, or it should search. With a parallel model, no itinerary is needed.

What is a *limited-capacity* parallel search model? It's a model in which the capacity of the system to support parallel search is restricted. As more elements clamor for activation, the rate at which each of them can accrue activation following presentation of a test stimulus dwindles, as if some resource is in short supply. No matter what that resource may be—oxygen, glucose, or something else—the activated elements compete for it.[14]

How does the competition work? Are the pre-activated elements doled out their needed elixir in inverse proportion to their number, or do the pre-activated elements duke it out, as it were, inhibiting each other to a degree that depends on how many of them there are?

I favor the "duke-it-out" option over the "doler" option because, with the doler option, you have to assume some special energy source distributed to the memory elements. What that neural tonic is, is a mystery. It might be oxygen or it might be glucose, both of which are needed for neurons to survive, but no one has ever been able to say what the mysterious resource might be. Studies of attention have failed to pinpoint any single resource for which mental elements compete. Another problem with the doler option is that someone or something must do the doling. Postulating such an agent begs the question of who's in charge. If activated memory elements inhibit each other, no homunculus is needed to determine how the doling should be done. So I prefer the duke-it-out view of memory, where all the pre-activated memory elements compete for recognition. The more of them that are pre-activated, the tougher the fight.

Stimulus-Response Compatibility

Deciding whether competition is really needed in a model of cognition can be tricky. In the context you've just been considering—the recognition task of Sternberg—competition can be avoided altogether, even granting a limited-capacity parallel search, by saying that the response selector has a harder time hearing a "Yes" amidst a chorus of many responses of "No" than hearing a "Yes" amidst a chorus of fewer responses of "No." Such a simple fact of discrimination may explain the data without the need for squabbling among cognitive contenders.

There are other tasks, however, where it's clearer that competition plays a role in shaping RTs. One is the task of pressing a left key if a left visual stimulus appears or pressing a right key if a right visual stimulus appears. Choice RTs are short in this circumstance. By contrast, if the mapping is reversed, so the left key must be pressed when a right stimulus appears, or the right key must be pressed when a left stimulus appears, the choice RTs are longer.

The ability to respond more quickly to same-side stimuli reflects a principle called *stimulus-response compatibility*. According to this principle, responses are quick and accurate if the stimuli calling for them arrive via "natural" or "compatible" stimulus-response mappings, but are less so stimulus-response mappings are "less natural" or "less compatible."[15]

What do the terms *natural* and *compatible* mean? Natural or compatible stimulus-response mappings are ones that have strong connections. Less natural or less compatible stimulus-response mappings are ones that have weaker connections. Accordingly, when responses that enjoy strong stimulus-response (S-R) associations must be made, those responses whisk through by virtue of their strong S-R bonds. Conversely, when responses that do not enjoy strong S-R associations are the ones that must be made, the *other* responses must somehow be made and the powerful S-R bonds must be inhibited. The left response "wants to go" when the left stimulus appears, so if the right response is necessary, the left response must be held in check. Likewise, if the right response "wants to go" when the left response is necessary, the right response (the response on the right) must be restrained.[16]

The Simon Effect

So great is the need for inhibition of prepotent responses that the inhibition may be necessary even when the relevant stimulus-response mappings are more indirect. Suppose you're instructed to press a left key if you see the letter *X* or press a right key if you see the letter *Y*. Where the *X* or *Y* appears is irrelevant to the task description. Nevertheless, if the *X* is on the left, the left-key response is quick, but if the *X* is on the right, the left-key response is slow, and vice versa for the right-key response to the *Y*. This phenomenon is known as the Simon effect, in honor of the psychologist who discovered it.[17]

What mechanism underlies the Simon effect? Why should the side of the stimulus affect choice RT when only the identity of the stimulus officially matters? Inner competition among response tendencies provides the answer once again. A left-side stimulus activates a left-side response independent of what the stimulus happens to be. Similarly, a right-side stimulus activates a right-side response independent of what stimulus happens to appear there.[18] A response is potentiated by the stimulus appearing on the responses' associated side. For the other response to occur, extra time is needed to resolve the conflict.[19]

Go/No-Go

Another RT task that reflects inner competition is a third one introduced by Donders on top of his simple RT and choice RT tasks. This third task lies somewhere between the other two.

Recall that in Donders' simple RT task there is just one possible response, whereas in Donders' choice RT task there is more than one possible response. The third, intermediate task that Donders also developed is the go/no-go task. Here participants are supposed to respond when one signal appears, but they are *not* supposed to respond when another signal appears. This is a familiar enough requirement. If you're driving and the traffic light is green, you're supposed to go. If the traffic light is red, you're *not* supposed to go. The red light means, literally, STOP!

Stopping is something you need to do even in simple RT situations. It's important not to jump the gun before the "go" signal comes on. Yet that demand is often violated. Swimmers poised to lunge into pools for their racing laps or sprinters leaning on their starting blocks sometimes start prematurely, reflecting a failure to fight the urge to lunge forward when the starting shot is fired.

Going only when you're supposed to takes self-control or, more specifically, inhibition. When the need to inhibit is small, RTs can be zero or even negative. RTs are zero when responses coincide perfectly with the stimuli that are supposed to elicit them. RTs are negative when responses come too early, leading rather than following the stimuli.

In Donders' go/no-go task, the need to refrain from responding is an explicit response alternative, not an implicit one. A useful feature of the go/no-go task is that within it, an experimenter can vary the probability that a response is called for. If a response has a high probability, it tends to have short RTs, but if a response has a low probability, it tends to have long RTs.

A natural way to interpret this finding is to say that a rarely-required response is greatly inhibited, whereas an often-required response is less greatly inhibited. Varying the degree of inhibition of a response is a way to match its likelihood. Go/no-go RTs depend on the probability of a response being called for or not.

Is this probability effect actually due to graded inhibition? An alternative view is that on each trial the participant simply predicts that the response will be required or not. If the prediction is correct, the RT can be quick and the accuracy high. If the prediction is incorrect, the RT will be longer and the accuracy lower.

Invoking an all-or-none prediction model has a problem, however. It suggests that RTs for a given response should either be very short (when the response that is predicted is actually required) or very long (when a response that's not predicted is required). But RT distributions don't usually have two clear humps.[20]

The other problem with the all-or-none prediction model is that it begs the question of what prediction is. Predictions aren't always made; sometimes one is in a don't-know state of mind. When one *is* in a predictive state of mind, it's very difficult, in my opinion, to understand what the neural representation of that state of mind could be. How exactly can the brain represent what might happen with some probability? I don't know, and I don't think anyone else does either.

An alternative, simpler, explanation is that activations of S-R alternatives grow with their frequency, and the inhibitory effects of those S-R alternatives on other S-R alternatives also grow with their frequency. Activation and inhibition, varying in degree, tell the whole story.

Stopping

Inhibiting responses is clearly required when you get ready to perform a response and then have to stop it. This situation has been studied in RT tasks where participants get a ready signal followed either by a go signal or by a don't-go signal. If there's a good chance a don't-go signal will come shortly after a ready signal appears, participants become adept at stopping the response. In fact, if the probability of a don't-go signal is *very* high, participants don't even bother to prepare the response, as shown by the relative lack of electrical activity in the muscles and in the brain compared to cases where the probability of the don't-go signal is more moderate.

For less probable don't-go signals, the dynamics are more interesting. If the don't-go signal comes on soon after the go signal, the participant can withhold the response. However, if the don't-go signal comes on late after the go signal but before the response has been made, the don't-go signal has no impact. The response occurs anyway, suggesting that the internal signals coalescing in the brain to permit a response reach a point of no return. Like a competitive swimmer who has leapt from the launch platform before the starting gun goes off, as soon as he or she is airborne there's no turning back.[21]

How long is the delay between a ready signal and a don't-go signal such that people can't suppress their responses? A particular time value is less important than the fact that the time is within the range of normal RTs. This is relevant to this discussion because if you think the tactics people use in the stopping procedure are very different from the tactics they use in normal RT tasks, you might expect the temporal point-of-no-return to be outside the normal RT range. The fact that it's within the normal range is consistent with the hypothesis that the inner workings of the nervous system are essentially the same when people are on the lookout for stimuli telling them which response to make or which response *not* to make. Inhibiting responses, by this line of argument, isn't something that occurs only in stop-signal studies. Rather, it happens all the time.

Why Are RTs So Long?

Just as it is instructive to compare RTs for different kinds of tasks—and we will consider still more of them momentarily—it is also instructive to consider the lengths of RTs themselves. A few paragraphs back, I mentioned that RTs can be zero or even negative when responses coincide with or lead their associated stimuli. RTs can also be positive when people react to stimuli after the stimuli are presented. Little attention has been paid to understanding why positive RTs have the values they do. Why are simple RTs about a quarter of a second, and why are choice RTs about a half to a full second? These questions are interesting because RTs are longer than might be expected. The reason, I'll argue, is that it's a jungle in there.[22]

The speed of nerve conduction is about 32 meters per second, or about 72 miles per hour.[23] Given this rate, you can ask how far nerve signals would travel in .25 seconds (a respectable simple RT time) or in .5 seconds (a respectable choice RT). Because distance equals rate times time, the neural travel distance for a simple RT would be .25 seconds times 32 meters per second, or 8 meters. The neural travel distance for a choice RT would be .50 seconds times 32 meters per second, or 16 m.

How do 8 meters and 32 meters compare to the length of the human body? An average-height American man is 1.73 meters (5 feet, 8 inches) tall, so 8 meters is 4.62 times the length of his body, and 32 meters is 18.49 times the length of his body. If you thought RTs reflect the distance traveled by nerve signals, you'd have to say that in simple RT tasks nerve signals cover nearly 5 times the length of the body, and in choice RT tasks nerve signals cover nearly 19 times the length of the body.

What's the use of these numbers? If you suppose a typical neuron, including its dendrites and axons, has a length of 1 millimeter, then 8,000 neurons are needed to cover the 8 meters for a simple RT, and 32,000 neurons are needed to cover the 32 meters for a choice RT. You've then got an awful of neurons lined up, doing what exactly? That's the puzzle. Too many neurons seem to be involved.

Why do there seem to be too many neurons? Think of a neuron as a switch. The nervous system might prepare for a simple RT task by keeping one switch open until a stimulus is detected, at which time the switch could close and the response could be triggered. Alternatively, the nervous system might prepare for a *choice* RT task by keeping *two* switches open, one per S-R choice. The added time for a choice RT compared to a simple RT could then be ascribed to the need for two switches rather than one. The problem with this scenario is that the time needed for an individual neuron to switch on is so short that the time is virtually unmeasurable.

A different way to address the question is to say that most of the time contributing to RTs is possibly non-neural. It could be, for example, that most of the RT is spent getting the muscles to physically generate the response. You could allow that more time is spent getting the muscles to move in choice RTs than in simple RTs, and you could assign the difference between choice RTs and simple RTs to muscle activation rather than to neural signaling. For example, you could say that in choice RTs, participants often need to relax some of their muscles that they initially tensed in order to generate the required response. All or most of the RT might then be taken up with relaxing and activating muscles rather than with sending signals down the neural transom. But it turns out that muscle activation times are very short relative to total RTs. Neurophysiologists have measured the times between neural signals in the motor cortex and subsequent button presses. The times are about 50–70 ms, and that's true regardless of whether the data come from simple RTs or choice RTs.[24] Thus, muscle activation can't account for the lengths of RTs.

Another possibility is that there's untold complexity in stimulus processing. To reach the point of finally throwing a neural switch one way or the other based on the detection of a stimulus in a simple RT task, it might be that a very long line of neurons is needed just to reach that point.

This possibility, like the possibility that muscle activation accounts for RT length, can be set aside. When neurophysiologists record from sensory regions of the brain, they pick up reliable differences in the neurons that fire depending on which stimulus is presented, and they pick up those differences in extraordinarily short times after the stimuli come on. The times are so short—on the order of a few milliseconds—that it's hard to believe the largest portion of RTs reflects sensory processing. Only a small portion of RTs actually reflect the differential registration of one stimulus among the alternative possible stimuli, at least if the stimuli are easily discriminated, which they have been in the tasks I've been describing—for example, when there's a light several centimeters to the left or right of a computer screen's midline.

So what's the best hypothesis about the length of the RT vis-à-vis the number of neurons underlying them? On the way to answering this question, let me say that you don't need to equate RTs with strings of neurons. It's useful to do so for the sake of discussion, but the main point of the argument I've been making has actually been to string you along, so to speak, to show that it's not especially helpful to equate RTs with neural strings. Linking RTs to some number of neurons working in a linear chain is not a profitable line of argument, not least because if any neuron in the chain malfunctions, the chain breaks. Nature seldom puts all her eggs in one basket; instead, she favors redundancy. If you allow for more than one linear string of neurons between a stimulus and a response—a possible way of avoiding putting all the eggs in one basket—it's not clear what each neuron in the chain actually adds. In fact, adding more neurons to a single chain might just add statistical noise. As in the game "whispering down the lane," the more communicators there are, the more degraded the signal.

We come, then, to an explanation that I think makes sense. Not surprisingly, the explanation relies on the idea that RTs are as long as they are because they reflect inhibition as well as excitation. Postulating inhibition provides the basis for saying why RTs are considerably longer than you'd expect if you merely considered the number of neurons operating at their normal speeds.

I haven't explained why RTs have the particular values they do, only why they're longer than expected. The reason they're longer than expected, I believe, is that it's a jungle in there. The time needed for any given S-R alternative to be expressed depends not just on that S-R alternative gathering activation for itself. It also depends on the S-R alternative inhibiting its competitors, not to mention overcoming whatever inhibition it had to endure as its competitors tried to suppress it. RTs are long, then, because of inner conflict. Were there none, we wouldn't take as long as we do to make the decisions we do.

Other RT Phenomena Due to Inhibition

So far in this chapter I have said why I think inhibition as well as activation needs to be invoked as a basis for RT results. I haven't stressed activation, since activation is hardly in doubt: To activate a response, activation (or excitation) is clearly needed. But to the extent that inhibition is in doubt, I want to give more reasons to identify it as a source of RT effects.

It turns out that a number of RT phenomena can be ascribed to inhibition. One of these is *negative* priming. Priming usually has a positive connotation. In cognitive psychology, that connotation is most famously expressed in the lexical decision task, where, as described earlier, you decide whether a stimulus is a word. It turns out that people are generally quicker to indicate that a stimulus is a word if it's preceded by a semantically related word than if it's preceded by a semantically unrelated word. The classic example is "doctor" priming "nurse." The time to indicate that "nurse" is a word is shorter if "nurse" is preceded by "doctor" than if "nurse" is preceded by some semantically neutral word like "boat." This *semantic priming* effect is due to automatic, unconscious facilitation.[25]

Semantic priming is an instance of positive priming. The priming is positive because the prime helps speed processing, reflected in shorter RTs. Negative priming, by contrast, *slows* processing, causing RTs to increase. Negative priming is manifested when a stimulus that was previously ignored is now supposed to be noticed but isn't noticed as easily as it would be otherwise. For example, if you've repeatedly reached for a red cup among other-colored cups, you're able to reach for the red cup more and more quickly—an example of positive priming. But if you next need to reach for a blue cup in successive trials, you'll get quicker at that, but, most critically for this discussion, if you next have to return to reaching for the *red* cup again, it will take you longer to reach for the red cup than if you hadn't reached for it before. The red cup gets marked as something to be avoided.[26]

Negative priming effects can also be obtained in word-naming tasks. Suppose you try to name the color of the ink in which words appear. This is the Stroop task, described earlier.[27] If you see the word RED in red ink, you'll be faster to say "red" than if you see the word BLUE in red ink. This benefit illustrates positive priming. You're quick because, as a skilled reader, you can automatically say "red" in response to seeing RED or "blue" in response to seeing BLUE. But if BLUE appears in red ink and you're still supposed to say "red," you must suppress your urge to say "blue" and your RT grows. Whatever active suppression or inhibition that you apply to your automatic response carries forward to the next trial. If in the next trial you see the word BLUE in blue ink, your RT becomes longer than it was before, when you hadn't previously suppressed your BLUE-"blue" production.[28] Such negative priming effect is consistent with the view that you inhibited the "blue" response, making it hard to say that word if it was needed next.

Another RT phenomenon that is likely to reflect inhibition is the slowing of RTs in task switching. When you perform a task, you follow a procedure. For example, if you indicate, over and over again, whether each of a series of numbers exceeds some target value, you follow a different procedure than if you indicate whether each of a series of numbers is odd or even. It turns out that you're slower to use a procedure if you just used a different procedure than if you use a procedure that's the same as the one just used. The slowing associated with task switching has been ascribed to inhibition of the just-used, but now unused, procedure.[29]

Redundancy Gain

In the discussion so far, I've suggested that to understand RT effects, you need to invoke inhibition as well as excitation. Neuroscientists won't be surprised by this claim because, in the nervous system, inhibition and excitation are pervasive. Neuroscientists would say there's no reason why only excitation or only inhibition should influence RTs. Given this fact of physiology, it's remarkable how strongly some cognitive psychologists have argued that inhibition doesn't underlie RT effects.[30] The zeal with which they've argued this point has surprised me because I don't understand what larger theoretical or practical issue is at stake. Nonetheless, I've taken their position seriously enough to devote a fair amount of space to the merits of inhibition in the analysis of RTs. Had there been an equally vociferous anti-excitation school, I suppose I might have devoted as much space to the defense of excitation.

My aim in endorsing inhibition (as well as excitation) as a basis for RT effects has been to emphasize the competitive basis for perception and performance, as indexed by RTs. To confirm that my aim is to endorse both excitation and inhibition, let me turn briefly to another phenomenon that can be explained perfectly well without appealing to inhibition. Interestingly, it is a phenomenon that can be explained by appealing to an inner "horse race."

The phenomenon is *redundancy gain*. It arises in visual search tasks when people look for one or more targets, typically in a field of one or more distracters. The speed with which participants can find targets is of practical interest because there are many real-world situations where finding visual objects is important. Spotting planes at air-traffic control centers is an example, as is spotting guns at airport security checkpoints. Redundancy gains appear when two targets are present, not just one. When two targets are present, detection times are usually shorter than when only one target is present.

To explain redundancy gain from the perspective of the jungle principle, you might be tempted to say that redundant targets form a kind of wrestling tag team. They gang up on their opponents, joining forces to quash the other targets' aspirations. That's one possible model, or one possible metaphor for a model that could be expressed with greater precision. Unfortunately for this model, it turns out that when it's compared to another model that does not use inhibition, the inhibition-free model does better.

The relevant research was done by Rolf Ulrich of Tubingen University (in Germany) and Jeff Miller of Otago University (in New Zealand). They showed that an inhibitory account doesn't accurately predict redundancy gain, whereas an inhibition-free "horse-race" model does.[31] Their idea was that each target's "horse" races to the finish as quickly as possible at a rate that's independent of the other target. Redundancy gain, they showed, could be understood simply by recognizing that when there are two horses, the chance that either one finishes below some short time is higher than when there is only one horse. No "warfare" is needed.

What's the larger point? As I said earlier in this section, not all RT effects need to be ascribed to competition. By extension, it would be a mistake to say that all phenomena that seem to embody competition or inhibition necessarily do. Sometimes, activation alone suffices, as when all the horses in a race get as activated as they can and run as quickly as they can. The more horses there are, the greater the chance that one of them reaches the finish line within a given period. This view doesn't deny competition, but it indicates that inhibition needn't always be invoked.[32]

Toward a General Theory for RTs

Is there a problem with embracing an activation-only model for some tasks while embracing an activation-plus-inhibition model for others? I don't think so. Redundancy gain arises when multiple targets are available for inspection. The other phenomena I've discussed are ones in which only one target was visible at a time and the other possible targets either didn't light up (in the case of lights atop buttons) or lit up only metaphorically, in the participant's mind. This difference in procedure helps explain the difference in outcomes.

A second reason not to be concerned about the difference in the results is that in all the cases I've considered, competition appeared to be the driving force behind the observed empirical effects. Whether in the search for a target in memory or in the search for a target in a display, the factor that emerged was rivalry among relevant elements. If the elements compete by racing against each other or inhibiting each other, that difference doesn't really matter from the perspective of establishing the broader principle of interest, which is that it's a jungle in there.

Third and finally, it turns out that the most successful recent attempt at theorizing about all RT data relies heavily on competition. This fact is remarkable considering that the most successful theory of attention was competition-based as well. Recall that I ended the last chapter by saying that the most successful, all-encompassing theory of attention was the biased competition theory of attention of Robert Desimone and John Duncan.[33] As we approach the end of this chapter on RTs, I can again point to a competition-based theory as the one that seems to provide the best overall account of the phenomena to be explained.

The theory to which I refer was advanced by Marius Usher and James McClelland.[34] I won't review their theory here because doing so would plunge us into more technical detail than is needed. Suffice it to say that Usher and McClelland's theory—the *leaky competing accumulator* model—is similar in spirit to what I've argued in this chapter. The main claim is that internal elements vie for selection and accumulate activation depending on how much evidence comes in for them, though the activation can leak, as would be expected for a biological system that has imperfect storage. The sweep of the theory is impressive, as is the precision of its predictions vis-à-vis obtained results.

Usher and McClelland's paper doesn't refer to jungles *per se*, but their claims are consistent with the jungle view. What I should add, given my tremendous respect for these authors (especially McClelland, who is an eminent researcher in cognitive psychology), is that the broad, discursive picture I have offered here is consistent with the model that McClelland and Usher introduced. Such consistency is hardly coincidental.[35]

6

Look Out!

You can find jungles in the ocean as well as on land. If you swim in one of these aquatic arenas, you'd better watch your back, not to mention your front, sides, top, and bottom. If you're a horseshoe crab trying to survive in such a wet world, you need to detect looming predators. An attacker from above could land you on its dinner plate.

Why do I refer to horseshoe crabs at the start of this chapter on perception, for that's what this chapter's about? The reason is that one of the most important principles concerning the neural basis for perception came from research on horseshoe crabs. The two biologists who conducted their research on these invertebrates won a Nobel Prize for their work.[1]

The feature of horseshoe crabs that attracted the researchers to these creatures was what attracts many people to creatures they find enchanting: their eyes. In the case of horseshoe crabs, the creatures' eyes aren't particularly beautiful, at least to us humans. Instead, the eyes are plentiful. Horseshoe crabs have slews of tiny, light-sensitive receptors atop their heads. These ensembles of mini-eyes are like the photoreceptors of mammalian retinas, but they're much larger and more accessible, making them attractive for study by physiologists.

The two physiologists who studied vision in the horseshoe crab reasoned that the way this creature's light-sensitive organs process light might shed light on the way human photoreceptors work. In taking this approach, the scientists gave a thumbs-up to a rule-of-thumb among biologists: Nature's solutions to physical problems get replicated in different species. What works for one species tends to work for others. This principle is congenial with Darwin's theory of natural selection.

Pursuing this line of thinking, the researchers used electrodes to record from the horseshoe crab's photoreceptors while the scientists projected different light patterns onto the receptors. What the scientists found was surprising. There was more neural activity for photoreceptors in the light than in the dark, as expected, but there was also an exaggerated response at the edges, which was more surprising. Where light and dark met, the response of the photoreceptors was especially strong.

Hypersensitivity to edges makes sense in hindsight. An edge can signal the boundary of a solid object, such as a hungry shark hovering above. The midsection of a dark or light area carries less information.

Being aware of life-threatening changes in the environment is one reason to speak of the visual system of the horseshoe crab, but it's not the only one. This creature's visual system also shows that it's a jungle in there as far as vision is concerned, and here's why.

The horseshoe crab's photoreceptors compete for access to neural units beneath them—to *ganglion* cells, as they're called. Each photoreceptor sends excitatory signals to the ganglion cell below. At the same time, each photoreceptor sends inhibitory signals to the ganglion cell to either side. The strength of these signals is proportional to the light energy the photoreceptor receives. The output of each ganglion cell is proportional to the sum of its inputs. Some of the inputs are positive, coming from the "friendly" photoreceptor just above. The other inputs are negative, coming from nearby, "unfriendly" photoreceptors. The exaggerated response of the ganglion cells near the shadow's edge reflects the differences between the positive and negative inputs.

The tendency of neurons to inhibit neurons they adjoin is called *lateral inhibition*. The discovery of lateral inhibition proved to be enormously important in neuroscience because it revealed how the interplay of neurons in simple circuits could give rise to adaptive and often surprising results, such as hypersensitivity to edges.

Inspired by the discovery of lateral inhibition, many neuroscientists embarked on the study of neural circuits. They appreciated that neural wiring diagrams, using lateral inhibition and other interactions, could underlie the workings of the brain.

The study of neural circuits has emerged as one of the most exciting frontiers of science. That said, my interest here is less on the details of the circuits than in the larger principle they embody—that the brain follows a neural dialectic, a balance of competition and cooperation from which mental and behavioral phenomena emerge.

Center-Surround Inhibition

Is the balance of neural cooperation and competition peculiar to the visual system of horseshoe crabs? Consider another phenomenon known as *center-surround inhibition*. This phenomenon also reflects the excitatory-inhibitory drama sketched above, but it is also evident in mammals, including people.

If you work in a neurophysiology lab and cast a spot of light on the eye of a cat or other mammal, the neural responses you can record from the animal's retinal ganglion cells are similar to those picked up from the horseshoe crab's ganglion cells. Ganglion cells called "on-center" cells are excited by light cast directly *on* them. But they're also excited by the relative *lack* of light cast *around* them. By contrast, ganglion cells called "off-center" cells are excited by the relative *lack* of light cast directly on them, and also by the presence of light cast in surrounding areas. The underlying mechanism in both cases is lateral inhibition.

Of what functional consequence are these two sorts of cells—these "rooster" cells that wake up to light and are turned on when their neighbors find themselves in the dark (the on-center cells), and their "vampire" cousins that revel in darkness and are turned on when their neighbors find themselves in the spotlight (the off-center cells)?

Having on-center cells and off-center cells promotes edge detection, which is no less important for landlubbers than for crabs and other aqua-dwellers. Edges help you identify objects and locate their boundaries. If you're unsure of the importance of edge detection for vision, ask any computer scientist who works on robot vision whether he or she thinks edges are important. The roboticist will tell you that without edges, it would be well-nigh impossible to recognize objects. Computer-vision systems designed to identify objects often exploit on-center and off-center units to detect object edges.

Is there evidence that on-center cells and off-center have observable consequences for visual experience, or are the consequences of these cells seen only in neurophysiology labs? It turns out that the effects of on-center cells and off-center cells can be observed in the comfort of your home.

Consider Mach bands, discovered by the Austrian physicist, Ernst Mach, who, among other things, was the first person to measure the speed of sound. Mach bands are illusory, but when you first see them, it's hard to believe they are (Figure 6).[2]

The physical display used to show Mach bands has adjacent regions that get progressively darker. Figure 6 shows a series of such regions. Wherever the regions touch, you may see a bright region on the dark side and a darker region on the brighter side. This may cause you to see depth. When you look at the image in Figure 6, you may see ridges at the boundaries.

This illusion is created by the visual system's reliance on lateral inhibition. On-center cells are bombarded by inputs that cause them to get excited in the light, causing you to see a white band. Off-center cells, meanwhile, are bombarded by inputs that cause them to get excited in the dark, causing you to see a dark band. Neither of these bands is actually present. They are figments of

FIGURE 6. Mach bands.

your imagination, as it were, or, more specifically, of the lateral inhibition in your visual system.

You can experience a similar visual illusion by looking at an image made up of black tiles with narrow white borders (Figure 7).[3] If you look at such an image, you will probably see gray squares at the intersections of the white boundaries. These gray squares are not present in the display. They are created by you, or by neural interactions in your visual system. Cells turned on by the large dark regions send massive excitatory inputs to on-center cells as well as massive inhibitory inputs to off-center cells. Meanwhile, the on-center cells are excited by the bright strips, and the off-center cells are inhibited by those same bright strips. The combined output of the on-center cells and the off-center cells is a weighted sum of the outputs of the two kinds of cells. The perceptual consequence is a shade of gray that, like Mach bands, reflects lateral inhibition.[4]

Color Aftereffects

Another perceptual consequence of "inner jungleism" is one that may be so startling you may break out in a sweat when you read this section. I confess

FIGURE 7. The grid illusion.

I was really quite shaken up when I learned what I'm about to tell you, so be prepared.

Presumably, you believe the world has color. Consider the following verse, however, which I composed for this occasion:

Roses are red,
Violets are blue,
Grass is green,
But all through you.

The world, it turns out, has no color! Nothing inherent in the wavelengths of light produces the colors we see.

You may not believe this. "What's that you're saying?" you may exclaim. "Are you color blind?" Fortunately, I do see color. I don't suffer from color blindness, though as a male I'm statistically more likely than females to have this syndrome. In saying the world is colorless, I mean that color is an emergent feature of brain activity. Only by virtue of the internal pulls and pushes of neural friends and foes do we see the colors we do.

The colors we see are due to three teams of neural elements in the retina. Some are activated by the wavelengths of light we call "red" (long wavelengths), some are activated by the wavelengths of light we call "green" (medium wavelengths), and some are activated by the wavelengths of light we call "blue" (short wavelengths). The interactions among these three elements produce all the colors we see. Especially important for the theme of this book, the interactions reflect cooperation among members of the same retinal team, as well as competition among members of opposing retinal teams.

Understanding color perception in its full form requires an *opponent-process* model of color perception. This model was first proposed by a nineteenth-century physiologist named Ewald Hering and was later refined by two vision scientists, Leo Hurvich and Dorothea Jameson, who spent most of their careers at the University of Pennsylvania.[5] The main idea of the opponent-process model is that neurons responding to different dimensions of visual input at levels higher than the retina send excitatory signals to their friends and inhibitory signals to their enemies. The dimensions of the opponent processes turn out to be red-green, blue-yellow, and black-white. These dimensions refer to the avenues of animosity. Red and green are opponents, blue and yellow are opponents, and black and white are opponents.

Having a model like this explains the so-called negative aftereffect of color. Stare at a green field for a while and then look at a white field. The white field will appear to be a shade of red. If you do the exercise the other way around, you will get the opposite result. If you stare at a red field for a while and then look at the same white field, it will appear to be a shade of green.

This is a strange outcome if you think about it. It's surprising that after seeing one color for a long time, you should see some other color. It's also surprising that the color you see on a chromatically neutral surface (a white sheet of paper, for example) after prolonged exposure to a chromatic hue such as red or green is some *other* particular color (red following green, or green following red).

What accounts for this? If one color is present for a long time, neural receptors for that color undergo a change due to their extended stimulation. It would be convenient to say that the receptors become fatigued, but that's a bit of an oversimplification. Among other things, saying that receptors get tuckered out doesn't explain why you continue to see a color as long as it's present. You'd expect the color to disappear if the receptors simply became exhausted. Claiming that receptors simply get tired also doesn't explain why you see a complementary color when the first, long-exposed color is replaced by a chromatically neutral stimulus.

So what actually happens? For present purposes, it suffices to say that there's a duel between receptors for one color and receptors for the color's opponent. If the receptors for green get stimulated for a long time, their ability to inhibit their opponents reaches some steady, low level. Then, when the green receptors get no more visual excitation, they stop inhibiting their red opponents. The perceptual result is perceived redness (or a tint thereof).

A number of other visual phenomena are explained by the opponent-process theory of color vision. I won't review them here because this book is meant just to give a taste of various mental and behavioral phenomena and the internal cooperation and competition that yield them. Nevertheless, I do want to mention that direct evidence has been obtained for the kinds of color receptors assumed in the opponent-process theory. That evidence has been obtained through physiological recordings similar to the ones taken in the study with which this chapter began—where recordings were taken from visual-processing cells of the horseshoe crab. The color-receptor studies were done in mammalian visual systems.[6]

Still more support for the understanding of color perception comes from color blindness, a topic I mentioned briefly. In some individuals, receptors for particular wavelengths are missing due to genetic mutations. These mutations happen to be sex-linked. In humans, the inability to see some colors is more common in males than in females. The way color blindness is tested is to determine whether an individual suspected of color blindness misses objects differing from other objects with respect to hue alone. Failing to notice those objects provides the telltale sign that receptors for that hue are missing. Which colors can and can't be seen by color-blind individuals, plus the negative aftereffects of color they do or don't experience, fit with the model of color perception sketched above, an opponent-process model that, as its name implies, relies on inner competition (and cooperation, too).[7]

Motion Aftereffects

In the last section, you saw that one form of evidence for opponent processes in color perception is the negative aftereffect of color. Because I adduced this phenomenon as a source of evidence for "inner jungleism," it would be useful to know that analogous phenomena exist for other aspects of perception. In this connection, consider the so-called negative aftereffect of motion. To a first approximation, this is the motion equivalent of the negative aftereffect of color.

To understand the negative aftereffect of motion, suppose you're in a tranquil place. Instead of dodging dangerous dogs or evading electrifying eels, you take a break. You sit down beside a peaceful waterfall, watching its languid tendrils descend from the brook above. You sigh. You relax. You enjoy the gentle summer breeze. At long last you've found a place where you can relax.

After watching the waterfall for a while, you look past it, glancing non-chalantly at the hill beyond, expecting to take in another calm vista. But the sight you behold baffles you. The slope beyond the stream seems to stream upward! It does so for several seconds. No earthquake has occurred. No gigantic UFO, à la *Close Encounters of the Third Kind*, has floated above, lifting the hillside to take it home for study.[8]

What accounts for this *waterfall illusion*, as it's called? The basis for the effect is similar to the one that produces color negative effects. Neural elements specially tuned to an aspect of visual stimulation—downward motion rather than specific hues—get excited, but because they're excited for a long time, their responsiveness declines. The continual signaling of downward motion ceases to be informative, so the outputs of the relevant cells diminish or are discounted by other neural subsystems. The result is that neural pools sensitive to motion in other directions contribute more to the global visual experience than they otherwise would. Neural pools for rightward and leftward motion continue to fire, but they oppose each another and their outputs cancel, but neural pools for upward motion get to have a much stronger voice than they normally would. As a result, there is an illusion of upward motion, a result that would be expected only if the contribution of the up-motion population carried more weight than the contribution of the down-motion population.[9]

Motion aftereffects are not limited to linear motion. They also arise after prolonged observation of rotary motion. Suppose you watch a swirling spiral that seems to move away from you. Later, when you look at a stationary object, it will seem to approach you. The opposite outcome occurs if you watch a swirling spiral that seems to move toward you and then you look at a stationary object. That stationary object will seem to recede.[10]

The neural dynamics of such effects are similar to the opponent processes for up and down motion. Cells for approach "bounce back" when cells for recession have fired for a long time and then stop being supported by external inputs. Similarly, cells for recession recover when cells for approach have been activated for a long time and then get no support from the external world.[11]

Perceptual Inference

In the waterfall illusion, you have the sense of upward motion, but you can tell the hill you're looking at isn't really rising. You have no basis for believing the hill's on the rise, and you have plenty of basis for believing it's staying put. Your gaze angle doesn't increase as you look at the cliff beyond the stream. Your head doesn't tilt up more between successive glances at the slope. You don't feel the ground rumbling before your feet or see rocks and pebbles sliding down the hill as they would if the earth were heaving.

Inference lets you know that motion hasn't occurred, but in other situations, inference lets you know that motion *has* occurred. A familiar example is noticing that the minute hand on an analog clock is not where it was before. You may not see the minute hand move, but you can infer that it must have because it's not where it was before.

Why am I speaking of inference? What does inference have to do with perception? Should inference be taken seriously as a factor in perceptual experience? How does perceptual inference, if there is such a thing, relate to the larger claim that it's a jungle in there?

Drawing inferences about visually sampled events entails drawing conclusions based on more information than first meets the eye. If you infer that a man is unmarried because he's a Roman Catholic priest, you've reached a point you weren't at initially. You got there without being told the priest is a bachelor.

The ability to draw inferences is what the Greek philosopher Aristotle pointed to when he drew attention to logic as a way of learning. Via logic, Aristotle argued, you can know more than you would from data alone. If Aristotle had commented on mechanical clock-watching, he would have said that you can infer from a clock that time has passed, because the clock's minute hand occupies a different position that it did a while back.

Inferring that a clock's hand has moved is one way of perceiving motion, but it's not the only way. The other is perceiving motion directly. If an object passes from one place to another before your eyes at a sufficiently high rate, its passage through space and time are immediately apparent.

Returning now to the example of the mysteriously rising hill, you can decide that the hill doesn't rise after watching a stream cascade downward because you don't get other information to support the hill-rising inference. By contrast, you *can* decide that the water is really descending because you can see bits of debris being washed down the waterfall, you can hear the water falling, you can stick your hand into the stream and feel the water running through your fingers, or you can ford the stream at the base of the waterfall and feel the water race around your toes.

The idea that perception relies on inference was advanced by an intellectual giant of nineteenth-century science, Herman von Helmholtz (1821–1894). Helmholtz invented the ophthalmoscope, the device used by doctors to view the inside of the eye. As mentioned in the last chapter, he also measured the speed of nerve conduction.[12]

Helmholtz argued that inference helps perception. He also suggested that perceptual inference is largely unconscious. In saying this, he pointed to cognitive processes beneath conscious awareness, much as Freud did, but Helmholtz's suggestion is less well known, perhaps because the subject of seeing is less sexy than the subject of sex. Helmholtz suggested that perception entails bringing together, without awareness, cues that enable us to make the best guesses we can about what's in the external environment.

The Ames Room

To help Helmholtz think through the nature of such perceptual detective work, he contemplated illusions such as the ones discussed here. Consider another illusion associated with a special room built years after Helmholtz's passing. The room was built by an American ophthalmologist named Adelbert Ames Jr.[13] The design of the room was meant to trick you. It looked, for all intents and purposes, like a perfectly ordinary room, but it was far from ordinary. Whereas a normal room is rectangular (or square), this room was trapezoidal. Owing to its design, if you peered into the room and saw two people of objectively equal size standing in it (one in the front and one in the back), one person would appear gigantic compared to the other. If the two individuals traded places, the one who looked large before would now look tiny, and vice versa.

The basis for the illusion is that the optical cues from the room indicate that the person who is farther away is closer than he or she really is. To make sense of the apparently greater proximity of that individual, the brain "says" in effect, "If the individual is only so high when he or she is so close, then he or she must be extremely short."

Cues like those used for the Ames room are exploited by artists to convey the impression that some depicted objects are farther away than others. This is a neat trick considering that the objects shown in drawings and paintings lie on flat planes. That the trick is of use to you in your daily life is shown by the fact that, at least to a first approximation, the retinas of your eyes are flat planes too.

The way you see depth is by relying, in part, on the visual cues just mentioned, which are monocular (one-eye) cues to depth. There are also *binocular* (two-eye) depth cues. The main binocular cue to depth is the disparity between the retinal projections of objects on your two retinas. The fact that you have two eyes not only provides you with cues to depth based on retinal disparity. Your two-eyedness also provides you with a whole raft of fascinating phenomena subsumed under the rubric of *binocular rivalry*. Rivalry is, of course, another word for competition. Inputs from your two eyes converge to let you see. Along the way, however, there is fierce antagonism.[14] Seeing as you do is due to the pushes and pulls of neural gnomes vying for a piece of the visual action.

Perceiving More Than Is There

Scientists who are attracted to Helmholtz's perspective have sought to further his inferential approach to perception.[15] It is worth listing a few examples of perceptual phenomena that convey the value of this approach because they illustrate how putative agents in the brain can exert considerable influence on perceptual experience.

Focus first on seeing more than is there. One example is related to the *blind spot*. It turns out that one part of your retina has no photoreceptors. This is the part of your retina where your optic nerve leaves your eye and courses inward toward your brain. Oddly, your optic nerve—the nerve that carries signals from your photoreceptors to your brain—doesn't begin *behind* your retina and travel back to your brain. Instead, it begins *in front of* your retina and then makes a U-turn, passing back through the retina toward structures within your brain. Because there are no photoreceptors where the optic nerve passes, there is literally no way to see whatever light might be projected there. Nevertheless, you have no awareness of such invisibility.

You can demonstrate the blind spot for yourself by stretching your arm out before you and holding your thumb up while staring at it with one eye open. As you slowly vary the angle of your outstretched arm, you'll notice that your thumb vanishes at some critical angle. When this visual amputation occurs, the image of your thumb is cast on the part of the retina where your optic nerve passes through your retina. The fact that you normally don't experience this blind spot indicates that your brain "fills in" the hole. Neural elements receiving inputs in the areas surrounding the blind spot extend their influence to the area where no visual input is received. The no-input area remains vulnerable to whatever its visually powerful neighbors signal. The result is seeing more than is there, as would be expected from massive cooperation and competition among neural elements involved in visual processing.[16]

Now consider nother exmple of seeing more thn's there. This is illustrted in the wy this prgrph is written. You probbly hve little trouble reding this. Your brin fills in the missing informtion though the first letter of the lphbet hs been removed.

This next paragraph—the one you're now reading—returns to proper spelling, and illustrates yet another example filling in. If you're focusing on the meaning this paragraph, you probably don't have much trouble reading it. You may not even notice that anything's wrong with it, but something is.

What was wrong with the last paragraph? You may have to go back to check. The answer is that I removed the word "of" twice. Quite possibly, you noticed only one the missing ofs. To keep up the mischief, I deleted yet another "of" just now, one sentence ago. Did you notice? If you didn't and if you had no trouble understanding the text, that's because your brain filled in the missing information. In terms of the metaphor running through this book—the metaphor of little demons seeking evidence for their favorite input—it wasn't critical that the letters "o" and "f" appeared. The contexts supporting "of" allowed their neural representatives to get so excited that they yelled loudly enough for you to be fooled into thinking the "ofs" were there.

This phenomenon is so robust that writers must be on guard for it. Otherwise, they fall prey to the *proofreader's error*, the tendency to miss textual mistakes because of expectations (conscious or unconscious) about what should appear. The proofreader's error can be maddening. You may be as vigilant as possible when you check for typos, but they escape your notice, as if there's a conspiracy in your head not to notice those bloopers. There *is* such a conspiracy! Often, it's only when you come back to text you've worked on for a long time and read it "with fresh eyes" that you notice mistakes you missed before. The reason why there's a higher chance of spotting errors later is that the dynamics of the inner ruckus have settled down.[17]

Filling in linguistic information isn't limited to reading. It also occurs in listening. You rarely hear speech in perfectly pristine acoustic conditions, with each syllable being pronounced with Shakespearean clarity. Imagine a short-order cook yelling to his helper, "Gimme a nummer 8!" The helper gets the message in the midst of clattering dishes, clanging spatulas, sizzling bacon, and whistling kettles. If some part of the message is masked by extraneous noise, it doesn't matter. The helper fills in the missing information.

The ability to fill in missing speech sounds is called the *phoneme restoration* effect. It's the auditory analogue of the proofreader's error. Like the proofreader's error, the phonemic restoration effect is clearest when the material that is removed is highly predictable.[18]

There are many other examples of perceiving more than is there. Imagine having a conversation with someone who happily chews bubblegum while speaking to you. At some point, your chewy chum blows a big bubble. The bubble conceals much of her face. Do you think the person's mouth and nose have vanished? Of course not. Your brain fills in the missing parts.[19]

The same thing happens if you see someone with his hand in his pocket. You don't see an arm ending in a stump. If the person pulled his arm from his pocket and no hand emerged, you'd be astonished. Only if you had reason to expect a lost hand would you be unsurprised by its absence.

A final example is less visually arresting. (Not all visual phenomena need to dazzle, by the way; part of doing science is learning to recognize that small, humble things are significant.) Here's the example. Are you ready? A child sees her dad pass behind a tree. That's the end of the demonstration.

The point of this humble example is that though the image of the dad is momentarily interrupted, parts of him being hidden by the trunk, the child doesn't see parts of her dad fade away and then come together again. What she sees is a coherent person. This is so unremarkable that it takes a moment to appreciate the sophistication permitting it.

Phenomena like these reflect *top-down* processing. The term refers to high-level interpretations biasing perception, so perception is not just dictated by immediate sensory data—*bottom-up* processing—but is also shaped by expectations.[20] A child expects to see her dad reappear after he, or part of him, momentarily vanishes behind a tree.

Using the terms top-down and bottom-up processing doesn't fully illuminate the mechanisms they rely on, or at least leaves many questions unanswered. I've sketched a way these mechanisms might work—namely, through cooperation and competition among relevant neural representatives. A sketch is just that, however—merely an outline. In science, it's useful to have sketches or overarching general conceptions of the ways systems work. Ultimately, though, it's important to work out the details. Toward that aim, the next section is concerned with a phenomenon that reflects top-down and bottom-up processing in a way that has been explained in specific mechanistic terms. As it happens, the model comports with the theme of this book and, indeed, helped inspire it.

The Word Superiority Effect

The phenomenon I'll tell you about now is called the *word superiority* effect.[21] The procedure used to demonstrate the effect works like this. In one condition, participants (university students, typically) are shown a single letter, such as *d* or *k*, which is immediately covered by a visual mask, such as #$*@. Two letters are shown afterward until the participant indicates which letter matched the letter he or she thinks was shown before, either the *d* or the *k*. People are pretty good at this. There is, after all, just one letter to perceive initially.

In another condition, the same participant is shown not one letter but four. In some cases, the four letters form a word. As in the one-letter case, the letters are masked and then the participant is shown two letters that remain on the screen until s/he indicates which letter appeared before. The test letter is shown at the same serial position as the letter whose identity is being queried, so, as in the one-letter task, there is no uncertainty about where the test letter appeared. Participants do worse in the four-letter condition than in the one-letter condition, which is not surprising since there were, after all, four letters, not just one.

The most surprising outcome of this experiment is that participants do worse in the four-letter condition than in the one-letter condition only when the four letters form a non-word. When the four letters form a *word*, participants actually do *better* than when they're presented with a single letter. So if the four letters form "work," participants do better at recognizing the *k* than if the original stimulus was just the letter *k*.

How can you explain this remarkable *word superiority* effect? Somehow the fact that the four letters form a word gives the letter identification process a leg up. A model that explains this outcome looks unruly, like a tangle of vines that you'd find in a jungle (Figure 8). The model looks so wild, so out of control, that you might wonder whether the cognitive psychologists who proposed it were in command of their senses. I assure you they were. What they realized was that out of the seeming chaos came a way of explaining the word superiority effect.[22]

According to the model, there are units tuned to particular aspects of experience—to line segments oriented in various ways, to letters, and to groups of letters comprising words. The units excite their friends (units with which they're consistent) and inhibit their enemies (units with which they're inconsistent). So a unit that's tuned to a diagonal line tends to excite an *A* unit or a *K* unit, but tends to inhibit a *G* unit or an *S* unit. A unit that's tuned to the letter *A* tends to excite word units containing that letter (words like ABLE, TRAP, TAKE, and CART) but tends to inhibit word units that don't contain that letter (words like TRIP and TIME). The same dynamic—consistent units exciting each other and inconsistent units inhibiting each other—is expressed throughout the network.

The network I've described is typically shown with three levels—a feature level, a letter level, and a word level—but there are no levels as such in the

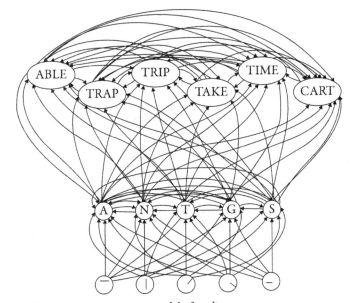

FIGURE 8. The interactive activation model of reading.

network. It's just a matter of convenience to show word units above letter units and letter units above feature units. The levels are implicit in the connections of the units. Crucially, and happily from the point of view of making as few assumptions as possible (always a tenet of good science), the interplay of units is no different within or between putative levels.

How does the model explain the word superiority effect? The dynamics of the model encourage constituents of words for which there is some evidence and discourages constituents of words for which there is no evidence. The constituents in turn encourage the words of which they're a part and discourage the words of which they're *not* a part. The constituents—the letters and the features they contain—also excite and inhibit each other depending on the history of their partnerships. Single letters have more diffuse partnerships than do entire words. Consequently, letters have a lower likelihood of being identified when presented alone than when presented with other letters in established words.

The model as a whole is called the *interactive activation* model of word perception. It provides a quantitatively confirmed account of the word superiority effect and other phenomena in reading. Its success attests to the promise of the general approach it embodies, which is that there are patterns of connectivity among neural elements whose mutual excitation and inhibition can account for key aspects of perception, including surprising results from perceptual research.

Features

You weren't born being able to read, so the neural network you use to do so is shaped over the course of development. So far, I've said relatively little about the role of development in this book, but this is a good place to say something about it, and more will be said in later chapters.

Consider how Darwin's ideas may hold promise for the development of perception. A useful place to start is with "young pirates," those children who wear eye patches for prolonged periods to help them see.[23] The rationale for this therapeutic procedure is to promote normal visual development in the unpatched eye. Covering the "good" eye can help the "bad" eye improve.

Why do doctors recommend this seemingly paradoxical intervention? In children for whom the treatment is prescribed, the poorer vision of the "bad eye" may be due to a problem with moving that eye. The eye-movement difficulty may make it difficult for the two eyes to focus on the same object simultaneously, forcing the brain to choose between the two eyes' inputs.

People who have difficulty bringing their eyes into alignment are said to have *strabismus*. In one form of strabismus, the bad eye points inward—toward the body midline. In another form, the bad eye points outward—away from the body midline. Having one eye point in a different direction than the other causes the brain to get two images rather than one. This situation forces a choice between the images—a choice that is normally unnecessary. If the choice consistently favors one eye, the brain's ability to process visual inputs from the other eye may gradually deteriorate to the point where whatever sight was available in that not-so-good eye gets even worse, to the point, in the worst-case scenario, that that eye goes blind.

The mechanisms behind these changes were elucidated by the two neurophysiologists, David Hubel and Torsten Wiesel, whose discovery of visual feature detectors was covered in Chapter 3. I'll expand on it here, both by considering visual development and, before that, by considering the role of visual feature detectors in visual perception.[24]

Recall from Chapter 3 that Hubel and Wiesel found that single cells in an area of the adult cats' brain (area V1) are tuned to particular stimuli. As discussed earlier, some of these cells are tuned to dark vertical lines standing against a light background, other cells are tuned to light vertical lines standing against a dark background, other cells are tuned to dark lines moving along a 45-degree axis, still other cells are tuned to dark lines moving along a 135-degree axis, and so on. Because the stimuli that activated the cells were simple, Hubel and Wiesel referred to these cells as *simple* feature detectors.

Hubel and Wiesel also found cells that responded to more complex ensembles of features, and they called those cells *complex* feature detectors. Hubel and Wiesel also found cells tuned to still more complicated stimulus ensembles, which they called *hyper-complex* cells.

Hubel and Wiesel were careful not to make claims about how simple, complex, and hyper-complex cells contribute to visual perception. But it was hard for others to resist suggesting that feature detectors might activate each other in such a way that their combined activity specifies real-world objects and scenes. According to this hypothesis, you can recognize a yellow Volkswagen, say, because the features for that vehicle activate relevant detectors in your brain.

This hypothesis runs into problems, however, at least if you insist that for a yellow Volkswagen to be recognized, the brain needs a yellow-Volkswagen detector.[25] The hypothesis isn't tenable because yellow Volkswagens, like virtually all objects, appear in infinitely many ways. If you needed a different yellow-Volkswagen detector for every possible yellow-Volkswagen stimulus, you'd be in trouble. In addition, if your recognition of a yellow Volkswagen depended on the firing of a yellow-Volkswagen detector, you'd have serious difficulty if that detector happened to die. "What's that lemon-like object approaching me at high speed here on the Autobahn?" you might ask if your one-and-only cell for recognizing yellow Volkswagens became dysfunctional. Putting all your processing eggs in one basket (in one neuron) is not a good idea. More to the point, since we want to eschew top-top design in the Darwinian scheme of things, it's not a design that's likely to survive for very long.

If you say that single high-level feature detectors are problematic for a theory of perception, you needn't conclude that feature detectors are useless. Sensitivity to stimulus features is crucial for perception. One way we know this is that camouflage is feature-based. The more features a target shares with its background, the harder the target is to spot. This is true for detection of soldiers in military theaters and, just as much, for detection of letters among distracters. It's much harder to find a capital *K* among a sea of *X*s, *A*s, and *H*s than among a sea of *C*s, *O*s, and *Q*s. When a *K* is in the midst of *X*s, *A*s, and *H*s, the time to find the *K* increases with the number of distracters, but when a *K* is in the midst of *C*s, *O*s, and *Q*s, the time to find the letter hardly depends on the number of distracters. The *K* just pops out from the display.[26]

When visual stimuli are shown very briefly and then are masked by other stimuli, the features may mis-combine. If you're shown a red circle and a blue triangle, for example, and these stimuli are quickly covered by a mask (a bunch of random symbols or hash marks), you may mistakenly think you saw a red triangle and a blue circle. Such illusory conjunctions are expected if the features of the stimuli are somehow extracted from the raw stimulus and then are reassembled. Reassembling the features in the wrong way can lead to illusory conjunctions.[27]

The mistaken joining of features can occur in the everyday environment. If you find yourself in a dark alley and witness a stabbing, you may mistakenly believe that the person wielding the knife was a guy wearing a red beret. If at the crime scene there was actually a guy wearing a red *baseball cap* and another guy wearing a *blue* beret, the illusory conjunction of red and beret could land the wrong guy in jail.

Visual confusions like these are explained by saying that neural representatives of perceptual features get activated by the appearance of the features to which they're tuned. Once this activation occurs, a contest follows. Features jointly activate other neural representatives to which they belong while inhibiting other neural representatives to which they don't belong. The higher-level representatives also activate the features feeding them and inhibit the lower-level representatives that don't. Illusory conjunctions and the other phenomena just reviewed can arise from those dynamics.

How do these results relate back to the young pirates described at the start of this section? Think back to Hubel and Wiesel, who wanted to know how feature detectors develop. They tested the hypothesis that feature detectors get strengthened if the features are supported by environmental input or get weakened otherwise. To study the fates of feature detectors, Hubel and Wiesel thought the effects of experience might be especially pronounced in young animals. They also thought that a convenient way to study the role of experience on perception might be to limit sight to just one eye.

To pursue these ideas, they sutured one of the eyelids of their kitten subjects so the kittens received patterned visual input only through the exposed eye.[28] Before the eyelids were sutured, the kittens' visual cortex cells were equally sensitive to visual input from either eye. A given cell that was tuned to a visual stimulus entering the *left* eye, say, was, on average, just as sensitive as any given cell tuned to a comparable visual stimulus entering the *right* eye.

After suturing, things changed. A given cell that was initially tuned to visual input from the eye that was sutured became less sensitive to visual input to that eye. This was shown in tests where the eye that was shut was briefly exposed to visual stimuli. Many of the cells that were originally sensitive to visual input to the previously open eye lost their sensitivity. Meanwhile, those same cells became increasingly sensitive to visual input to the *other* eye, the one that stayed open.

What do these results reveal? They show that it's a jungle in there. Inputs from the eye that remained open always "wanted" to connect with neurons that, initially, were mainly connected with the other eye. But without consistent input from the other eye (the eye whose lid was sutured in the experiment), those neurons became easy targets for inputs from the open eye.

Now you know why young pirates inhabit daycare centers. Kids with medically prescribed eye patches need help strengthening sight in their "weak" eyes. The strengthening can be achieved by pursuing the counterintuitive practice of restricting input from the stronger eye. When the stronger eye no longer dominates because it fails to receive visual stimulation, the weaker eye has a chance to strengthen its connections within the brain.[29]

A further aspect of the eye-patch procedure bears mentioning. This is the *critical period* effect. Within a certain time frame, the possibility of changing neural connectivity is high, but later it declines. One way to understand the critical period effect is to say that beyond some point in development, cooperation exceeds competition. Neural birds of a feather stick together so strongly that it's hard to pull them apart. Owing to the critical period effect for vision, the pirates I've told you about are young rather than old. Older individuals are less likely to benefit from visual retraining.[30]

Late Development of Depth Perception

Just how critical is the critical period? It would be a mistake to conclude from the last section that the critical period is all-or-none. A safer conclusion is that the critical period is statistical. The chance of gaining or regaining use of an eye is higher during the critical period than afterward, but that doesn't imply that the chance of regaining use of an eye drops to zero.

A demonstration of this more encouraging outcome came from a professor of neuroscience at Mount Holyoke College in South Hadley, Massachusetts: Susan Barry. Barry was cross-eyed as a child. Because of the misalignment of her eyes, the images coming from her left and right eyes failed to fuse in the normal way. As a result, her depth perception was askew.[31]

Recall from earlier in this chapter that retinal disparity provides a cue to depth. In fact, retinal disparity is the main binocular depth cue. The slight offset of images cast on the left and right retinas by objects at different distances supplies observers with the most reliable source of visual information about how far away objects are. In the case of Susan Barry, retinal disparity was always huge, and as a result it didn't provide a reliable cue to depth. As a girl, Susan learned, given this large retinal disparity, to alternate her attention from one eye to the other—a common strategy among cross-eyed people. Given this alternation of attention, she could see with each eye, but with only one eye at a time. Deprived of the usual retinal disparity cues to depth, she saw a flat world.

Classical research in visual neuroscience, such as the research reviewed earlier in this chapter, suggested that individuals like Susan Barry would have no chance of gaining depth perception in adulthood. According to the classical, all-or-none, critical-period view, her neural connections relevant to depth perception would be choked off by the time she reached maturity. But Susan Barry disproved the classical conception.

As an adult, she embarked on a training procedure in which she learned to coordinate her eyes in a new way so she could aim both her eyes at the same place at the same time. What she discovered, as told in her book, *Fixing My Gaze: A Scientist's Journey into Seeing in Three Dimensions*, was that she learned to see in 3D.

Susan Barry's success in this venture proved that neural plasticity allowing for recovery of visual depth perception does not shut down once a putative critical period ends (around the time of puberty). Neural plasticity extends into adulthood.[32]

More on Visual Training

The effects of cooperation and competition on perceptual learning are not limited to inter-ocular communication. They also extend to other aspects of vision, and to other modalities. Within the visual modality, developmental changes similar to those described for the two eyes have been mapped out for sensitivity to visual tilt. The pioneering study was done by two neuro-physiologists at Stanford University whose approach followed logic similar to Hubel and Wiesel's.[33] Instead of suturing single eyelids of kittens, the Stanford researchers restricted the visual inputs to each of their kittens' eyes. The kittens wore special goggles that allowed one eye to see only horizontal lines and the other eye to see only vertical lines.

The result was that the receptive field properties of neurons in the kittens' visual cortices became sensitive to the orientations to which each eye was exposed. If an eye was exposed to vertical lines, neurons with receptive fields for that eye became tuned to vertical lines. If an eye was exposed to horizontal lines, neurons with receptive fields for that eye became tuned to horizontal lines. Thus, the cells' orientation sensitivities changed based on experience.

Effects like these are not limited to long-term learning via selective rearing methods in kittens. They're also demonstrated through perceptual learning studies with people. In one experiment, adults with normal visual acuity judged the offsets of two vertical line segments.[34] One line segment appeared above the other but was shifted slightly to the left or right. The observers' task was to indicate whether the top line segment was to the left or right of the line below. After pressing the associated button, the observers got feedback about the accuracy of their responses. With practice, their visual acuity improved. The offsets the observers could detect got smaller and smaller. The same thing happened if the orientation of the line-segment pairs was horizontal rather than vertical. Now, after indicating whether a left line was higher or lower than a right line, observers were again told whether their decision was correct. The offsets they could detect got smaller and smaller with practice, indicating finer discrimination for line height.

The most interesting outcome came when the participants switched from judgments about vertical offsets to judgments about horizontal offsets, or vice versa. You might think that with practice at judging offsets, people would become experts at offset judging, no matter what the orientation of the stimuli. This is not what happened, however. After observers made judgments about horizontal offsets, they did poorly at making judgments about vertical offsets—worse, in fact, than observers who had never made the same vertical-offset judgments. The same thing happened for observers who first made vertical-offset judgments. They improved on those judgments, but if they switched to horizontal offsets, they did worse than observers who had never made those judgments.

How can you make sense of this outcome? You can infer that perceptual learning can be remarkably specific. It doesn't always have to be, of course. Someone who develops a clear sense of what constitutes a good painting of a *landscape* may become adept at judging the quality of painted *portraits*. But in the case of judging offsets, people develop remarkably specialized perceptual abilities. The reason for this specialization is rooted in the neural basis of these judgments. Neurons get recruited for the specific judgments that are required. As a result, there is greater acuity for that kind of judgment but not others. Other, related judgments may be even become harder to make than usual if their neural territory was co-opted.[35]

Many other studies have been done on perceptual learning, and they, in turn, have demonstrated improved discrimination abilities that are often remarkably restricted. Models that have been developed to account for such changes have invariably resorted to internal competition and cooperation among neural elements coding aspects of the inputs, typically in a redundant fashion. The models have assumed selective pressures causing some connections to get stronger and others to get weaker. As a result, someone who becomes an expert at judging certain kinds of stimuli can be said to house mental creatures that have become adept at responding well to those stimuli. Like creatures in the wild who become specialized for the niches they occupy, specialized neural ensembles develop to cope more expeditiously with some stimuli than others. The stimuli that are handled well are the ones that are regularly encountered. Seldom-encountered stimuli aren't handled so well because few neural teams can claim those stimuli as niches.

These comments are meant to show that the jungle principle applies to perception and perceptual learning. I should mention in closing that I focused on vision in this chapter, but the jungle principle applies equally well to all sensory modalities, at least as far as I know.

7

Move It!

While I was preparing this book, I attended a conference at a bucolic research institute in Bielefeld, Germany—the Zentrum für interdisziplinäre Forschung, also known as the ZiF, or the Center for International Research. The institute is located on the edge of a forest. It's nestled among tall trees, and it fulfills most people's idea of a scholar's paradise. It's lushly carpeted, beautifully furnished with a world-class library, and has a lobby adorned with paintings and sculptures honoring deep thinkers. Scholars at the institute work intently on their books and manuscripts, unfazed, apparently, by the outer jungle.

Even at a place like ZiF, however, just thinking isn't enough. At the end of a scholar's stay there (typically at the end of a sabbatical), he or she is asked to submit a list of accomplishments. "Had deep thoughts" doesn't get lots of credit. "Wrote six journal articles and a book" carries more weight.

I'm telling you this partly to dispel the myth that scholars merely think for a living. They don't. They write grant applications, scramble for book contracts, angle for speaking engagements, and so on. Even the deepest thinkers must communicate their ideas. Being lost in thought does scholars little good—as little good, in fact, as for anyone working in the "real world."

Doing nothing because you're lost in thought is quite different from doing nothing because you can't move. If you can't express yourself no matter how much you want to, that can be frustrating. If you can't reach for something that you must take hold of, that inability can cost you your life.

Stories of people who can't move can be gripping. You may have seen the movie *127 Hours*, a film about a mountain climber whose arm gets caught under a boulder. What the climber does to finally free himself is hard even to contemplate: He cuts off his own arm. This awful act takes incredible bravery. The planning the climber must do to carry out the unspeakable act reflects the need for painstaking, not to mention pains-*making*, problem-solving. To complete the self-amputation, he has to solve many problems, some physical and others emotional. In the end, he has to bring himself to a mental place where, to escape from where he was—literally between a rock and a hard place—he must do what few of us can even imagine doing.

Not all physical problems require such intense preparation. If you reach for a glass and move it to another location, you have a physical problem to solve, though you hardly notice that you do, at least if you're an adult with normal neuromuscular control. You can grasp the glass virtually anywhere, and you can take hold of the glass with any of an infinite number of body positions—with your elbow extended or with your elbow bent, with your hand high on the glass or with your hand low down, and so on. You don't need to think about which grasp to use, but by the time you've grasped the glass, you've implicitly chosen one of the infinite number of grasps that was possible.

It turns out that where and how you grasp a glass depends on what you plan to do with it. If you plan to carry the glass to a high position, you'll probably grasp it low, but if you plan to carry it to a low position, you'll probably grasp it high.[1] This change of behavior reflects planning of future body states. Similarly, if you plan to turn the glass over, rotating it 180 degrees in order to fill it with water, you'll probably grasp the glass with your thumb pointing *down*—a posture you'd be unlikely to adopt otherwise.[2] Young children don't appreciate this rule for grasping. They tend to grasp glasses or other objects thumb-up as they prepare to turn the glasses over, even if this leaves them in a relatively awkward thumb-down posture at the end.[3]

These observations suggest that everyday physical actions require planning.[4] How well you plan reflects how skilled you are, and how skilled you are is manifested in virtually everything in you do. In athletics, for example, what makes a basketball player great is not just that s/he can make foul shots reliably. It's also that s/he can determine, on the spur of the moment, how to get the ball to a teammate or to the basket. What makes a skier skillful is not just that s/he can descend the same slope over and over again without falling. It's that s/he can cope with the vicissitudes of the snow, the vagaries of the wind, and the variations of his or her own body. If the skier has just sprained an ankle but can still slalom down the course in record time, s/he's a champion.

Star basketball players and Olympic skiers make perceptual-motor creativity especially clear. At the other end of the quality-of-performance spectrum, young children who don't yet know how to get dressed remind us that everyday skills take practice. People who have had strokes or other neural or muscular insults teach us the same thing, as do modern robots, not by dint of their great abilities but by virtue of their woeful inadequacies. Robots today can't do what most young children can do routinely—climb trees, tie simple knots, or scamper through jumbles of toys strewn over bedroom floors.

Regarding robots, consider two displays of computer prowess that wowed the world. The first was IBM's "Deep Blue" computer, which in 1997 played chess against the best player in the world, Gary Kasparov. To the chagrin of many, Kasparov lost the match. Then, in 2011, another IBM computer called "Watson" beat Ken Jennings and Brad Rutter, the two best *Jeopardy!* players in the world before Watson came along.

What Watson and Deep Blue did was impressive. These computers displayed remarkable abilities to solve problems when symbols were manipulated and verbal information had to be looked up as quickly as possible. On the other hand, few people paid attention to the fact that Deep Blue couldn't set up the board or move the pieces. Watson, likewise, couldn't understand the host's speech; the test items were presented to it as digital text. Nor could Watson make its way to the studio, doing things like opening a door, walking down the street, hopping on a bus, grabbing a seat, getting off the bus, and sprinting to the studio in time to record the show. These physical tasks may have been considered too humdrum to warrant IBM's attention. Still, if these tasks had been included in the repertory of things the computers had to do, there would have been no match between the humans and the IBM machines. The humans would have won hands down.

Errors

Recognizing that the planning of skilled physical action doesn't just happen but instead relies on considerable intelligence (not to mention quick nerves and resilient muscles) raises the question of what processes allow those skilled actions to appear. How are movements planned and controlled? And how, relatedly, is stability managed? How, in other words, do you stand while riding a crowded, bumpy subway, and how do you stand your ground while waiting for a traffic light to turn green in a howling wind? Are the processes that allow for these impressive feats of motor control compatible with the jungle principle?

One way scientists have studied motor control has been to analyze errors. By examining mistakes, they have pursued the idea that the *faux pas* people commit betray the inner workings of their nervous systems.

Suppose, for example, that you're groggy and intend to turn off a light but instead turn off a radio. This error tells you something about how you control your behavior. Similarly, if you're distracted and answer someone's question about what you're doing by telling them, "I'm writing a mother to my letter," that slip of the tongue reveals something about what's going on in your mind.

Errors like these, where you say or do something that doesn't line up with what you intend, share an important feature. They reflect competition. Consider the example of turning off the radio rather than the light. Were it not for inner "demons" campaigning for radio termination, there'd be no reason to expect you to turn off a radio when a light needs dousing. Likewise, for the mother-rather-than-letter example. If it weren't for inner "elves" campaigning for saying "mother" when the next noun to be said was "letter," there'd be no reason to expect you to say "mother" too soon or "letter" too late.

Mistakes of this kind have fascinated psychologists for over a century. Such bloopers can be amusing but, more important, they can be revealing. Sigmund Freud believed slips of the tongue reveal pent-up urges.[5] According to Freud, if a man says "mother" too soon, it may be because he has an unresolved Oedipus complex. For language scientists, a more mundane account suffices. The mental representation of "mother" happens to be assigned to the wrong slot in the cue of forthcoming words, possibly because that mental representation competed too vigorously for the slot already reserved for another noun awaiting pronunciation. The fact that "mother" changes places with "letter" suggests that competition is strongest among words of the same grammatical class. Nouns exchange with nouns, verbs exchange with verbs, and so on. This fact grants grammarians gravitas they might not have enjoyed otherwise. Teachers of grammar who implore their students to learn about nouns, verbs, adverbs, and adjectives can take heart in the fact that those grammatical classes are real mental categories, not just artificial divisions used for socializing kids about rules for writing.[6]

Errors don't only involve speech. They also involve nonverbal behavior. When someone accidentally turns off a radio rather than a light, the mixed-up actions share the "turn-off" feature. If you decide to turn off a light, the associated intention can trigger a different action that satisfies the same general need. Inner demons that contribute to turning off the radio jump up and down, as it were, when information comes in that something needs terminating. If their activation is too high relative to the activation of demons associated with light extinction, the radio rather than the light is turned off.[7]

Editing

It's tempting to say that when you screw up, you do so because a little supervisor in your head temporarily loses it. Think of an editor who checks the text that's supposed to appear in a magazine. Reporters supply stories to the editor. The editor needs to ensure that every word is correct. When a mistake appears in print, it's the editor's fault. The buck stops with him or her.

Is there an editor in your brain? From the perspective of parsimony, it would be better to say there's not. Saying there's an inner evaluator begs the question of how that agent knows what's right and wrong.

But can the absence of errors, and the occasional presence of errors, actually be explained without appealing to an inner editor? A cognitive psychologist at the University of Illinois, Gary Dell, argued that they can be. He devised a neural-network model consisting of nodes that interact more or less as neurons do. Excitation passes between some nodes while inhibition passes between others.[8] According to Dell, the nodes that pass excitation or inhibition to other nodes are identified on the basis of which sentence is supposed to be produced. By Dell's way of thinking, the reason someone makes the mistake of saying, "I'm writing a mother to my letter" is that the "mother" node out-excites (or out-inhibits) the "letter" node. This may happen every so often by chance alone.

The sort of neural network Dell endorsed can support nonverbal behavior as well as verbal behavior. Therefore, just as the model needs no editor to explain slips of the tongue, neither does it require an editor to explain slips of the hand. I made such an error on the morning I first wrote this. Just after waking, I turned on the radio and then turned on the water to brush my teeth. The radio volume was too low, so what did I do in my half-asleep stupor? I turned up the tap! I knew I wanted to turn something up. I wanted to make something more intense. The thing I applied turning-up to was incorrect, however.

"Now wait a minute," you might say. "Shouldn't there be some sort of internal supervisor who helps with things like self-control?" Holding back is often crucial. Without self-monitoring, civilization would crumble. People would tell others off more often than they do, they would hit others more often than they do, they'd rape others more often than they do, and so on. Given the clear introspective evidence all of us have that we can control ourselves, is it right to say no editor resides in our brains?

Suppose for a moment that there *is* an inner editor. You might have one if you're a reasonably self-controlled person who checks what you say and do. Freud named the editor the *superego*.

One reason to grant credence to an internal editing process is that sometimes you know you've made a mistake even when you're making it. Consider releasing a basketball at the free-throw line. You may know as you release the ball that the ball won't go in. Experts viewing free throws can make such judgments even when they see the ball only at the moment of release, so it's plausible that the shooter him- or herself also knows whether a shot will go in from the moment the ball leaves his or her hands.[9]

A more subtle phenomenon that reveals the same principle is that during typewriting, incorrect keystrokes are made less forcefully than correct keystrokes.[10] From this simple observation an interesting implication follows. If you respond less forcefully with keystrokes that are wrong than with keystrokes that are right, then at some level you know those keystrokes are wrong even while they're happening. Some internal process tries to inhibit the keystroke, but the inhibition comes too late.[11]

Another source of evidence that there can be internal checking of actions comes from the fact that some verbal and action slips occur because, ironically, you check your performance *too* carefully. If you monitor how you're behaving too much, the vigilance can interfere with how you perform. This point is well known to anyone who suffers from stage fright. Worrying about the way you perform is a kind of editing. When the self-monitoring gets too overbearing, the wrong mental creatures are turned on and may exert inhibitory effects on the ones whose outputs are actually adaptive.

Another hint that self-monitoring can be harmful comes from research showing that focusing on your own behavior can hurt your performance. Athletes and musicians often say it's better not to think too much while performing, and recent research bears this out.[12] Sian Beilock of the University of Chicago and her colleagues asked experienced golfers to putt in two conditions. In one, the golfers were asked to attend to extraneous stimuli that diverted attention from the putt. In the other, the golfers were asked to direct attention to the step-by-step nature of their putting. Golfers in the step-by-step condition did worse than golfers in the attend-elsewhere condition.[13]

How do these results bear on the question of whether an editor is needed to explain errors? They show that inner supervision can occur and can be detrimental. On the other hand, saying that inner supervision can happen doesn't imply that there really is an intracranial being whose job is to legislate. Inner creatures can have collective effects that give the appearance of editing. None of the phenomena reviewed here actually needs an editor to explain them. Appealing to neural creatures that become more or less active suffices to explain the effects just covered.

Population Coding

When neuroscientists have delved into the neural dynamics of movement preparation and control, they have found that the brain relies on a process more akin to democracy than dictatorship. Consider research from a team of neuroscientists led by Apostolos Georgopoulos, working at the time at Johns Hopkins University.[14] Georgopoulos and his colleagues made recordings of neurons in the motor cortex of monkeys. The monkeys moved one hand to each of a number of targets in a circle from a central home location. When a target appeared, the monkey was supposed to move its hand to the target in order to get a reward. All the movements were made in the horizontal plane.

By recording neural activity in the motor cortex, Georgopoulos and his colleagues demonstrated neural democracy. Their discovery was embodied in a principle called *population coding*.[15]

Population coding works much as an election does (Figure 9). In the case of manual positioning, it relies on several facts. First, individual neurons fire most strongly to particular directions of movement. Second, all the cardinal directions (0 degrees, 45 degrees, 90 degrees, etc.) have neurons that prefer them. Third, particular directions of movement arise from the votes of all the neurons.

Consider each of these facts. Regarding the first one, that individual neurons fire most strongly to particular directions of movement, Georgopoulos and his colleagues found that individual neurons in the motor cortex fired the most when particular directions of arm movements were made. The more the

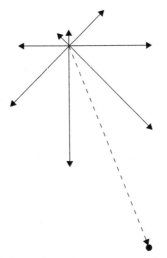

FIGURE 9. Population coding. Each solid arrow corresponds to a neural pool. The angle of each solid arrow shows the favorite direction of a neural pool, and the length of each solid arrow shows the strength of activation of that neural pool given a target (the dot). The dashed arrow shows the sum of the solid-arrow vectors (the population-code vector), pointing in a direction that none of the neural pools prizes the most.

direction of arm movements deviated from a neuron's preferred direction, the less the neuron fired.

How did this play out? When a monkey moved its arm straight ahead toward the 12 o'clock position, a neuron that was tuned to that position fired the most, but when the same monkey moved its arm toward 11 o'clock or toward 1 o'clock, the same neuron fired less. The neuron fired still less when the monkey moved its arm toward 10 o'clock or toward 2 o'clock. It fired still less when the monkey moved its arm toward 9 o'clock or toward 3 o'clock, and so on. Each neuron had a preferred direction and an associated tuning curve (a bell-shaped function relating activation to direction, with the peak at the preferred direction), but different neurons had different preferred directions.

Just as every neuron had a preferred direction, every cardinal direction had a neuron that preferred it. So 12 o'clock was the favorite direction of one neuron, 2 o'clock was the favorite direction of another neuron, 4 o'clock was the favorite direction of another neuron, and so on. There was no large portion of the direction range that remained unpreferred by any investigated neuron. That was the second fact, a fact reminiscent of what I wrote about at the end of Chapter 2, that "no stone goes unturned" when it comes to natural selection.

Third, the direction of actual movement turned out to be a weighted sum of the activations of all the neurons. In other words, when all the activations were summed up, the total vector was one whose direction depended on the preferred directions of all the neurons, weighted by their activations.[16] This outcome made it possible for the arm to move in a direction that wasn't strongly preferred by any neuron. The graded outputs of all the neurons made it possible to go in any direction, even if no neuron was specifically tuned to it.

Population coding is an elegant method for making decisions and enacting them. Not only does it not require an executive, it is also robust to degradation. If a few neurons in the "electorate" happen to fail, the system as a whole can still function. Finally, in case it's unclear, there's no reason why population coding can apply only to arm movement directions. It can apply to any aspect of decision-making and control for which neural "voters" can chime in to a degree reflecting their fit to the challenge at hand.

The proven power of population coding shows that skilled performance emerges from competition and cooperation among neurons. In the case of arm movements, competition is at play because neurons unsuited for needed directions get less weight than neurons that are well suited for those directions. Cooperation is at play because the collective output of all the neurons reflects all the neurons' contributions to the ensemble.[17]

Reflex Modulation

Competition and cooperation among neurons are also seen in reflexes. You're familiar with reflexes from your everyday experience. When you withdraw your hand from a hot stove, you make this motion without deliberation. You start and finish the motion in a fraction of a second.

Reflexes are vital for survival. Their neural underpinnings have been built up over eons of evolutionary time. In what sense are they reflective of an inner jungle?

Consider another kind of reflex that has been studied by neuroscientists—the response made by a cat when it feels pressure on its paw during walking. If the pressure is applied to the sole of the cat's paw at the moment the cat steps *down*, the cat presses down a bit harder than usual. But if the pressure is applied to the sole of the cat's paw when the cat steps *up*, the cat *raises* its foot a bit higher than usual.[18] These opposite responses, made to the same mechanical stimulus at different phases of the step cycle, occur with such short latencies that they qualify as reflexes. The differing responses reflect internal switching. The neurons activated by extra pressure on the foot cooperate with the neurons for foot *lowering* in one phase of the step cycle. But in the other phase of the step cycle, the neurons activated by extra pressure on the foot cooperate with the neurons for foot *raising*.

Cats aren't the only creatures that display such neural nimbleness. People do too. Consider what your lips do when you make a "b" sound. Your top and bottom lips come together to interrupt the flow of air escaping from your mouth. Curious about how this works in detail, some researchers carried out an experiment whose logic was similar to the one just described. They used a specially designed torque motor to tug down gently on the lower lip of an experimental participant who agreed to say "ba, ba, ba," over and over again. The speaker's lower lip was pulled down painlessly and by just a few millimeters. The time of the perturbation was unpredictable for the speaker.[19]

The researchers who performed the experiment wondered how the upper lip would respond when the lower lip was mechanically lowered. They found that the upper lip did just what it had to do to achieve bilabial closure. As soon as the lower lip was pulled down, the upper lip raced down after it, descending more quickly than usual in a way that had a good effect. The two lips came together just when they should have to achieve the "b." The latency of the upper lip's response was so short—less than 100 ms—that the response qualified as a reflex.

In another condition, the researchers didn't have the participants say "ba ba ba." Instead they had the participants say "fa, fa, fa." In this case, the downward tug on the lower lip didn't result in rapid descent of the upper lip. Instead, when the perturbation was applied, the upper lip was unaffected.

So just as the cat responded differently to the same mechanical stimulus depending on what task it was performing at the time—either lifting or lowering its foot—the human speaker in the lip-pull experiment responded differently to the same tugging on the lower lip depending on what sound s/he was trying to make—saying either "ba, ba, ba" or "fa, fa, fa." Thus, the reflex was tuned to the current task demands in both situations.[20]

Such tuning of reflexes is essential for adaptive behavior. Suppose you're in a state of high arousal when you walk down a dark alley. The slightest touch or sound can make you startle. If you're not on guard—if, say, you're lying on a hammock dozing beneath a pair of pines—the same touch or sound will have little effect.

A related phenomenon concerns the excitability of the muscles in the lower back and legs. The excitability of these muscles depends on what movement you're planning to make. If you're about to reach for an object, the excitability of your spinal reflexes related to postural control increases dramatically. Which muscles get activated before the reach depends on the properties of the reach to come.[21]

It's possible to model results like these with a simple neural network model that relies on cooperation and competition.[22] Focusing exclusively on the "ba" or "fa" experiment, imagine that one neural unit propels the lower lip upward and another neural unit propels the upper lip downward. The two units inhibit each other when the sound to be made is "b" but not when the sound to be made is "f."

Such context sensitivity can be modeled by supposing that there is another unit that either excites or inhibits an interneuron mediating the inhibition between the lower lip and upper lip. When the sound to be made is "b," the mediating interneuron is excited, so it lets the lower lip inhibit the upper lip to an increasing degree the farther the lower lip progresses in its upward journey. However, when the sound to be made is "f," the mediating interneuron is inhibited, so the lower lip's activity has no effect on the upper lip. Through this balance of cooperation and competition among neurons, you can account for context sensitivity in the two-lip perturbation study. Applying the same basic logic to other behaviors makes it possible to account for context sensitivity in response to perturbations for them as well.

The fact that a simple neural-network model can account for task-dependent reflex modulation suggests that the neural machinery underlying that modulation is well established, both phylogenetically (in terms of evolution) and ontogenetically (in terms of individual development). The bottom line is that shifting alliances among neurons can account for the modifiability of reflexes.

Trial-and-Error Learning

So far in this discussion, I've suggested how cooperation and competition can shape motor output, but I've said little about learning. If the control of physical action relies on a Darwinian process, loosely conceived, the control of physical action should adapt to the demands it faces via trial-and-error learning. The reason is that natural selection is a trial-and-error process. Research on the learning of action skills bears out the expectation that trial-and-error learning plays a key role in the acquisition of action skills.[23]

Consider the development of locomotion in toddlers. These youngsters excel at exploring ways of moving. A charming example concerns toddlers in Jolly Jumpers.[24] A Jolly Jumper is a baby-friendly seat suspended from a beam via a pair of elastic bands. Thanks to these big rubber bands, a baby in a Jolly Jumper can bounce up and down, provided his or her feet touch the ground. At first, the baby has no idea s/he can bounce this way. Over time, however, s/he discovers that a gentle step here, a more powerful step there, leads to jolly jumping.

Why babies find jumping so enjoyable is an interesting question to which there is no known answer, as far as I know. Setting that aside, the feature of the Jolly Jumper that makes it important here is that no instruction manual tells the baby what to do. No Mommy or Daddy stands there explaining to the infant how to get the most bang for the buck. The baby simply discovers, through trial-and-error learning, how and when to push on the floor to bounce most bountifully.[25]

Improving on a Jolly Jumper takes time, and during that time, babies mature. It is conceivable that maturation alone accounts for the greater efficiency of jolly jumping over time. If that were the case, however, you wouldn't expect babies to adapt to this gizmo as quickly as they do; large gains can be observed in a matter of hours. Similarly, babies of different ages brought to the Jolly Jumper for the first time take time to get the hang of it. If jumping in this device were all a matter of maturation, older, more mature babies wouldn't need a warm-up period. Finally, if developing the ability to jolly jump reflected only maturation, you wouldn't expect babies to vary as much as they do in another behavior, which, like jumping, is related to walking. That behavior is crawling.

Crawling takes many forms, as documented by Karen Adolph of New York University.[26] Every infant seems to have his or her own way to crawl. Some babies crawl on their hands and feet, keeping their bellies above the ground. Other babies sit up as they scoot along, letting their heels serve as yanking hooks and their arms serve as balancing poles.

Such variability would not be expected if the development of walking were a matter of lockstep neural maturation, with all infants following the same hard-wired growth path.[27] Instead, each child follows his or her own opportunistic journey. Much as species take different forms depending on the environments they occupy, the behavioral tendencies of different individuals vary, whether the behavior is crawling or some other form of action.[28]

Karen Adolph, the investigator who has played up the variability of crawling, has not explicitly emphasized trial-and-error learning in her description of motor development, but trial-and-error learning is compatible with her notion that motor development is a dynamic process not guided by a predetermined maturational schedule. Trial-and-error learning provides an effective way of gearing organisms to their environments, both at the level of speciation (the subject that interested Darwin) and at the level of behavior (the subject of interest here).

Given this double-duty usefulness of learning by trying and then succeeding or failing, it's unsurprising that trial-and-error learning has proven to be such a powerful method of learning in a wide range of contexts.[29] Trial-and-error learning underlies virtually all forms of perceptual-motor learning. To name just a few domains where it has proven useful, it plays a role in learning how to trace patterns viewed in a mirror, how to compensate for distortions in visual feedback caused by prisms or other optical displacements, how to make foul shots on the basketball court, how to develop track-and-field skills, and how to enhance robot learning.[30]

Spaced Practice

Because trial-and-error learning is prototypically Darwinian and because I want you to judge my Darwinian thesis critically, I invite you to consider the ostensive limitations of the trial-and-error approach. There are aspects of skill learning that trial-and-error learning seems unable to explain, at least at first blush. If those difficulties are real, you might feel that the inner jungle hypothesis is doomed, and you might then want to hunt for a better theory.

One seeming limitation of trial-and-error learning is that the simple cycle implied by that phrase—try, then err, try, then err—isn't entirely apt. That phrase makes it sound like trial-and-error learning is as rhythmically regular as a polka. It's not. The learning of perceptual-motor skills works best when practice occurs in clumps rather than continuously. If you want to learn to touch-type, for example, you might be tempted to spend large amounts of time at the keyboard, concentrating for hours on end to learn to hit the right keys without looking at them. It turns out, however, that you can develop your typing skill more efficiently if you engage in spaced practice rather than massed practice. Spaced practice means practicing with many breaks. Massed practice means practicing for extended periods with few breaks.

Spaced practice, in general, allows for more rapid learning than does massed practice. For example, a study of learning to touch-type showed that typing students could learn more efficiently if they practiced two times a day for one hour than if they practiced one time a day for two hours.[31] That's a happy outcome, isn't it? It's nice to discover that you can be relieved of hours of needless drudgery if you want to learn a skill. You can get a kind of free lunch by taking a break—and maybe literally going out for lunch—between practice sessions.

What accounts for the superiority of spaced over massed practice? For one thing, nonstop practice is tiring. Whether it's your muscles that ache or your head that throbs, after concerted effort on a task, you can feel yourself fading.

Interleaving different kinds of practice—switching between learning to type and learning to fiddle, say—also exposes you to more kinds of information. As a result, spacing leaves you prepared for more kinds of challenges. That's undoubtedly helpful in the outer jungle, where you never know exactly what challenges you'll face.

But the most important reason for the superiority of spaced over massed practice is one that fits with the jungle principle. Spaced practice lets some internal agents get strong at the expense of other internal agents, without letting any internal agents get so strong that they "kill off" the others, leaving them unable to deal with the challenges they would handle otherwise. Becoming a complete master of one task rather than a jack-of-all-trades at several can leave you insufficiently prepared for the challenges that may come along for the tasks that are les practiced. The brain's internal dynamics favor balance between specialization and diversification.

Skinner, Chomsky, and Bayes' Rule

Another seeming limitation of trial-and-error learning is that it appears to ignore innate dispositions and preferences. The domain where this seeming failure has played out most dramatically is in the debate about whether language learning relies mainly on innate mechanisms or on learning based on trial and error. The latter idea was advanced by the American behaviorist B. F. Skinner.[32] The former idea was advanced by the American linguist Noam Chomsky.[33] No issue in cognitive psychology has sparked more heat than the debate between these two thinkers and their disciples.

Chomsky's view leads to the position that trial-and-error learning cannot explain language learning in children. Consistent with this idea, Roger Brown, a psychologist at Harvard, reported that parents do not reward children for speaking grammatically; instead, they reward children for speaking agreeably.[34] Brown found, in effect, that when a child said, "Wuv you, Mommy," the mom is more likely to come back with, "Mommy wuv you, too" than she is to scold for the child for speaking unprofessionally. When Sarah, my daughter, declared at the age of 4 that she wanted to go "tennising"—saying this while holding a tennis racquet that was nearly as large as she was—my wife and I didn't correct her English. Instead, we beamed at her cuteness. Through her language, Sarah showed that she had over-generalized a rule of English. Over-generalization is hard to explain in terms of trial-and-error learning, a point emphasized by Chomsky and his followers.[35] Chomskians argue that over-generalization of grammatical rules reflects an innate affinity for those rules. On this view, very little input is needed to trigger the rules, which, once triggered, obviate trial-and-error learning.[36]

Grammatical rules aren't the only kinds of knowledge that can be acquired with little input, however. Semantic concepts can be acquired this way as well. For example, after just a few exposures to pictures of elephants, children can learn that the word "elephant" refers to a large-nosed pachyderm rather than some other sort of animals. How can such learning occur?

To pursue this question, first consider that if trial-and-error learning helps you learn concepts, then this capacity reduces the need to appeal to less direct explanations, like saying genes alone account for these abilities. You do, of course, have language-related genes in the sense that you, as a human being, are more likely to develop the capacity for language than to develop the capacity for flying or the capacity for photosynthesis. But saying you have language genes begs the question of what neural mechanisms, allowed by those genes, let you become a language user. Explicating those neural mechanisms remains a supreme challenge of science.[37]

Second, it turns out that there is a way that trial and error learning can account for the capacity to learn at surprisingly rapid rates, even with sparse inputs. The method relies on a powerful statistical principle called Bayes' Rule.

Thomas Bayes was an eighteenth-century Presbyterian minister whose rule relates four quantities: (1) the probability of an event, (2) the probability of the source of the event, (3) the probability of the event given the source, and (4) the probability of the source given the event. The formula is simple, encouraging the belief that students in statistics courses can learn it and, more importantly, that neural networks can embody it.[38]

If neural networks embody Bayesian statistics, then learning can be hastened by exploiting Bayes' Rule. For example, by having an estimate of how likely pachyderms are and how likely the word "elephant" is, a child can use Bayes' Rule to determine the probability that a new word such as "elephant" refers to pachyderms rather than other beasts. It turns out that Bayesian inference—that is, reliance on Bayes' Rule to determine which source is most likely—may make it possible to induce linguistic rules to learn new words and concepts and to perform perceptual-motor tasks, even when sensory conditions change dramatically.

Regarding perceptual-motor tasks (those being more closely aligned with the kinds of tasks that have mainly been discussed in this chapter), suppose Sarah, now grown up, is on a tennis court. She's out there enjoying the game, but a fog suddenly descends on the court and the scene is less visible than it was before. It turns out that Sarah and her tennis partner can continue to play despite the reduced visibility. They can do this thanks to their ability to exploit Bayesian statistics, as shown in an experiment that used a computerized analogue of a tennis game played in conditions of high or low visibility. Without Bayesian inference, the participants in the study might have been unable to adapt as well as they did, but with Bayesian inference—with the ability to use Bayes' Rule implicitly—they could easily adjust to conditions analogous to the sudden settling of a fog.[39]

Given the power of Bayesian inference, interest in the topic has swelled.[40] Scientists who endorse the view that people and animals behave as if they rely on Bayesian inference believe that people and animals don't *explicitly* calculate probabilities using Bayes' formula. Instead, they believe that the nervous system acts *as if* it is making those calculations, doing the statistics implicitly.[41]

How does this conclusion relate to the jungle principle? It indicates that neural networks with known properties can cope with sparse data. No hidden rule system is needed to explain how, with relatively little input, the nervous system can act as if it is endowed with a privileged way of learning in special domains. Trial-and-error learning can occur, but it can occur more efficiently than might be imagined were it not for the capacity to exploit Bayesian inference.

Modeling

On the list of possible problems with trial-and-error learning, the final one is that a lot of learning seems to occur without any trial and error at all. Sometimes observation alone leads to learning.

The most influential demonstration of observation-based learning came from Albert Bandura at Stanford University. In Bandura's experiment, children watched a video of another child striking a Bobo doll—a big rubber clown, filled with air and weighted on its bottom to keep it from toppling over when it was bopped. Children watched a child on a video playing with the Bobo doll. In one condition, the observed kid hit the doll a lot. Later, those who observed that behavior did likewise. By contrast, child observers who saw the model *play* with the Bobo doll were less likely to hit it. Instead, they played with it, too.[42]

Bandura was interested in observation because the prevailing view of learning prior to his study was the one espoused by B. F. Skinner—that learners can learn only by engaging in behaviors that lead to success or failure. Merely imagining behaviors or watching others perform the behaviors shouldn't work, Skinner's theory implied. Bandura showed otherwise. Via his Bobo-doll experiment, he showed that modeling is an effective way to learn.

Learning through observation doesn't occur only by watching Bobos get bopped, however. It can also be observed in other contexts. Students of musical instruments watch and listen to their teachers play their trumpets, trombones, or tambourines to get a sense of how they themselves should play. Dancers watch choreographers demonstrate the steps and gestures the dancers should perform. My daughter, Nora (Sarah's non-identical twin), learned to walk by watching Sarah stand and fall, over and over again. When Nora finally became convinced that walking was possible, she stood up and did so. So while her sister used trial and error to learn to locomote, Nora used modeling. Trial-and-error learning isn't necessary, therefore, at least for walking in children. Modeling is another option.[43]

Action-Related Perceptual Suppression

Is modeling a blight on Darwinian learning? If modeling works well, should Darwinian learning be dumped? Not at all! Learning how to act by watching others is an outcome you would expect if you thought the brain mechanisms involved in acting cooperate with the brain mechanisms involved in perceiving. There is abundant evidence that such cooperation exists. At the same time, equally strong evidence exists for *competition* between mechanisms for acting and for perceiving. The competition, like the cooperation, is so tight that the linkages bespeak nurturing niches for perception-action relations.

Take the case of blink suppression. When you blink, which you do every 2 seconds or so, your eyelid covers your cornea for about .2 seconds. This means that for much of your waking life, your eyes are covered and you literally see nothing. Yet you are completely unaware of this momentary darkening. The reason is that when your brain issues a command to close your eyes, your blink command center also sends signals to your visual center to disregard the darkness.

How can you be sure this claim is correct? You can rely on one of the most imaginative studies in experimental psychology.[44] The researchers who carried out the experiment asked volunteers to allow an optic fiber to be placed in their mouths. The end of the optic fiber lightly touched the roof of the volunteers' mouths. The researchers delivered flashes of light through the optic fibers. In case you didn't know—and why would you?—it turns out that you can see red when light is directed to the roof of your mouth even if your eyes are closed. You can confirm this with a flashlight. Light manages to make its way to your retina through the blood-infused passages within your head.

In the study of blinking, light flashes were briefly presented through the roof of participants' mouths at random times. Meanwhile, the blinks of the participants were recorded. This made it possible to determine after the fact when the flashes were delivered relative to the participants' blinks. The experimenters found that sensitivity to light was dramatically reduced during the blinks. For a light to be detected around the time of a blink, it had to be brighter than at other times. This outcome suggests that the brain centers for blinking inhibit the brain centers for seeing. The inhibition allows the brain to distinguish between darkening of the world due to blinking and darkening of the world due to external dimming.

Other examples of action-related perceptual suppression have also been found. Another is saccadic suppression. Just as you're less able to detect flashes when you blink, you're less able to detect flashes or locate pinpoints of light when you shoot your eyes from one place to another. Such eye jumps are known as saccades. The perceptual attenuation that accompanies these ocular hops is called *saccadic suppression*.

You can demonstrate saccadic suppression by looking into a mirror and trying to see your own eyes move. You will fail. You can't see your own eye movements. Yet a friend watching you carry out the saccades can easily see your eyes dart from place to place. Therefore, your eyes don't move too quickly to be seen while moving. Instead, it's that you, the agent of your own saccades, can't see the saccades you generate. If you're unsure whether you can see eyes moving quickly, you and your friend can change places. If you watch your friend attempt to see his or her own eyes moving in the mirror, you'll be able to see his or her eyes flitting about, though he or she won't be able to see those same saccades. So you can see rapid eye movements. You just can't see your own eyes move when you perform saccades.

What accounts for this curious outcome? The answer is that the swoosh of the visual scene across your retina is suppressed when you move your eyes. "Pay no attention to that swoosh," your eye-movement command center tells your visual center, much as the Wizard of Oz tells Dorothy and her accomplices not to pay attention to the man behind the curtain. The competition implicit in this communication has a cooperative effect on a larger visual scale. By not seeing visual swooshes as you perform saccades, you experience the world as a coherent whole, not a jittery jumble.[45]

Another example of inner competition related to perception and action concerns tickling. No matter how much you might like to be tickled, you can't tickle yourself. The reason is that when you try to tickle yourself, your brain centers that issue tickle commands tell other brain centers sensing touch to disregard the sensations coming along for the ride. The sense of self-touch isn't completely eliminated, of course, but the unexpectedness of the stimulation diminishes, so the giddiness you'd otherwise enjoy is diminished.[46]

Action-Related Perceptual Enhancement

Acting doesn't only *suppress* perception; it can also facilitate it. This possibility was noticed in the nineteenth century in Germany by Hermann Lötze and in America by William James.[47] James wrote about imagining himself getting out of bed and then carrying out the just-imagined action. In much the same vein, he suggested that the mental image of his own writing triggered that writing, that the mental image of his own speaking triggered that speaking, and so on. The notion that the idea of what you want to achieve triggers the action for achieving it came to be known as the *ideomotor* theory of action. It's a theory that has attracted "Lötze" interest lately.[48]

In one experiment that supported ideomotor theory, people wrote a single letter of the alphabet as quickly as they could. In one condition, the letter to be written was designated visually. In a second condition, the letter to be written was designated auditorily. In a third condition, the same participants *said* the letter after seeing it. In a fourth condition, the same participants said the letter after *hearing* it. In general, the time to start producing the letter was less when the letter was going to be produced in the same modality as the modality signaling its production. The interaction between the modality of the stimulus and the modality of the response—quicker responding with speech for a heard stimulus and quicker responding with writing for a seen stimulus—can be explained with ideomotor theory: Perceptual inputs that resemble perceptions produced by actions trigger those actions more quickly than inputs that don't resemble those actions' perceptual outcomes.[49] Relatedly, actions that yield simple perceptual consequences turn out to be easier to perform than actions that yield complex perceptual consequences.[50]

Mirror Neurons

Another source of support for ideomotor theory pertains to mirror neurons. These are neurons that fire when you observe actions you can carry out. For example, if you're a monkey and a neuron in your brain fires when you eat a banana, if that same neuron fires when you see someone else eat a banana, that neuron can be considered a mirror neuron. Mirror neurons have not yet been directly observed in humans, but many researchers are convinced they exist in people.[51]

The existence of mirror neurons has led to interesting speculations about their role in cognition. According to some researchers, mirror neurons might provide the neural substrate for empathy. The apparent indifference to the humanity of others by some has been ascribed to the possible absence or malfunction of mirror neurons in their brains.[52]

Regardless of whether you think mirror neurons underlie empathy, the existence of such cells makes a lot of sense in the jungle scenario. It's congenial with the jungle hypothesis that a special niche is occupied by neurons that fire in the way that mirror neurons do, being activated both by the perception and by the production of particular actions. The reason this expectation is

congenial with the jungle view is that neurons that contribute to the production of actions also benefit from the perceptions those actions provide, as
suggested in Chapter 2. To the extent that rich opportunities exist for neurons with these properties, it makes sense that mirror neurons should grace
the brain. I would venture to say, based on the arguments just given, that the
presence of mirror neurons will turn out to be more the rule than the exception in the animal kingdom.

Another expectation one might have about mirror neurons is they have
the status they do at least partly by virtue of experience. If the production of actions benefits from the perception of those same actions, and
vice versa, then the more often actions co-occur with their associated perceptual consequences, the greater the expected strength of the connection
between them.

Several studies have yielded data consistent with this hypothesis. In the
most famous one, dancers with different kinds of expertise—dancers of ballet and dancers of the Brazilian dance, capoeira—watched videos of ballet
dancers or capoeira dancers. The ballet dancers' brains showed more activity
when they watched ballet dancers than when they watched capoeira dancers,
and the capoeira dancers' brains showed more activity when they watched
capoeira dancers than when they watched ballet dancers. This outcome fits
with the hypothesis that ballet dancers have mirror neurons for ballet but not
for capoeira, whereas capoeira dancers have mirror neurons for capoeira but
not for ballet. The brain areas where the differential responses were recorded
were consistent with the known anatomy of mirror neurons in monkeys.[53]

Personal experience also points to the plausibility of mirror neurons. I'll
report some of my own personal anecdotes that are suggestive of mirror neurons in my own brain. None of the anecdotes proves that my brain has mirror
neurons, but I find it useful to reflect on the stories to keep alive the possibility that they do.

One occurred while I was giving a lecture. During the lecture, while holding a microphone in one hand, I held an empty water glass in the other. A gentleman in the first row kindly offered to fill the glass for me. He indicated,
through a gesture he made, that he would gladly pour water from a large
pitcher into the glass I was holding with one hand while I held the mike with
the other hand and continued to speak. While I watched him pour the water
into the glass, I stopped talking. I couldn't talk! There was no way I could!
That's how great my concentration was, though, of course, I didn't need to
concentrate on the pouring because I wasn't pouring. All I had to do was stand
still, or perhaps not even that, for if I moved, the generous gentleman would

have compensated for my inadvertent moves and kept the water flowing into the glass. The truth was that I was also pouring the water, if only vicariously. My mirror neurons, if I have them, were triggered and their activity spilled over into my behavior.

A second example came from an experience I had with my wife, Judy, in connection with filling out a long, complicated form for a financial transaction. Each of us had to sign and date the form on a number of pages. I had done all my signing. Then I brought the form to Judy and stood by her as I watched her leaf through the pages, searching for the places to sign. As she prepared to turn one page after another, I found myself licking my right index finger, getting ready to turn the next page as well, albeit in thin air and with no contact with the page itself.

A third example concerned my walking pace as I saw a car approach an intersection as another car approached on a perpendicular street. High bushes prevented the two drivers from seeing each other, except at the last moment. The car I was especially concerned about was traveling at a high speed. In my mind's eye I saw the fast-approaching car about to crash into the other car. What did I do? I slowed my walking! In hindsight, this made no sense. Slowing my walk wouldn't slow the fast-moving car, but slowing is what I did, apparently reflecting my desire for the driver of the fast-moving car to slow down. Here again, I vicariously carried out an action, quite possibly because of mirror neurons.

A final example concerns an experience I had at a dinner with some colleagues. One person there, a normally loquacious cognitive psychologist, had laryngitis and couldn't speak. Gradually, the two people to one side of her got into a conversation that left her out, and the two people to the other side of her (one of whom was me) got into a conversation that also left her out. We had urged our hoarse friend to write down what she wanted to say, but after a couple of attempts at this, her motivation waned. I noticed this and thought of mirror neurons, so I suggested we write down messages to her, which of course was unnecessary because all of us had perfectly healthy voices. Yet the ploy worked. When our friend was handed a note, she smiled and wrote back. This went on for the rest of the evening. The method might not have worked if it weren't for mirror neurons.

None of these examples proves that there are mirror neurons in the human brain. Still, they are consistent with the hypothesis that such neurons exist. That they do is, at the very least, expectable from the perspective that neurons opportunistically form bonds with other neurons if such liaisons are useful.

Typing

The final class of phenomena I'd like to consider in this chapter on action concerns the parallel, interactive nature of action control. Consider typewriting. For typewriting to work, your fingers must land on the keys in the right order. The sentence I just typed, for example, required that I hit the shift key first, the "f" key second, the "o" key third, and so on. If you think about how this behavior is managed, you might suppose that a typist's fingers start moving toward their respective keys in the same order as the keys are pressed. The first finger to move might be the one that hits the first key, the second finger to move might be the one that hits the second key, and so on. This expectation is reasonable, except that it turns out to be wrong. As shown in movies of skilled typists, their fingers start heading toward their respective targets as soon as they can.[54] Each finger seems to be driven by a little demon that's intent on moving its finger to that finger's next target as soon as possible. Saying this another way, each target tries to attract its associated finger as soon as it can, wooing it like a Greek-myth siren.

What's to prevent the fingers from colliding? Why don't the fingers just launch *en masse* to wherever they must go? The answer, according to a model of the serial ordering of behavior that I find particularly compelling, is that behaviors that are supposed to occur late are inhibited more than behaviors that are supposed to occur early (Figure 10). According to the model, it's the degree of inhibition among behaviors that defines their serial order.[55] In the model, the last element is inhibited by the element before it, by the element before that, by the element before that, and so on. The penultimate element is inhibited by all the elements preceding it but not by the one to come afterward. Similarly, the element before the penultimate element is inhibited only by the elements preceding it but not by the two last elements.[56]

This model is elegant because its principal assumption is that serial order is embodied in patterns of inhibition. It doesn't say that response elements are linked to serial position tags, such as "position number 1," "position number 2," and so on. Claiming that there are position tags begs the question of how serial positions are represented. So does saying that keystrokes are defined by their positions in a hierarchical control structure, such as a tree whose bottom nodes can be read from left to right. That symbolism might be helpful for teaching, but it leaves unanswered the question of how the behaviors are actually controlled.[57]

Building on this inhibitory model of behavioral control, David Rumelhart and Donald Norman, working together at the time at the University of California (San Diego), modeled the timing of keystrokes in typing.[58] The

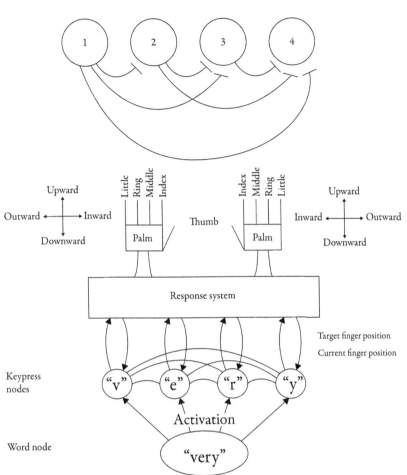

FIGURE 10. Ordering of events with an inhibitory network.

details of their model are less important than its general flavor, which, again, is "jungle-like." Each key beckons its associated finger or, said another way, each finger tries to reach its attracting key as soon as it can, being held up only by inhibition from other responses and by physical interference.

After Rumelhart and Norman introduced their model, a great many studies showed that motor output is not a single, unitary activity but instead reflects a kind of conglomerate of pulls and pushes, all occurring simultaneously. So, for example, when people reach for a target, their hands can be heavily influenced by the sudden appearance of another target.[59] Similar results have been obtained for eye movements and for speaking.[60] Tug-of-war is the rule rather than the exception when it comes to action control. Effectors are drawn in parallel to targets in the external environment.[61]

Back to the Institute

All of the foregoing suggests that the way we move comports with the idea that it's a jungle in there. Warring factions and, not to be forgotten, mutually supportive factions yield the patterns of activity that characterize our voluntary and involuntary actions. Theories of action control that proffer headmasters or headmistresses are unnecessary. Pushes and pulls, operating at the neural level, can account for the dynamics of action control, or that, at least, has been what I have hypothesized here.

As we approach the end of this chapter, I ask you to turn your mind back to the Center for International Research (ZiF), where this chapter began. At the conference I attended there back in June 2010, one of the speakers reviewed the research of a leading scientist in the field of perception and action. That earlier pioneer was Erich von Holst, the director of a Max Planck Institute in Germany. von Holst showed that the signaling of perceptual centers by motor centers, as discussed here in connection with blink suppression, saccadic suppression, and tickling, held in animals as well as humans.[62] He also showed that limbs interact so that, in humans as well as in fish, if a limb starts wiggling more quickly than it did before, other limbs wiggle more quickly as well. The nature of the interactions is remarkably similar over species, attesting to the deep-seated nature of these effects.[63]

In the lecture at the ZiF conference, the speaker summarizing von Holst's contributions, Michael Turvey, a distinguished researcher at the University of Connecticut and Haskins Laboratories (New Haven, Connecticut), reminded the audience that von Holst summarized all of his work with one pithy statement:

$$\text{Coordination} = \text{Competition} + \text{Cooperation}$$

The right-hand side of the equation maps onto the subtitle of this book, *How Competition and Cooperation in the Brain Shape the Mind*. This is hardly coincidental, in my opinion. Much as von Holst saw fit to summarize all that he knew about perception and action by referring to the combination of competition and cooperation, I see fit to say that these two forces are the ultimate mediators of *all* experience. Shaped by evolutionary pressures, not just over the eons of evolution but also over the span of individual lives, competition and cooperation within the brain shape the way we act. It could not be otherwise, in my view, since the control of action is one of the most basic functions of the nervous system.

8

Learn the Ropes!

When I turn to the topic of learning and memory in the class where I first said, "It's a jungle in there," I show a cartoon from *The New Yorker* featuring "Mr. Total Recall," a fictional character who seems to remember everything. In the cartoon, this figure recollects every bit of a long-past meeting with the other character in the cartoon, a puzzled-looking man who clearly is unable to remember the perfect-memory freak. The man with imperfect memory is like the rest of us. He remembers some things but not others. What he remembers matters to him. What's unimportant to him has vanished from his mind, if it ever entered.[1]

Though perfect recall is a joke, many people crave it, spending fistfuls of dollars on memory-improvement books and other aids to help them remember names of people they've met, facts they think they'll need for exams, and so on. Forgetting someone's name can be bad for business, just as forgetting facts for exams can be bad for GPAs. In the outer jungle, forgetting what a sickening mushroom looks like can be deadly, as can forgetting that a patch of ground was quicksand.[2]

While it helps to remember things in some circumstances, in others forgetting can be a boon, not a bane. If you were raped—of course I hope you weren't, though the statistics concerning sexual abuse are all too high—you may wish you could forget that terrible event. If you were a soldier who saw a buddy blown up in battle, that horrific image may stay with you no matter how hard you try to forget it. Ironically, the more you try to forget awful experiences, the harder it is to do so. Trying to forget something specific can, ironically, increase the odds of remembering it.[3]

Examples like these suggest some of the questions a theory of learning and memory should answer: Why do we remember some things but not others? What happens when we forget? When we do forget, does information vanish entirely, or does it just become hard to find? When we remember something but don't remember it exactly, is that a worrying sign of impending senility or just a result of normal processes? When we try to forget something but can't, why can't we?

Forgetting much more than you want can, of course, be a cause for concern. On the other hand, occasional lapses of memory are just what you'd expect if you thought learning and remembering reflect internal competition and coopera-tion among neural agents. Accordingly, I'll argue that memory representations generally get strong when they develop friendly associations, or they get weak otherwise. Saying this another way, the chance that a memory survives depends on how well it fits its environment: The better the fit, the better its fate.[4]

Retrieval Difficulty

Consider a librarian who does her best to keep all the books in her library where they belong. Despite her best efforts, some books get misplaced. Absentminded readers move volumes to errant locales. Mischievous visitors hide books in secret spots. When a book can't be located, the problem isn't that the book has left the library. It's that it has become buried somewhere and is hard to find.

A challenge in studying learning and memory is to determine whether forgetting is due to loss of information or to difficulty of retrieval. Like a mis-placed library book, a memory may be "somewhere in your brain" but hard to locate. The challenge for all of us going about our lives is to retrieve what we want to, though some of it may be hard to find. The further challenge for memory researchers is to find out whether memories that seem to be gone forever are merely elusive.

Showing that forgotten material actually exists is a little like searching for life on other planets. Not finding it doesn't prove it's not there. Little green men or women could be wandering around their extraterrestrial worlds. Not spotting them doesn't prove they don't exist. They could be sailing their Saturnian seas or roving their Jovian jungles. They could be remembering where safe mushrooms can be found and where quicksand pits can be avoided. If they remember where strong vines can be grasped for swinging, that knowledge can help them survive. Learning the ropes, by this fanciful example, is truly a universal concern. But more to the point, not finding something doesn't prove it doesn't exist.

Brain Stimulation

If you don't remember something, it could be that a little librarian in your head has a hard time finding what she's looking for. That proposal sounds outlandish, but to some degree you may subscribe to it when you say things like, "I'm searching my memory," or "I'm trying to remember." When you say such things, it's as if you're claiming that you're rushing around in your own head, scanning mental shelves for something you think is present. This claim is fraught with problems, of course. *You* can't be inside *your* own head!

How can you make headway on this problem? Consider what determines whether memories can be found. Presumably, memories can be located if they're strong, which they are if they're powerfully activated. Memories are activated when relevant cues come along, and the activation is powerful when it doesn't take much cuing for the memories to sally forth. Having many reliable friends can help memories achieve this status. Having few adversaries can help as well.

To make more sense of how this works, consider some methods that have been used to bring memories to the fore. One is electrical stimulation of the brain. This method has been used in neurosurgery. It was pursued most famously by the Canadian neurosurgeon, Wilder Penfield, whose medical achievements became so influential that a boulevard was named for him in Montreal, the city where he practiced.[5]

Penfield treated epileptic patients for whom drugs were ineffective. To help his patients, Penfield performed brain surgery on them, attempting to deactivate the sources of the seizures or at least to retard their spread. Penfield wanted to make sure he didn't cut nerve tracts that were crucial for basic functions like moving or talking, so he used electrodes to record from brain sites in the patients. The other technique he used was to stimulate those sites to determine what roles they played. His patients volunteered for the procedure, were awake while it was performed, and felt no pain from the brain treatment itself.[6]

Penfield found that electrical stimulation of the brain elicited long-lost memories. Patients who had not thought of events for years reported re-experiencing those events when their brains were stimulated. Based on the apparent release of seemingly lost memories, Penfield suggested that more information is stored in the brain than is evident from ordinary recall. He even hypothesized that everything we experience is retained.[7]

Hypothesizing that nothing is forgotten is a strong claim, of course. It may be too strong, for if *some* memories can be activated by electrifying the brain, it doesn't follow that *all* memories can be reignited.[8] Nevertheless, the hypothesis is intriguing. Penfield was surely correct in suggesting that more is available in memory than might be imagined at first.

Recognition and Recall

Trying to revive long-lost memories through electrical stimulation of the brain isn't the most practical means of reawakening memories in everyday life. Another way is to rely on recognition rather than recall. In recognition, you indicate whether you've encountered something before. In recall, you reveal what you remember by recounting your experience, typically by describing what you saw or heard.

Recognition is generally easier than recall. A famous demonstration of this truism was provided in a study of memory for former high-school classmates.[9] Healthy people of various ages were asked to recall the names of people with whom they went to high school. In another condition, they were asked to recognize faces in yearbooks. Some yearbooks were from the participants' own high schools. Other yearbooks were from other high schools whose student populations had similar demographics.

The older the participants, the worse their recall, a result that is understandable from the standpoint that older people may have poorer recall abilities than younger people. Alternatively, it could be that older people had to go farther back in time than the younger ones. Young people don't have classmates from 50 years ago. Senior citizens do. Older folks also have more stuff to remember. An 80-year-old has roughly 4 times as much experience as a 20-year-old, assuming experiences—however they might be defined—come at a roughly constant rate.

The most striking result of the study was that, no matter how old the participants their recognition remained steady and very high (close to 90%), even 50 years hence. So people who had graduated from high school half a century before could recognize pictures of their classmates, even though they could not recall those people when asked simply to say who their classmates were.

This remarkable finding shows that recognition can be extremely durable though recall may slip. Another lesson from this study is that basing appraisals of memory on free recall can lead to underestimates of how much is stored. Relying on recognition shows that more is there than might at first be apparent.

Cued Recall

Why is recognition generally easier than recall? To pursue this question, imagine an elderly lady looking at a picture of a teenage boy in a yearbook photo. The boy is dressed and coiffed as teenage boys were back in her day. The senior-citizen subject has a vague feeling she recognizes the boy, but she's not sure. Then she's given a cue. "School orchestra," the experimenter whispers. Suddenly she recognizes the youth. He played the trumpet in the high school orchestra. She played the French horn. The verbal cue boosts her memory enough to move her from a vague feeling of knowing to a surety of knowing. Now she recognizes the boy and recalls something about him. He once arrived late to a rehearsal and the teacher scolded him. What was the boy's name again? She can't quite remember, but other facts come back to her in a flood—what the room looked like, what it felt like to hold her French horn, and the memory that her friend Bea told her she thought the boy was cute.

What all this shows—though the anecdote is fictional—is that memories have aspects. For the lady looking at the yearbook, some of those aspects were activated by sight of the boy. When an extra cue was given to her ("school orchestra"), other aspects were activated. The result of the refresher was more vivid recollection.[10]

Here's another demonstration of the way cuing can help. The demonstration concerns bringing people from a state of not being able to recall to a state of being able to recall. I use the demonstration in my cognitive psychology class. First, I read aloud a list of words, and then I ask the students to recall as many words as possible. Here's a typical list:

yacht, canoe, raft
celery, carrot, cucumber
skunk, raccoon, squirrel
Pabst, Sam Adams, Budweiser
salmon, trout, flounder
Poland, Germany, France
psychiatrist, dermatologist, cardiologist
plum, peach, grapefruit
Colorado, Idaho, Wyoming
elbow, shoulder, neck

Of the thirty items in the list, the students typically recall half of them. After the students have written down as many words as they can, I call out a cue word and ask the students to write down any additional words they can think of. If I say "fish"—the category name for a triplet on the list ("salmon, trout, flounder")—a few students write down those words if they omitted them. If I say "beer"—the category name for another triplet on the list ("Pabst,

Sam Adams, Budweiser")—some students write down beer terms they may have left out. Apparently, with a little help from their friends, memory items can be "brought to the surface."

Notice that the cues that helped in the demonstration were words that conveyed the meaning of a *set* of words in the list. Even though the word "fish" was not in the list, three of the words were "fishy enough" that the "fish" cue triggered recall of the fish words. From this you can infer that memory demons whose niches included the fish concept were turned on by other memory demons whose niches included particular fishes. Once the fish cue activated those demons, it became possible to recall the relevant terms.

Cues that enable recall needn't be names of semantic categories. They can be words that sound like words to be remembered, tunes associated with words to be recalled, strokes on the cheek that relate to words to be remembered, olfactory stimuli (smells), and so on.

Smells, it turns out, are especially evocative, perhaps owing to their ties to primordial needs like eating, drinking, and nuzzling up to mommy. A famous account of odor-based cuing came from the nineteenth-century French author, Marcel Proust, whose novel, *À la recherche du temps perdu (In Search of Lost Time)*, which he wrote between 1909 and 1922, described the awakening of childhood memories by the smell of a cake. In the incident, the adult character in the novel smells something he hasn't smelled since childhood—a cake baked by his aunt when he was a little boy. The smell of the cake—*le petit madeleine*—released memories pent up in his mind. Suddenly, upon smelling le petit madeleine, he remembers experiences that, ostensibly, had been lost forever.

Proust's character became talkative when he transitioned from not remembering to doing so. The opposite of talkativeness is being unable to say what you want, and being tongue-tied also provides clues about memory.

Consider the tip-of-the-tongue state. When you have something on the tip of your tongue (not literally, of course), you know you know it, but you can't recall it. You may recall a bit of it, like the fact that it's a short word or a long word or that it has a sound like a short "e" or a long "i." If a cue comes along that activates a hidden feature of the word—its meaning, perhaps, or some sound it contains—you may be able to move from being tongue-tied to being loquacious. What was stuck on the tip of your tongue comes out, often with accompanying excitement.[11]

The tendency of cues to liberate tip-of-the-tongue words provides evidence that memories may persist even if they're hard to access. The cuing power of specific features of words points to the componential nature of memories.[12] Memories have features that, when provoked, conjure cognitive confreres.

Implicit Memory

Cuing is an explicit means of prompting recall or recognition. Recall and recognition can also be encouraged through more indirect means, as in *implicit* memory tasks. Here, memory isn't tested by asking someone to recall or recognize as many words as possible. Instead, memory is tested more subtly, by having people complete word fragments in whatever way they like. The instruction can take the following form: "Just write down whatever pops into your head to complete these word fragments."

al_____
hot_____
wal_____

The words you generate tend to be ones you saw before. If you saw "alligator," you might be inclined to write "ligator" when completing "al____." Your chance of writing "alligator" is higher if you saw "alligator" than if you saw "alimentary." This outcome shows that memories for previously encountered words persist. The method used to show this result is called an *implicit* memory test. It's called *implicit* because memory is probed implicitly or indirectly rather than explicitly or directly.

The word-completion task allowed two psychologists, Peter Graf and Daniel Schacter, to make an amazing discovery.[13] They found that amnesic patients who showed no evidence of remembering via recall or recognition could nevertheless complete word fragments. The amnesic patients displayed the sort of bias outlined in the example given above. They often completed "al____" as "alligator" if they saw "alligator" before. If they saw "alimentary" before, they completed "al____" as "alimentary." (I offer these as illustrative examples, not as exact results from the study.) When the same subjects were explicitly asked to recall or recognize words they had seen, they couldn't. So when they were asked to recall, they drew a blank, and when they were asked to recognize, they performed at chance. The fact that they could do the word completion task in ways that reflected actual retention of the words shows that more information was stored than would have been expected based on standard recall or recognition tests.

Another demonstration of implicit memory is that people generally prefer familiar items to unfamiliar ones. Even if you're not sure you've encountered something before, you're inclined to say you like it.[14] This is a useful fact for memory researchers, for it shows that a way to find out what people remember is to find out what they prefer. It's also a useful fact for businesspeople, for it suggests that familiarizing customers with products and services leads them to like those commodities. Businesspeople know this, of course, which is why they advertise so much, often without telling much about the products or services themselves. As a result, there are on TV at the time of this writing, a witty lizard with a Cockney accent serving as a mascot for an insurance company (Geico) and irascible but lovable Vikings acting as mascots for a credit-card company (Capital One).[15]

Savings

There's still another way to show that more is stored than first meets the eye. This is with the method of savings, a method that comes into play when you try to relearn something you learned before. You can learn facts or procedures a second time more quickly than you could at first. The reduction in time spent learning the material is the measure of savings. If savings occurs, something must have been stored.

Suppose you lived in a foreign country when you were a child and later, as an adult, believe you've forgotten the language spoken there. I encountered such a student one year in my Intro-Cognitive class. She told me she lived in Germany between the ages of 2 and 6 and that she then moved to the United States and entered a world where no German was spoken. When I asked her if she remembered any German, she insisted she did not.

Did this student actually forget all her German? A way to find out would be to have her take a German class along with others whose ignorance of German was not in question—people who had never (or hardly ever) been exposed to that language. If her knowledge of German was as lacking as she thought, she would have been able to learn German no more quickly than the others.

In fact, she'd probably be able to learn German much more quickly than her classmates, for most people relearn foreign languages more quickly than they learn them the first time around.[16] The savings they enjoy shows that some knowledge of the language was there all along, albeit in hidden neural niches.[17]

The phenomenon of savings has been demonstrated in a wide variety of contexts, including classical conditioning (discussed in the next section), word learning, and skill learning.[18] Savings is relevant to the jungle principle because it suggests that some information may not be truly lost but instead may be weak, inhibited, or hard to access for other reasons.

The resilience of such out-of-the way information has another implication besides the ones already mentioned—that information may not be lost though it seems to be, and that seemingly lost information can be aroused through indirect means. The other implication is that it takes a lot to wipe out information once it has been learned well.

In this regard, there is a striking parallel between the durability of well-learned memories and the durability of well-adapted species. As I learned from a Wikipedia article on extinction, "...it is estimated that 99.9% of all species that have ever existed are now extinct." However, the same article mentioned that "a typical species becomes extinct within 10 million years of its first appearance."

It may be that 99.9% of the memories formed by an individual are lost forever, but if you ask what the personal analogue of 10 million years is, it's hard to know for sure. But whatever the exact value may be, it's a pretty long time, judging from the research that has been done on savings, implicit memory, cued recall, and recognition.[19]

Classical Conditioning

One domain in which savings has been shown is classical conditioning. You've been exposed to classical conditioning in your daily life. Every time your mouth has watered at the smell of a roasting turkey every time you've broken into a cold sweat when you found yourself growled at by a menacing dog, every time you've felt some longing in your loins when you've seen an attractive person, you've experienced the effects of classical conditioning.

In classical conditioning, an innate response (a so-called "unconditioned response") that is automatically triggered by some stimulus (a so-called "unconditioned stimulus") comes to be predicted when another stimulus (a so-called "conditioned stimulus") is encountered. The prediction becomes worthwhile to the extent the conditioned stimulus reliably heralds the unconditioned stimulus. The smell of a roasting turkey on a Thanksgiving morning is a good predictor of a meal to come, for example. The smell makes you salivate because you've learned that the aroma of roast turkey is followed by ingestion.

All Intro-Psych students learn that classical conditioning was discovered by Ivan Pavlov, a Russian physiologist who won the Nobel Prize in Physiology or Medicine in 1904 for his discovery of classical conditioning in dogs.[20] In his work, Pavlov noticed that when he prepared to feed his canines, they began to salivate before the food was delivered. The strength of the salivation grew on successive occasions as Pavlov prepared the food before delivering it. The sights, sounds, and smells related to Pavlov's food preparation became conditioned stimuli for the dogs.[21]

Because the dogs in Pavlov's lab salivated more as the conditioned stimuli reliably preceded the unconditioned stimulus, you might be tempted to say that the dogs predicted food delivery during the pre-feeding routine. In a sense, they did predict that they would get fed. But you should be careful not to proclaim that the dogs explicitly predicted anything. A mechanistically simpler account is that the neural ensembles related to eating were activated by the sights, sounds, and smells of the events culminating in meals.

What would happen if Dr. Pavlov stopped his normal feeding routine? Suppose he headed for the cupboard and then walked away. If this happened repeatedly, the dogs would stop salivating when Dr. Pavlov entered the kitchen. Their salivation would be "extinguished," the term used in conditioning research for the cessation of previously conditioned responses. Extinction was, of course, what I just spoke about at the close of the last section.

Extinction bears on the necessity, or lack thereof, of explicit mental prediction. Suppose that in extinction, the dogs in Pavlov's lab stop predicting that Pavlov will feed them and predict instead that he will not. A problem with this proposal is that a mechanism is needed to switch from one prediction to the other. Another problem is that the prediction, as just portrayed, is all-or-none: Pavlov will either feed the dogs or not, with no in-between. But that's counter to everyday experience. We have graded expectations. We can have varying degrees of confidence in the likelihoods of various events. Our confidence that it will storm will be lower when it's partly cloudy than when it's fully overcast and there is frequent, loud thunder.

Another interpretation of extinction vis-à-vis prediction is that when extinction occurs, prediction stops. According to this interpretation, Pavlov's dogs cease predicting and do so again only when prediction becomes useful again. This proposal has an obvious problem, however. How can prediction be triggered by its own usefulness?

Yet another interpretation of extinction in connection with prediction is that no explicit prediction *ever* occurs—neither when the dogs are fed, nor when they are not. Dogs simply behave *as if* they are predicting. This interpretation is the one advocated by radical behaviorists, who say that attributing mental states to animals, including humans, is misguided.

I am not a radical behaviorist, to be sure. However, I appreciate the warning not to re-describe phenomena in terms of what you're trying to explain.

If you're trying to explain mental states, it's not satisfying to explain those states in terms of other mental states. In connection with prediction, it's better to say that neural systems embody prediction by virtue of their collective actions than to throw up your hands and say that prediction just happens at a mental level.

This point is further reinforced by considering what happens when extinction is undone. Suppose Pavlov returns to his normal feeding routine. Now, every time he nears the cupboard, he feeds the dogs again. Soon the dogs resume their mouth-watering when the good doctor arrives. Critically, the dogs start salivating more quickly when Pavlov reinitiates his feeding routine than when he first started it. Thus, the dogs exhibit savings. The fact that they do so shows that savings is a basic phenomenon, not one seen only in complex tasks like relearning languages.

What does the phenomenon of savings imply about prediction? For Pavlov's dogs, it can logically imply any of the following: (1) the dogs returned from not predicting to predicting more strongly than they did before; (2) the dogs switched from predicting non-feeding to predicting feeding, and they made this switch more quickly than they did before; (3) the dogs' neural machinery governing the salivation response went from being weak or inhibited to being strengthened or released from inhibition.

Which of these accounts is best? The first and second accounts are complicated; each of them requires ancillary assumptions to make them work. The last account is simpler. It's the account I favor. I prefer it not just because it straddles the explanatory divide between neural and psychological events, but because it also echoes and supports the mantra of this book, that it's a jungle in there.[22]

Blocking

Other phenomena of conditioning provide further support for the view that learning and memory can be usefully understood in terms of the jungle principle. I'll review two such phenomena now. One is blocking.[23] The other is captured by an important model in this area of study, the Rescorla-Wagner model.[24]

Suppose one of Pavlov's dogs learned to associate Pavlov's arrival with Pavlov's subsequent food delivery. The dog learned to associate Pavlov's features—his beard, his white lab coat, and so on—with the provisions he provides. One day, Pavlov comes to the lab with a flower on his lapel. He still feeds the dog. Nothing has changed. Only the flower has been added. A few days later, after having fed the dog while wearing the flower, Pavlov goes on vacation. Two other lab workers take over for him, each coming in repeatedly but at different times. Neither newcomer has a beard or a white lab coat, but one wears a flower. As it happens, only the flower-wearing newcomer feeds the dog.

Does the dog quickly learn to salivate more intensely when the flowered attendant arrives than when the non-flowered attendant does? The canine should show this selectivity to the extent that the flower is predictive of food. But this expectation is not borne out. It takes a long time for the selectivity to be shown. The dog doesn't have trouble learning to link flowers to food. If Pavlov, from the beginning, fed the dog only while wearing a flower, the dog would learn quickly to salivate only when Pavlov wore the flower.[25]

The tendency to miss the added information provided by the flower worn by the newcomer is illustrative of a phenomenon called *blocking*. It's a phenomenon discovered by Leon Kamin, a psychologist at Princeton University.[26] The term "blocking" refers to the fact that new conditioned stimuli don't promote learning when they're added to other conditioned stimuli that have already been associated with an unconditioned stimulus. The new conditioned stimuli are blocked.

Blocking, like so many phenomena described in this book, can be understood in terms of inner agents competing and cooperating with one another. When conditioned stimuli are just being learned, there's plenty of room for new connections (cooperation). Later, when those connections have become entrenched, the network is less plastic; competition rears its head. New information is harder to integrate because potential niches have been spoken for. The agents within those niches have become so well adapted that they strongly resist challenges to their domain. Agents attempting to enter the niches (speaking metaphorically, of course) have little chance of doing so. They are blocked.[27]

The Rescorla-Wagner Model

Blocking can be viewed as a phenomenon of late learning, a phenomenon that suggests little openness to new information. Early learning and mid-course learning reveal greater openness to new information, as captured by another principle of conditioning, the Rescorla-Wagner model. According to this model, the strength of a conditioned response grows over time, but the rate of strengthening decreases as learning continues (Figure 11). The model was proposed by Robert Rescorla of the University of Pennsylvania and Alan Wagner of Yale University.[28]

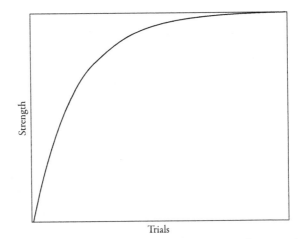

Trials

FIGURE 11. Strength of associations for conditioned stimuli as a function of number of learning trials according to the Rescorla-Wagner model.

How can the Rescorla-Wagner model be explained? Suppose there is some number of neural connections that need to be formed for a classical conditioning task to be fully acquired. Early in learning, the chance of forming a connection is high because there are many available slots, but as learning continues, the chance of forming a connection gets smaller because fewer slots are open. If each new connection strengthens the response by some amount, the increase in response strength should decrease as fewer connections can be made.

The Rescorla-Wagner model is visually described by a curve that rises steeply at first and then levels off (again see Figure 11). This same shape arises in other learning contexts, a fact that may be taken to suggest that the same dynamic underlies them as well. Not surprisingly, I think that dynamic is the one captured by the jungle principle.

The Power Law of Learning

Consider another context in which learning more and more is associated with gaining less and less. The context is skill learning. There, it turns out, the speed of performing a task increases a lot in the early phase of practice but then increases by smaller and smaller amounts as practice continues (Figure 12). Saying this another way and focusing not on the speed of performing a task but on its inverse, the time for task performance, the time to perform a task decreases a lot at first but then decreases less and less as practice goes on.

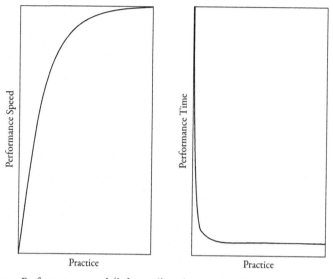

FIGURE 12. Performance speed (left panel) and, equivalently, performance time (right panel) as a function of amount of practice.

This relation was made famous in a study of the time taken by factory workers to roll and place cigars in cigar boxes.[29] The time to complete the cigar-rolling task dropped precipitously at first but then decreased at a lower and lower rate as the workers continued to perform the task over and over again.

This same pattern has been observed in many other tasks, including elementary button-pressing tasks,[30] reading inverted and reversed text,[31] justifying mathematical proofs,[32] and writing books by a prolific author (Isaac Asimov).[33]

The curves posited in the Power Law of Learning and the Rescorla-Wagner model look similar. Given the resemblance of the curves, it's tempting to think they might be rooted in the same neural changes. I think they are. The idea, consistent with the jungle principle, is that early in learning, the chance of forming a connection is high since there are many available slots, but as learning continues, the chance of forming a connection gets smaller, owing to the smaller number of slots still available. If each new connection strengthens the response, the increase in response strength is large at first but gets smaller as fewer connections can be made. Similarly, if *speed* of performance is related to response strength, then performance speed increases a lot at first but continues at a declining rate as practice goes on, for the same reason.[34,35]

The Forgetting Curve

In the last section, I expressed interest in the fact that the form of the relation between response *strength* and amount of practice is similar to the relation between response *speed* and amount of practice. In both cases, the curves are steep at first and then flatten out. In this section, I focus on the fact that forgetting behaves in much the same way.

Recall from earlier in this chapter that the longer ago someone graduated from high school, the smaller the number of classmates he or she could recall. The function relating number of names recalled to time since graduation plummets at first and then levels off. Again, there is rapid initial change followed by smaller and smaller change. This pattern has been observed so often that psychologists speak of it as "the forgetting curve" (Figure 13).

Why does the forgetting curve have the form it does? Might it be that the sheer passage of time accounts for it? This is doubtful, because time itself doesn't account for degradation. In physics, with its famous radioactive decay, it is electrons fleeing the coop, not time *per se*, that accounts for time-related decay. In biology, where rotting is a fact of life (or its aftermath), bacterial infestation does the dirty work; time *per se* doesn't. In both domains, things fall apart because of processes occurring *in* time.

In psychology, experiments have likewise shown that time *per se* does not account for forgetting. In one experiment, students at the University of

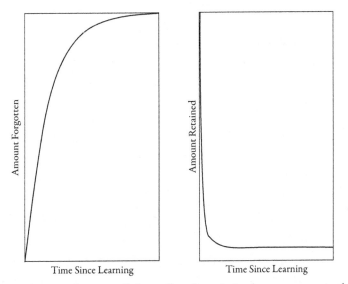

FIGURE 13. Amount forgotten (left panel) and, equivalently, amount retained (right panel) as a function of time since learning.

Michigan were asked to learn a list of words.[36] After being exposed to the words, some participants spent several seconds listening for a tone, tapping a key whenever they heard it. Other participants, after being exposed to the same words, spent the same amount of time listening for a syllable that sounded like one or more of the words in the to-be-remembered list. The syllable-monitoring participants were likewise supposed to tap a key when they heard the target. When both groups were later asked to recall the words, those in the tone-monitoring condition did much better than those in the syllable-monitoring condition. The same amount of time passed in both cases, so it was not the sheer passage of time that predicted forgetting. Rather, it was what happened during the retention interval.

The same result was reached in another study, conducted in the 1920s.[37] Participants were presented with a list of words, either at the beginning of a normal, busy day or before going to sleep. The subjects retained far more words if they learned the words before going to sleep than before going to work. The amount of time between study and test was the same in the two conditions, so once again it wasn't the sheer passage of time that predicted forgetting. What occurred during the retention interval determined how much was retained. When fewer things happened—in sleep rather than in daily activity—more information could be recalled later.

If the passage of time doesn't account for forgetting, what does? Radioactive decay and bacterial infestation aren't plausible answers. The best answer, I believe, is *interference*.[38] Here, competing material crowds out what's to be learned. The more competitive the material, the greater its crowding effect. So in the first study mentioned above, listening for a syllable like one in the list created a more competitive environment for the to-be-remembered words. In the second study, pursuing one's daily activities created a more competitive environment for the words to be remembered than did sleeping.[39]

A great deal of additional evidence supports an interference account of forgetting. At the same time, no evidence that I'm aware of contradicts the interference account.[40] I won't rehearse all the research here. I'll just mention one other demonstration of interference that attests to its importance. It is described in the next section. What makes the study noteworthy is that it provides an exception to the rule that recognition is easier than recall.

Conditions of Learning and Test

When you try to recall something as opposed to recognizing it, you've got much more to do. Recall requires generating a response—saying the item's name or typing it or signing it or singing it. By contrast, recognition requires generating a less specific response—saying "Yes, I saw it," or "No, I didn't," for example. As mentioned earlier, recognition is generally better than recall, but can actually be worse when interference is intense.

My favorite demonstration of this outcome is a study in which college students were asked to learn paired associates such as "river-bank." Later, the students were tested with a cued-recall procedure in one condition or with a recognition procedure in the other. In the cued-recall procedure they were given the first word in a pair and were asked to come up with the second word. When they were cued with "river," most subjects managed to recall "bank." In the recognition condition, the students were shown two words and were asked to indicate whether they recognized either one. When the word pair was "river-bank," they reached high levels of recognition, but when the word pair was "piggy-bank," recognition failed miserably. Though the word "bank" was in the original list, the meaning of "bank" was different when paired with "piggy" than when paired with "river." Cuing the wrong sense of "bank" caused participants to miss it. Evidently, the original memory of "bank" was obstructed by the new one. The interference was so strong that recognition failed in this instance.[41]

The "river-bank/piggy-bank" study is a clever demonstration of the extent to which conditions of test need to match conditions of study for memory performance to thrive. If conditions of test differ radically from conditions of learning, retrieval can suffer.[42]

Another study that made this point involved navy divers who studied lists of words on land or underwater. When the divers were later tested on the words, they did much better if the conditions of test matched the conditions of learning. Words learned on land were recalled better if they were tested on land than underwater. Similarly, words learned underwater were recalled better if they were tested underwater than on land. Thus, switching the context at the time of recall interfered with recall.[43]

Results like these lead to both theoretical and practical conclusions. Theoretically, the results indicate that memory performance reflects inner competition and cooperation among cognitive elements. When those elements have access to the system responsible for reporting them or for conveying whether the elements seem familiar, they can easily make their presence felt, allowing for robust memory performance. On the other hand, when they *don't* have such good access to the response system, they have a harder time announcing their presence.[44]

The results also have practical applications. The findings indicate that if you want to able to recall or recognize something, you should do what you can to minimize competition among potentially relevant memories. You should also do what you can to maximize cooperation among the memories. You can minimize competition by avoiding experiences that are similar to the ones you hope to remember. Don't expose yourself to different words that are closely related to the ones you need to remember. If you need to remember a phone number and are engaged in saying it over and over to yourself until you get to a phone, try to avoid hearing other numbers. Similarly, after attending a lecture on emotion, go for a swim. Don't head next to a class on affect.

Mnemonics

In terms of what you can do to maximize cooperation among memory elements, seek conditions of test that are similar to conditions of learning. If you absolutely *must* learn a list of words underwater, try to be tested for them there rather than on dry land. If the registrar of your university schedules your exam in a different room than the one in which you took the course, petition the registrar to keep the test in the same room as the lectures. If you employ mnemonics for studying (special tricks to aid memory), use mnemonic aids that uniquely and reliably trigger the memories you want. For example, medical students often learn the names of the twelve cranial nerves by memorizing a phrase unrelated to the nerves themselves but whose words' first letters cue the nerves' names: "**O**n **O**ld **O**lympus' **T**owering **T**op, **A** **F**inn **A**nd **G**erman **V**iewed **S**ome **H**ops." The twelve cranial nerves are the **O**lfactory nerve, the **O**ptic nerve, the **O**culomotor nerve, the **T**rochlear nerve/pathic nerve, the **T**rigeminal nerve/dentist nerve, the **A**bducens nerve, the **F**acial nerve, the **V**estibulocochlear nerve/Auditory nerve, the **G**lossopharyngeal nerve, the **V**agus nerve, the **A**ccessory nerve/**S**pinal accessory nerve, and the **H**ypoglossal nerve.[45] For those facing law-school exams rather than med-school exams, I can share the following mnemonic trick, which my daughter, Sarah (the same Sarah who years ago asked me and my wife if we wanted to go "tennising"—see Chapter 7), came up with while studying for the California Bar Exam: "**L**ove **f**orces **e**very **p**erson to **b**elieve in **r**ainbows." The first letters correspond to the initial letters of the ways to analyze a contracts question: "**L**aw, **f**ormation, **e**nforcement, **p**erformance, **b**reach, **r**emedies."[46]

A final mnemonic technique that can be very effective is the method of loci. Here, you associate successive items in a list with places you routinely visit, one after the other, such as the rooms in your house. The method of loci has been used since ancient times and can be highly effective even today.[47] Drawing on knowledge of a familiar routine like walking through your house can help you strengthen memories for things you need to do. Suppose, for example, you need to remember the following duties: "Buy turpentine at the hardware store and then pick up Q-tips at the drug store." You can remember this to-do list by forming an image in your mind of a can of turpentine sitting prominently in the room you enter when you come into your house, and by forming an image in your mind of Q-tips lying on your dining room table if the dining room is the room you enter next. Both images are weird, so they stand out against the familiar context in which they appear. That distinctiveness can help you remember them later on.

False Alarms

This chapter began with the story of a cartoon character—Mr. Total Recall, who recollected everything that transpired when he met some other person many years before. That other person was like the rest of us in that he remembered imperfectly at best.

If our memories are indeed imperfect, do they crumble randomly or do their frailties follow regular patterns? Might it be that the ways memories fail can be understood in terms of some memory demons growing weaker while other memory demons grow stronger?

Consider the ostensibly simple task of recognition. This is a good task to think about here because, with recognition being generally easier than recall, recognition might be impervious to inner competition and cooperation. That would be damaging for the jungle hypothesis. It would be troubling if the jungle principle failed to apply to the everyday task of indicating, or trying to indicate, whether something or someone has been previously encountered.

I've already described one demonstration of recognition gone awry in a manner consistent with the jungle principle. It was the study in which university students failed to recognize the word "bank" when asked to recognize one or both words in the pair "piggy-bank" after being exposed to "river-bank." Subjects in the study failed to recognize "bank" when the context shifted, as if the demons for the original sense of the word were deflated or inhibited by demons rallying in a new test situation that happened to turn them on especially strongly.

Failing to recognize something encountered before is one of the four possible outcomes of a recognition test, a "miss" The other three are recognizing an item correctly (a "hit"), recognizing something that wasn't actually encountered (a "false alarm"), and failing to recognize something that wasn't originally presented (a "correct rejection"). Because I'm concerned here with misremembering, and because I focused on one type of misremembering above (misses), I'll focus next on false alarms.

Suppose you witness a crime in which some no-good-nick grabs someone's purse and runs off. Later, at the police station, you're asked to view a lineup of eight individuals and you're supposed to point to the culprit. If you saw eight people at the robbery, the *a priori* chance of your identifying any one of them as the perpetrator of the crime is 1 in 8. But if the "perp" isn't in the lineup and the only person in the cue who actually was at the crime scene was an innocent bystander, you'll finger that innocent bystander at a rate significantly higher than 1 in 8, or at least you'll do so if you perform as others did who have been tested in laboratory mockups of this situation.

What accounts for this result? The jungle principle provides an answer. Inner elves get excited by the sight of someone from the crime scene. "I've got it covered," each of them shouts, as it were. Meanwhile, as you try to answer the question, "Do you see the criminal here?" there's a ruckus in your head and you infer from the ruckus that whoever looks most familiar in the lineup must have been the culprit.

The crime you witnessed had three victims. One was the person whose purse was snatched. The other was you, who, in a sense, become a victim of overzealous critters in your head. The third was the bystander who now finds him- or herself in the unfortunate position of potentially facing charges. Sadly, people have been wrongly convicted on the basis of such misunderstandings.

Other demonstrations of false alarms in recognition show that people sometimes recognize things they never encountered. Consider a study by John Bransford and his colleagues at Vanderbilt University.[48] They presented people with sentences like the following:

The shirt looked terrible because George ironed it.
The floor was dirty because Diane used the mop.

When you read these sentences, you may infer that George couldn't iron and that Diane used a mop that was dirty. If you form such inferences, there's a good chance you'll later think you saw "George couldn't iron" and "Diane used a dirty mop." You didn't see those sentences, but later you'll think you did. You might even *swear* you did.

A similar result is obtained with simple word lists. If you're shown a list such as "milk, sugar, cup, Starbucks," there's a good chance you'll later say you saw the word "coffee." You didn't! You *thought* of coffee while reading the list and then, having come up with the word yourself, are likely to false-alarm to it later.[49]

A last point about false-alarming is that you can be provoked to false-alarm to inferences you drew long *after* you take in stuff to be remembered. This *post-exposure* effect, as it's called, was discovered by Elizabeth Loftus, then at the University of Washington in Seattle and now at the University of California, Irvine.[50]

In one of her experiments, Loftus showed people images of a car stopping at a stop sign or at a yield sign. Other participants saw images of the same car merely slowing down at the same stop sign or yield sign. A given participant saw only one of these four combinations.[51] Later, Loftus asked the participants, "Did the car stop at the stop sign?" or "Did the car stop at the yield sign?" She posed these questions both to participants who actually saw the stop sign but did not see the yield sign, and to participants who actually saw the yield sign but did not see the stop sign.

Loftus found that when participants were later tested for recognition of scenes they hadn't actually seen, they falsely recognized pictures implied by the leading question. So if a participant didn't actually see a yield sign but Loftus asked whether the car stopped at the yield sign, the participant would later be inclined to say that s/he did indeed see the yield sign when shown an image of the car standing by it. Similarly, if the participant didn't actually see a stop sign but Loftus asked whether the car stopped at the stop sign, the participant would be inclined later to say that s/he saw the stop sign when shown an image of the car beside it.[52] This outcome wasn't due to participants paying no attention to the sign at first. Other tests showed that they successfully recognized the sign that was shown. Likewise, they successfully rejected the sign that wasn't shown if it wasn't suggested by a deceptive leading question.[53]

Such results are explained by the jungle principle in terms that will now be familiar. Demons turned on by stop signs or demons turned on by yield signs are activated by leading questions presupposing their favored elements. Later, when recognition is tested, those demons yell loudly when their contexts are cued. Memory is biased, therefore, because demons activate themselves and their allies, and they also deactivate their foes. What you remember, then, is less accurate and more malleable than what you might expect. If you subscribe to the jungle principle, however, you won't be surprised to learn that your memory is a wild and wooly place.

Contents of Recall

The final part of this chapter is concerned with the contents of recall. These, I will argue, reflect elfish selfishness.

What you recall isn't always a faithful reflection of what actually happened but instead can be a *reconstruction* of what occurred. Such re-rendering of past events stems from mental elves acting like members of a mob trying to throw their weight around, adding their two cents (or more if they can) to their sense of what happened in a cued context. Each time an elf gets to have its identity expressed, it gets a bit stronger (or at least it gets no weaker). Consequently, recall tends to be influenced by the interests of the elves who are most active, and recall obeys an epistemic rich-get-richer scheme.

What I've just said amounts to the claim that recall is reconstructive. This idea was advanced by the British psychologist, Sir Frederic Bartlett, whose impact was so great and his esteem so high that he was knighted for his contributions—hence the "Sir" before his name. Bartlett asked British subjects to listen to a story called "The War of the Ghosts." The story was weird, at least compared to typical British tales. On the other hand, it wasn't weird for Kwak'wala Indians who live on Vancouver Island, from whom the story came. Bartlett's English subjects had a hard time recalling the story. They transformed it when recalling it, retelling it in a way that fit standard British storylines. The Kwak'wala did no such thing. They recalled it as presented. Seeing his British subjects normalize the scripts rather than repeat them exactly, Bartlett concluded that recall is reconstruction, not rote regurgitation.

Bartlett's insight laid the groundwork for the work of Elizabeth Loftus and others. One of them was Ulric Neisser of Cornell University and Emory University, who is often credited with coalescing the field of cognitive psychology chiefly through his 1967 book by that name.[54] Some of Neisser's work was on memory and continued along the line established by Bartlett. Here is what was said about Neisser's work on memory in an obituary that appeared for him:

Dr. Neisser's work showed that memory is a reconstruction of the past, not an accurate snapshot of it.... The mind, he said, conflates things. In a much-publicized experiment the day after the space shuttle Challenger exploded in 1986, Dr. Neisser asked students to write down their immediate experience upon hearing the news. Nearly three years later, he asked them to recount it. A quarter of the accounts were strikingly different, half were somewhat different, and less than a tenth had all the details correct. All were confident that their latter accounts were completely accurate. Another memory experiment compared the testimony of John W. Dean III, the former aide to President Richard M. Nixon, during the Senate Watergate hearings with tapes of Mr. Dean's conversations that the president had secretly recorded. He found discrepancies in detail after detail. But Dr. Neisser said the testimony was accurate about the most important truths: that there really had been a cover-up, and that Nixon did approve it.[55]

As the obituary indicates, misremembering reflects normalization. It can also reflect prejudice. In seminal research on the effects of prejudice on memory, other researchers showed people pictures of socially charged events. One image showed a white man holding up a black man at gunpoint. When the participants were later asked to recall what they saw, many of them recalled a black man holding up a white man. Prejudice led to the false memory. If the event had been real, the wrong person might have been accused of the crime. False arrests and convictions have occurred all too often for this reason.

Remembering wrongly can be affected by biases wrought *after* events are experienced as well as before. This possibility was demonstrated in another series of studies by Elizabeth Loftus. Here, she and John Palmer, both at the University of Washington at the time, showed participants a film of one car apparently having an accident with another.[56] Later, the researchers asked different participants different leading questions, with the assignment of questions to subjects being random. The questions included the following. I have italicized the word that distinguished the questions from one another to help you see the differences. The experimenters did not change their vocal stress.

About how fast were the cars going when they *contacted* with each other?
About how fast were the cars going when they *hit* each other?
About how fast were the cars going when they *collided* with each other?
About how fast were the cars going when they *smashed* into each other?

The question the researchers were interested in was how fast the participants would say the cars were going depending on the word used in the question. The average speed estimates the participants gave were 31.8 miles per hour (mph) for "contacted," 34.2 mph for "hit," 39.8 mph for "collided," and 40.8 mph for "smashed." Thus, the more forceful the verb used to describe the event, the more quickly the participants remembered the cars as having traveled. Because the verbs were presented *after* the movies were watched, the subjects revised their memories after their memories were formed. This effect applied not just to speed but also to the appearance of the accident scene. The more forceful the verb, the higher the likelihood that subjects recalled seeing broken glass on the road. No broken glass ever appeared, however.

Results like these are unsettling if you believe you can trust your memories. If you, or your identity, *are* your memories but you can't trust your own memories, who can you trust? That's a question I can't answer for you. All I can is say that this question is one each of us asks from time to time as we consider the rough-and-tumble world we live in. As if it's not unsettling enough to remember that we live in a tough *outer* world, I'm now telling you that you live in, or house, a tough *inner* world as well. Perhaps inner toughness is optimally suited for the tough outer world we live in.[57] If the same sorts of dynamics capture what goes on internally as well as externally, the way we remember may be best for both worlds.[58]

Summing Up

As with the other chapters of this book, I tried in this chapter to review the results of research on the topic at hand—learning and memory in this case— to see whether they could be understood in terms of Darwinian dynamics. What I presented can indeed be understood in Darwinian terms. The fact that this is so is hardly surprising given that the concepts and abilities acquired over the lifespan are adaptive; they are likely to help in everyday life. More importantly, the building blocks of these concepts and abilities get mixed and matched in ways that can give rise to the kinds of learning and memory phenomena reviewed here. These were only a subset of all the phenomena that could be discussed, of course. But no other phenomenon that I'm aware of in the domain of learning and memory vitiates the Darwinian view.

As a final remark, I want to mention that while I was preparing this chapter, I found out about a book I was unaware of before, *Beyond the Learning Curve: The Construction of Mind*, by Craig Speelman and Kim Kirsner (2005). Near the end of the book, the authors wrote the following:

> The general principle in our theory of entities competing for survival, with the winners surviving to undertake future competition, and losers dying off, is wholly consistent with natural selection.... Thus, while biological evolution involves intergenerational changes or adaptation in species characteristics, intelligence and changes therein enable intra-generational adaptation in the behaviour of individuals [p 228].

Taking stock of this statement, we see once again that other investigators, after summarizing their field of specialization, appealed to Darwin's theory. That Darwin's idea extends so far and wide can hardly be accidental.

9

Aha!

The sight of a man running through the streets wearing nothing but a bath towel and screaming deliriously is usually cause for concern. But if the man is yelling "Eureka!" and he happens to be an ancient Greek who has spent months pondering a problem for his king, his running through the streets and shouting at the top of his lungs could be cause for celebration.

The ancient Greek to whom I refer—Archimedes by name—had been approached by King Hiero II to determine whether a crown the king had received was solid gold. The question arose because the king had handed pure gold to a goldsmith for the crown's creation, but when the king got the crown back, he suspected the goldsmith may have filched some of the precious metal, replacing it, the king feared, with some cheaper alloy. How to check the content of the crown without damaging it? That was the problem Hiero handed Archimedes. Hiero turned to Archimedes because Archimedes was the smartest of Hiero's subjects. Archimedes, meanwhile, had his reputation on the line.

Archimedes thought long and hard about the problem, but to no avail. No matter how hard he thought, he always came up dry. Then one day, while settling into a bath, he noticed that the water rose as he lowered himself into the water. Such a common observation would have gone unnoticed by most people, but Archimedes' mind had been preoccupied with matters related to volume measurement. Archimedes knew that the density of an object equals its volume divided by its mass. He also knew what the mass of the crown was and what the density of pure gold was. Archimedes understood that he could divide the mass of the crown by its volume to see whether the ratio of mass to volume—the crown's density—matched the density of pure gold. What Archimedes didn't know was how to estimate the crown's volume. Archimedes and his fellow Greeks knew how to measure the volumes of regularly shaped objects like cubes and spheres; the formulas for doing so were among their proudest achievements. But they didn't know how to measure the volumes of irregularly shaped objects like crowns for kings, or bodies for mathematicians. The problem had befuddled him for months.

When Archimedes lowered himself into the tub and saw the water rise, he realized that the height to which the water rose was related to how much he displaced it. The water would rise more for a more voluminous body, Archimedes realized, and he appreciated that this would be true no matter what the body's shape.

So excited was Archimedes by seeing the connection between water displacement and volume that, according to legend, he jumped out of the tub and ran through the streets shouting "Eureka!" That term means something like, "Whoopee! I'm so happy! I just figured out how to solve a nasty problem that's been bugging me for ages!"

The history of problem-solving is filled with examples of people reaching solutions in the seemingly paradoxical way that Archimedes did—being unable at first to solve the problem and then having the solution come to them as if from the blue. Solutions don't come from thin air, of course. They come from gray matter and white matter in the brain. How this happens is the problem cognitive psychologists have sought to solve while bathing, so to speak, in their own data and theories.

Cognitive psychologists have used the word "aha" to refer to the moment when the transition happens from not seeing a solution to seeing it. A challenge for cognitive psychologists is to understand how aha moments come about. Another challenge is to check whether aha moments are epiphenomenal. Are they, in other words, extraneous moments of joy that happen to coincide with finding solutions, or are they events critical to hitting on the solutions themselves? Are problems solved in bursts, or are they solved gradually?

In considering this question, I had something of an aha moment when I realized that the jungle principle could shed light on problem-solving itself. I realized it could because the jungle principle provides a useful metaphor for thinking about the search for solutions. The idea was that cognitive demons can collectively embody solutions to problems, but for the right cadre of cognitive demons to form, they must be activated to the point that they yield insights that previously were out of reach. Groups of cognitive demons that represent solutions may be suppressed by other more dominant demons, not because those other demons feared the repercussions of the solutions about to unfold—the solutions were not yet recognized, after all—but because the business of the demons already in control was more pressing, more worthwhile, than the business of the demons not yet unionized. If the neural environment fails to favor unions that permit problem solutions, they're not selected for. But once a coalition of cranial creatures comes together in a way that's fortuitous, the system as a whole can move from a state of "Yuk, I'm stuck!" to a state of "Aha, I'm in luck!"

Incubation

When Archimedes dipped into his bath and had his eureka moment, he was not, as far as I know, filthy from weeks of non-bathing. Presumably, he had taken baths prior to the bath that figuratively knocked his socks off. When he bathed prior to his eureka experience, Archimedes was unimpressed by the waxing and waning of his bathwater. Merely seeing the water rise and fall in those earlier ablutions didn't trigger his recognition of the solution he sought. But something changed in Archimedes' mind when he saw the solution. What was it?

Cognitive psychologists who study problem-solving say that problem-solving benefits from *incubation*. Their idea is that solutions not yet found are like chicks not yet hatched. A hen sitting on her egg provides the egg-bound chick with the heat and protection it needs to grow and ultimately break out of its shell. Cognitive psychologists say that solutions to problems are like that. Like chicks in their eggs, solutions to problems not yet solved need the right milieu to spring forth. Only when solutions are sufficiently mature will they be realized.

Other anecdotes besides the one concerning Archimedes provide further support for the incubation view. Consider an experience of the great French mathematician, Henri Poincaré. This giant of mathematics, whose work laid the foundations for modern dynamical systems theory, worked on a difficult problem for a long time and couldn't solve it. Faced with this frustrating state of affairs, Poincaré did what any reasonable Frenchman would do: He went on vacation. The holiday had a happy effect, as Poincaré later reported:

> Then I turned my attention to the study of some arithmetical questions apparently without much success and with a suspicion of any connection with my preceding researches. Disgusted by my failure, I went to spend a few days at the seaside, and thought of something else. One morning, walking on the bluff, the idea came to me, with just the same characteristics of brevity, suddenness, and immediate certainty, that the arithmetic transformations of indeterminate ternary quadratic forms were identical with those of non-Euclidean geometry.[1]

It turns out that Poincaré was not alone in having a solution find him, so to speak, rather than the other way around. Other notable thinkers have had similar experiences, and they continue to do so. For example, while I was working on this chapter, *Science* magazine ran an advertisement for a website created by its parent organization, the American Association for the Advancement of Science. The advertisement showed the inventor of the vaccine patch, Carl Alving, along with a quote about how he came up with his medical breakthrough. "A dream told me to do it," Alving said in the ad, which ran for several issues.[2]

Experiments have shown that incubation is a real phenomenon and not one limited to luminaries like Archimedes, Poincaré, or Alving. Incubation helps ordinary folks solve mundane problems like crossword puzzles, riddles, and other amusement problems.[3] Take the "cheap necklace" problem. The challenge here is to create a single necklace out of four 3-link segments given three constraints: (1) It costs 2 cents to open a link, (2) it costs 3 cents to close a link, and (3) no more than 15 cents can be spent altogether. Think about this problem and see if you can solve it. It's challenging. There's a good chance you won't be able to find a solution immediately if you're like most people. The solution is given in the note referred to here.[4]

A psychological study of the cheap-necklace problem showed that incubation helps lead to its solution. College students were assigned to three groups. One group worked on the problem nonstop for half an hour; 55% of the students in this group solved it. A second group worked on the problem for 15 minutes, had a half-hour break during which they did other things, and then worked on the problem for a final 15 minutes; 64% of the students in this group solved the problem. A third group had a 15-minute work period, a 4-hour break filled with other activities, and then a final 15-minute work session; 85% of the students in this group found the solution.[5]

These results show that the more time a group had with a problem, the more likely they were to solve it. The outcome wasn't due to the fact that participants who had more time to work on the problem came back with the solution; that wouldn't have been interesting. What happened was more informative. Participants with breaks came back without having already solved the problem, but soon after returning to it were able to get it. It was as if, with more time away, there was more chance for the chick to nearly hatch.

Set Effects

I've likened working on problems to hens keeping their eggs warm, but what mechanism actually underlies incubation? It's insufficient to say that the mechanism is keeping potential solutions warm, for that doesn't answer the question of what the warming does. It also leaves unanswered the larger question of how new solutions arise, which is the main question of interest.

The time to solve a problem reflects the time for neural cooperation and competition to reach a point where a solution becomes possible. The appropriate balance of power must be reached among ideas or idea components for solutions to emerge. Are there findings about problem-solving that shed light on this process?

Consider an activity that any child would love—pouring water into and out of jugs. The aspect of this activity that might challenge the youngster despite the initial appeal of the water play is the need to end up with a specific quantity. The target volume differs from the volume of any of the jugs, and no extra measuring cups are available. To solve the problem, what's needed is a series of "jugular" additions and subtractions.

The table below shows a series of problems that a group of participants was given in a famous study of problem-solving that involved jug-to-jug water transfers.[6] All the problems except the eighth could be solved by first filling jug B, then emptying jug B into jug C, then emptying jug C and filling jug B again, then emptying jug B into jug C once more, and finally pouring jug B into jug A. The amount left over in jug B would be the target amount, given by the equation $B - 2C - A = 100$.

Problem	Jug A	Jug B	Jug C	Desired Quantity
1	21	127	3	100
2	14	163	25	99
3	18	43	10	5
4	9	42	6	21
5	20	59	4	31
6	23	49	3	20
7	15	39	3	18
8	28	76	3	25
9	18	48	4	22
10	14	36	8	6

When this series of pours proved useful—that is, when it was adaptive to pour according to the procedure $B - 2C - A$—participants came to rely on it, using the procedure over and over again because it worked, as it did in problems 1–7. "If it ain't broke, don't fix it," the participants seemed to say to themselves, which was fine until the procedure no longer satisfied the task demand, in problem 8. Then things fell apart. Many participants failed to solve the eighth problem even though they had gotten better and better on the problems before.

What does this finding reveal about problem-solving? It shows that when a procedure proves useful, it dominates. This is fine as long as the procedure helps. But when it doesn't help, despite having proven useful before, it still tries to rule the roost, so to speak, inhibiting the method that would work if given a chance.

Persisting with a method is called a *set* effect. The word "set" refers to the fact that you can get stuck in your ways. This can be helpful if the method proves useful, but it can be detrimental otherwise.[7]

Here's another example of a set effect. Try to unscramble each letter string so it makes a word.

kmli

recma

graus

foefce

teews

ikrdn

Once you get the idea that the solutions pertain to coffee-drinking, the solutions come in a rush, bursting forth like froth from an espresso machine. The time to solve anagrams like these, which are semantically organized, is much shorter than the time to solve anagrams that are not.

Functional Fixedness

The effect I've just summarized illustrates a positive set effect. There are also negative set effects. One was illustrated earlier in the difficult transition to the eighth step of the jug-pouring exercise. Negative set effects are also seen in studies of *functional fixedness*. Here people tend to get mentally fixed in the functions they assign to problem elements.[8]

Consider the problem of joining two hanging strings that are too far apart to be grasped simultaneously with outstretched arms. Present in the scene, besides the two hanging strings, are various objects: a chair, a jar with tacks, some other tacks lying on the floor, some pieces of paper, and a pair of pliers. How would you solve the problem?[9]

An initial temptation might be to move the chair midway between the strings and climb up before reaching either one. But that does you no good. The distance between the strings is just what it was before. Whichever string is farther from you is just as out of reach as it was before you mounted the chair. Tossing things at one of the strings to drive it toward the other is a method that might cross your mind, but that strategy is iffy at best.

Eventually, people figure out what to do, but their ability to do so depends on their seeing that one of the extraneous objects in the scene can serve a function other than the one it normally does. Pliers are normally used for squeezing, but you can also tie pliers to a string and set the string in motion. Once the weighted string swings to and fro, you can walk to the other side, catch the pliers as they swing toward you, and join the cords.

Seeing the pliers as a tool for gripping rather than as a tool for swinging leaves you stuck, suffering from functional fixedness. Overcoming blindness to the alternative function that pliers can serve—being a weight rather than a squeezer—lets you solve the problem.

Blindness to novel applications is just what you'd expect if you subscribe to the view that it's a jungle in there. Mental demons with narrow self-interests get excited by relevant stimuli. The sight of pliers activates demons related to gripping and squeezing, and they inhibit other demons with which they normally compete, such as demons that swing rather than squeeze.[10]

Helpful Hints

If the source of functional fixedness is what I've just said—cognitive creatures squelching other cognitive creatures—then there's a theoretically motivated anti-dote to such functional fixedness. By activating mental creatures who get turned on by swinging, it should be possible to help would-be problem-solvers overcome the fix they're in. This expectation is borne out: Giving hints to participants in problem-solving tasks helps them find solutions more quickly. For example, encouraging people to swing their arms helps them solve the two-string problem.[11]

Another example of a hint helping to fix functional fixedness comes from another problem studied by cognitive psychologists. This is the problem of mounting a candle on a wall. Part of the challenge is to leave the candle on the mount, burning brightly for as long as the wick will last. The materials you can work with are a candle, matches, and a box of tacks. Think about the problem for a while. The solution is given a few paragraphs from now.

One of the things that make the candle-on-the-wall problem hard is the way it's presented. The way the objects are shown can obscure the path to its solution. Showing the box filled with tacks makes the problem harder to solve than showing the box empty, with the tacks lying beside it.[12]

What makes the tacks-free box less taxing? When the box is filled, you're more likely to see it just as a container. But when the box is empty, you're more likely to see it as something that can serve some other relevant function, such as providing a base of support. Once you realize the box can support the candle, it's relatively easy to see that the tacks can be used to pin the box to the wall. If the box is pinned right-side-up rather than upside-down, it can even collect the melted wax, which may be appreciated by the homeowner whose residence you've turned into a haunted house.

Framing Effects

The discovery that people are more likely to solve the candle-on-the-wall problem when the box is empty than when it's full is a classic finding in the problem-solving literature. It was one of the first demonstrations of functional fixedness. As it happens, the demonstration can also be seen as one of the first indicators of an important finding that led to a Nobel Prize in Economics. The finding came from two cognitive psychologists, Amos Tversky and Daniel Kahneman, who showed that the way a question is framed strongly affects the answer it receives.[13]

A dramatic example of this framing effect, as it's called, pertains to the probability that people express willingness to donate their organs in case of traffic accidents. When you renew your driver's license in the United States and Germany, you check a box to indicate that you're willing to donate your organs. The acceptance rate, on average, is 14%. In other countries, such as France and Poland, when people renew their driver's licenses, they check a box to indicate that they're *not* willing to donate their organs. Then only 10% say they'd be unwilling to donate, so 90% of the respondents say, in effect, "Sure, you can have my organs if I die."[14] Amazingly, then, the logically equivalent question—"Are you *willing* to donate your organs?" or "Are you *unwilling* to donate your organs"—yields totally different outcomes.

What accounts for this amazing effect of the way the same question is framed? The surface features of the problem activate demons who take over the thought process. Demons for willingness to donate take over in one framing, whereas demons for unwillingness to donate take over in the other. Similarly, in the candle problem, demons favoring containment are activated by the sight of a box holding thumbtacks, and those agents inhibit agents favoring support. Conversely, demons favoring support are activated by the sight of a box *not* holding thumbtacks, and they inhibit demons who favor containment. Framing effects are expected, then, if it's a jungle in there. Creatures given a leg up try to tie down creatures who get no helpful kick.

Think Outside the Box

Solving problems benefits from the openness of mind called "creativity." Consider one form of creativity that arises in connection with another problem commonly studied in cognitive psychology—the 9-dot problem. The problem begins with an innocent-looking diagram—a 3 × 3 array of dots. If you undertake the problem, you try to connect the 9 dots with 4 straight lines. A further constraint is to do so without lifting the tip of your pencil from the drawing surface. Try the problem if you wish. Here, for your drawing enjoyment, are the nine dots.

```
.   .   .

.   .   .

.   .   .
```

People are often flummoxed by the 9-dot problem. They try paths that leave them frustrated. No matter how the series of four straight lines is drawn—whether it includes a diagonal from the top left to the bottom right or a diagonal from the bottom left to the top right—the lines fail to intersect some of the dots. This is true as long as all the lines fit within the imaginary box joining the outer dots of the matrix. But it's that imaginary box that hems you in. Your imagination limits you, for you see a box, or your mind imposes one. A box is for containment, for keeping things inside. Once you think outside the box, you can solve the problem. If you let your pencil go beyond the box's borders (a box that was never mentioned), you can join the nine dots with four straight, connected lines.[15] This example is often used in creativity workshops. When people are encouraged to "think outside the box," the box referred to is often the one from the 9-dot problem.[16]

It's important not to blame yourself for failing to think outside the box. If you attempt the 9-dot problem and can't solve it, you're unlikely to become more creative by castigating yourself for being less creative than you'd like. In fact, a damning attitude is likely to curtail creativity, not inspire it. Being down doesn't help the creative juices flow. Being up and lighthearted has the opposite effect. People exposed to comedy routines display measurable increases in creativity, as do people tipsy from alcohol.[17]

Analogies

Disappointingly, it often takes in-your-face directives to help people solve problems. This fact about thinking was established in relation to the problem of killing a tumor with radiation beams. The challenge was to kill the tumor without damaging the surrounding tissue. The researchers who did this study told people who would work on the problem a story about multiple invading armies attacking a fort from many sides.[18] The multiple armies could slip through enemy lines on the way to the fort and could then join the other forces at the fort to capture it. Would people hearing the story see the connection to the radiation problem?

Many people who were told the story did *not* make the connection. On the other hand, when people were explicitly told that the tale about the invading armies bore on the problem, more of them could see that the tumor could be killed by shooting weak beams at the tumor from many angles. This finding about the explication of analogies shows that sometimes you've got to "hit people over the head" to help them use their heads more wisely. Why some people need this more explicit advice and others don't is, as far as I know, not well understood.

True Creativity

What really matters in problem-solving is the ability to solve problems that truly matter, that can change the course of history, hopefully for the better. True creativity is a great asset. It's one of the things that define genius. This doesn't mean that creativity can be shown only in lofty spheres where geniuses strut their stuff. It can also arise in the context of the little party-game problems that are often studied in cognitive psychology labs, always with an eye toward shedding light on the ability to solve more important problems.

Consider, for example, the 9-dot problem again. I once read about a solution to this problem that was so clever it made me swoon. Whoever came up with the solution realized that the 9-dot problem could be completed with just *one* line! His or her solution didn't rely on the implicit premise that the 9-dot surface is flat. "Suppose, instead," this person must have said to him- or herself, "that the surface is curved, like the Earth's surface. On the Earth's crust, straight lines are actually curved, which is why, if you keep going in a straight line on Earth, you end up where you started." Based on this insight, it became possible to solve the 9-dot problem with one straight line, or a line that would appear straight from the perspective of an earthling. A spiral going

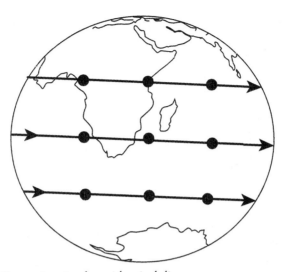

FIGURE 14. Connecting nine dots with a single line.

around Earth, passing through all the dots of the 9-dot problem, satisfies the problem and then some (Figure 14). Whoever came up with this solution was a particularly inventive person. I have no idea who it was. If he or she is reading this book, "Hats off to you!"

This'll Do

Perhaps the ultimate form of creativity is seeing a solution to a problem that wasn't even recognized as a problem before. A wonderful example concerns a man wandering through a field in Switzerland with his dog. While walking past some thistles, the canine brushed against some burs, which then clung to the dog's fur. Had this happened to you or me—had a thistle clung to your sweater or mine—you or I might have been annoyed to the point of proclaiming, "Damn thistles!" or words less fit for print. The man in the story had a different reaction. He realized that having objects stick to fabric could be useful. Based on this insight, he invented one of the most common and useful items known: Velcro.[19]

It's inspiring to learn the story of the invention of Velcro. You may even say to yourself, "I'll be on the lookout for things that may solve problems." But feeling inspired and saying that inspiration is the source of problem-solving isn't all that useful from a scientific perspective. Deciding to be more creative is about as useful, scientifically speaking, as saying that problems are solved through insight. Saying you'll be open-minded may get your creative juices flowing (whatever they are), but the statement doesn't have much explanatory power. As Thomas Edison so famously declared, "Invention is 10% inspiration and 90% perspiration."

Hard work is indeed important for invention because it keeps you involved with a problem for a sustained period of time. The longer you work on a problem, the greater the chance you'll hit on a solution. An egg kept warm for a long time is more likely to hatch than an egg warmed briefly. Merely declaring that you'd like to lay an egg is fine for starters, but it hardly cracks the surface of what's needed to go from a bird in the bush to a bird in the hand.[20]

Improvisation

If invention takes time, you should be able to find evidence for it brewing. As a practical matter, though, it's unlikely that you can actually catch an invention when it first comes to mind because inventions come along rarely.

Not to be deterred, two researchers, working at the National Institutes of Health at the time, managed to devise a way of seeing invention in progress. The researchers—Charles Limb and Allen Braun—scanned the brains of jazz musicians as the musicians improvised at the keyboard.[21] The scientists reasoned that during jazz improvisation, invention goes on continually. Consequently, they hypothesized that the brain activity of jazz improvisers might provide a glimpse into the neural basis of invention generally.

Limb and Braun studied their jazz-pianist participants in two conditions. In the experimental condition, the pianists improvised at the keyboard. In the control condition, the pianists played a piece they had memorized. The memorized piece was composed by the researchers to mimic in critical ways the keyboard sequences the experimenters expected the jazz musicians to play while improvising. The number of notes, the fingers used, the transitions between the notes, and so on were expected to approximate those in the "improv." This expectation was borne out, so Limb and Braun went on to compare the brain activity of the pianists in the play-from-memory condition and in the "improv" condition.

Consistent with the researchers' expectations, they found that different areas of the brain were active when the pianists recalled or improvised. One area of the brain, the medial prefrontal cortex, which is associated with self-expression, became more active in the improvisation condition than in the play-from-memory condition. The other area of the brain, the lateral prefrontal cortex, which is associated with conscious self-monitoring and inhibition of one's own behavior, became *less* active in the improvisation condition than in the play-from-memory condition.

Limb and Braun's results are consistent with the inner-jungle perspective in that some neural creatures turned out to be better suited for some tasks than others. Nonetheless, that finding is far from the full set of results needed to trace all the steps needed to go from the origin of a musical idea to its full musical expression. More work is needed on this difficult problem, including checking whether the results of the Limb and Braun study really got at invention *per se*. It could be that these scientists picked up brain differences related to the *attitudes* needed for musical invention versus musical recall but not for the spawning of new note sequences versus the recall of old ones.

Whether there is or could be a site for the spawning of new musical sequences is an open question. According to the perspective offered in this book, there needn't be (and probably isn't) a specific site where new ideas are formed. Rather, the formation of new ideas (and the destruction of old, not-very-useful ideas) is likely to occur everywhere in the neural jungle and, for that matter, all the time.

Recombination

Just as it is hard to tell where ideas come from in the neural population of a brain, it is hard to tell where an idea comes from in the population of people on the planet. In this context, a fair question is this one: How original am I, the author of this book, in advocating a Darwinian view of creativity? My unabashed answer is not very. Other authors have seen this connection before. One who did so a little more than half a century ago was the American social scientist, and once president of the American Psychological Association, Donald Campbell. He argued that creative thought relies on Darwin's mechanisms of random variation and selective retention.[22] Other authors have made similar arguments.[23]

Some who have pursued this approach have used sophisticated computational methods to test and refine their claims. One such method relies on *genetic algorithms*. The idea is to recombine rule elements to produce new "offspring" and to continue to do so the more adaptive the offspring turn out to be.[24] This approach has been used in a wide range of applications, including the development of new commercial products by computers.[25] Researchers who have worked on these systems have explicitly likened them to evolutionary processes. I've said only a few words about this approach here because the approach gets computationally intensive very quickly, and this book is not a technical treatise.

Genius

Another author who has likened creativity to Darwinian selection is Dean Keith Simonton of the University of California, Davis.[26] Simonton wrote a book, *Origins of Genius: Darwinian Perspectives on Creativity*. My mention of Simonton's book is meant to show that I feel, as concerns creativity, that I have merely continued the tradition established by Simonton and others. Where I have tried to go a bit further is to focus on a broader range of cognitive phenomena, many from the lab.

Building on Simonton's insights, however, I would venture to say that all cognitive phenomena can be profitably analyzed in Darwinian terms, not just those associated with problem-solving, whether done at the genius or ordinary-person level.

Speaking of geniuses, there is, at the end, someone who fully anticipated the point about problem-solving offered here. That genius was none other than Charles Darwin. His writings, it turns out, hint at his appreciation that his own theory might apply to thinking itself, including his own.[27]

It would be stunning if Darwin had not seen this connection, for in hindsight it is obvious. Once Darwin cleared the path for this simple way of understanding thinking, it takes considerably less genius, I believe, to see that just as species or series of species manage to solve the problems they face through trial and error in environments where they compete and cooperate, so inner (mental) species or series of species do the same.

10

Onward!

As I wrote in the Preface, the first time I used the phrase "It's a jungle in there," I was teaching Introduction to Cognitive Psychology at Penn State University. It occurred to me one day in the midst of a lecture that the phrase "It's a jungle in there" might convey the essence of what I was trying to say about a particular cognitive phenomenon. When I mentioned the phrase, not sure how it would go over, I was surprised to see how well it was received. It aroused more interest than I usually got, so I felt encouraged to repeat it. Soon the saying took on a life of its own. As the course went on, before I got to the explanation of an experimental result, some students would call out, "It's a jungle in there, right?"

I told this story about the birth of this book's title in the Preface and repeat it here in case you didn't read the Preface or don't remember it. My added reason for mentioning the origin of the phrase is to set the context for another phrase I often use in my teaching. It's a phrase that establishes the tone for this final chapter. Besides saying "It's a jungle in there," I often say, with my arms outstretched and with a beseeching expression on my face, "I stand before you intellectually naked."

When I refer to my intellectual nakedness, I don't mean to arouse images of nudity. Being a professor with a classic "professor body," one formed by hours of sitting and writing rather than by hours of running and lifting weights, I don't have a physique most people pine for. So when I say, "I stand before you intellectually naked," I mean to express humility, not hubris.

My humility applies to the explanation given for the cognitive phenomenon I happen to be describing in the lecture I am giving. At such times, whatever research problem I've just broached begs for a solution. I explain that I have no true solution to the problem, and neither does anyone else.

Here's an example. When I introduce language production, I invite my students to stop and think about how remarkable it is that they can form thoughts and express those thoughts with words produced through the movements of their tongues and lips. "How on earth do you do this?" I ask them. I confess that no one has any idea how thoughts originate. No one really knows what thoughts are, at least at the neural level. At such times, I offer my confession, standing before the students palms up, admitting my intellectual vulnerability. I then go on to say, "Maybe, one of you will solve this deep problem."[1]

It is with this same frame of mind that I must tell you now, as I begin the last chapter of this book, that I stand (or sit) before you intellectually naked, humbled by all that remains to be done with the idea offered here. What I have suggested—the so-called jungle principle—is more a sketch than a complete theory. Were I to proclaim that the jungle principle fully explains all that needs to be explained, I would be stretching things too far. "The emperor wears no clothes," you might rightly proclaim.[2]

I wish I could say in detail how the jungle principle makes us who we are, how it explains our creativity, our joviality, our agility. In truth, I can't provide such a detailed account. Nor can I map out in detail how the jungle principle yields hostility, avarice, or jealousy—emotions that are less fun to think about but define us just as much. Neither can I say precisely how mental illness arises from the competitive and cooperative processes in the brain. Why schizophrenia, paranoia, or autism beset some people are topics I can't really answer. The jungle principle allows for these syndromes, but how it does so, or why it does to different degrees in different people, is something I can't answer.

My expression of humility may seem at odds with the boldness of the pronouncement given earlier in this volume, that I have an idea for a global theory of cognition—or rather that I think such an idea has been available since the mid-1800s. There's no contradiction between hopefulness and humility, however. The main impetus for the theory I've sketched is the acknowledgment that the field of cognitive psychology (or cognitive science more generally) is in need of an all-embracing principle. As I said in the Preface, cognitive phenomena are generally presented as a rag-tag collection of curiosities—what might be found at a psychologists' tag sale. It takes humility to say that this is the state of affairs and that we should try to do better.

How can you and I search for a fuller account than the one given here? In the remainder of this chapter, I'll try to point the way by addressing several issues that haven't been addressed yet. For all of them, I'll argue that the Darwinian approach is promising. First, I'll discuss concepts and conceptual development. Then I'll consider emotions, sex, and altered states of consciousness. In the section after that, I'll comment briefly on social cognition. Consciousness and qualities of experience (qualia) will be the focus of the subsequent section. The section after that will be concerned with evolutionary psychology, an important area of contemporary research to which this book bears similarities but also important differences. The transmission of ideas between individuals will be covered in the next section. The origin of language will come up in the section to follow. In the penultimate section, I will say more about the sort of theory we should strive for. Here I will defend the view that the sort of theory offered here, inspired by Darwin, is the kind of theory we should pursue. In the final section, I will review how the jungle view could be applied to all the topics covered here and end with an urge for a critical consideration of the general proposal offered in this book.

Concepts

A topic I didn't cover before was the mental representation of concepts. An early proposal about concepts was that they are mental entities that can be captured by rules. An *animal*, for example, is a living thing that eats, breathes, and so on. A *bird*, meanwhile, has those attributes and others that other animals don't. Birds have feathers, for example. Because of this exclusive feature of birds vis-à-vis other animals, it's possible to entertain the possibility that in people's minds, the concept of *bird* is a subset of the concept of *animal*. If that's the case, it should be possible to place the concept of bird beneath the concept of *animal* in a neat and tidy tree diagram of the sort an executive of a large corporation would approve.

If this hierarchical structure does indeed characterize the way concepts are mentally organized, less time should be needed to affirm that a bird has feathers than to affirm that a bird eats. In other words, if you read a sentence like "A bird has feathers" or "A bird eats," you should need less time to press a "Yes" button following the first sentence than the second. The reason is that "has feathers" is more directly linked to *bird* than is "eats."

This prediction was confirmed in an experiment designed to test it for a broad range of sentences, not just the pair given above. In general, the more levels that had to be accessed to arrive at a correct "Yes" answer, the longer people took to give that response.[3]

This outcome is consistent with the hierarchical model. However, other findings called the model into question. These other results showed that concepts are not mentally organized in a neat, tidy hierarchy. Rather, they occupy a much "wilder forest" where they engage in a kind of free-for-all, clamoring for recognition.

What findings challenged the hierarchical model? Two were especially damaging. One was that verification times were not always best predicted by the number of levels that supposedly existed. For example, the time to confirm that "Apples are eaten" was less than the time to confirm that "Apples have dark seeds."[4] This outcome goes against the hierarchical model because "have dark seeds" should be stored directly with apples. By contrast, "are eaten" should not (or need not) be stored with "apples."

The obtained result—that people are quicker to confirm the "are eaten" proposition than the "dark seeds" proposition—makes sense from the perspective of how often people say things about those concepts. You've probably said, "I like to eat apples" or "Apples are good to eat." It's less likely that you've said, "Apples have dark seeds." It makes intuitive sense that if you've said something often, your saying it over and over helps you confirm it quickly. Yet according to the hierarchical theory, at least in unelaborated form, how often you say something shouldn't affect the time you need to say it's true.

The other result that's problematic for the hierarchical model came from studies of typicality. If an example of a concept is typical (usual) or atypical (unusual), that shouldn't affect how easily you can confirm that the example illustrates the concept, at least according to the (unelaborated) hierarchical view. However, typicality matters. If you think of examples of birds, you're more likely to think of "robin" or "canary" than "kiwi" or "ostrich."[5] Likewise, if you indicate whether a picture is an example of a category like "bird," you'll probably take longer to indicate that an ostrich is a bird than that a robin is a bird.[6] Finally, if you rate how sensible sentences are, you'd probably give a higher sensibility rating to the sentence "A robin flew down and began eating" than you would to the sentence "An eagle flew down and began eating."[7] This difference would not be expected if you checked propositions hierarchically.

One way cognitive psychologists have dealt with these results is to say that concepts are mentally represented in terms of stored instances. With enough stored instances, you can identify a most typical or "prototypical" example. You can also represent concepts with abstract generalizations—blanket overviews that apply to all members of the corresponding sets. Abstract generalizations are often expressed in statements like "an even number is a number that leaves a remainder of 0 when divided by 2."

There is no *a priori* reason why abstract generalizations and prototypes can't both be used by people in their everyday lives. In fact, it appears that both of them are. So you may understand what an even number is in the sense that you can generate an abstract sentence like the one I just offered, but you'd be more likely to say "2" when asked to name an even number than you would be to say "438."[8] Neither number is any "more even" than the other, of course.

How a concept is mentally represented can be affected by how it's learned. A demonstration of this principle came from a study in which two groups were taught the same concept in different ways. One group was taught the concept in a way that favored the stored-instance method. The other was taught the same concept in a way that favored the abstract-generalization method. Brain scans of the participants in the two groups, taken after they learned the concepts, showed that different areas of their brains became active depending on how they learned the concepts. For the stored-instance group, the occipital visual areas and cerebellum "lit up." For the abstract-generalization group, the prefrontal cortex became active.[9]

How do this result and the others just summarized bear on the jungle principle? First, the results suggest that concepts are not represented in terms of neat, tidy hierarchies, as already mentioned. Second, the results suggest that concepts are represented by teams of self-interested parties. All the team members metaphorically express their enthusiasm or relative lack of enthusiasm all the time. Their "votes" converge on the output system that ultimately interfaces to the outer world.

Where this leads, in my view, is that there are no concepts *per se*, or none in the sense that any concept can be equated with a specific neural state. What there are, instead, are neural networks that tend to become excited or inhibited given inputs they receive. Which neurons become excited or inhibited and to what degree defines the behavior that, from outside, suggests particular concepts within.

The Development of Concepts

Concepts do obey at least one clear and powerful constraint: They build on each other. You can't grasp a concept in tensor calculus without understanding the basics of arithmetic. You can't design advanced electrical circuits if you don't know the rudiments of electronics. It would be strange to encounter someone who understands higher concepts without appreciating the concepts' foundations. No matter how obvious this is, it provides still more evidence for the jungle view. As I'll try to show below, concept development doesn't follow the course it does just because concepts are logically dependent on one another. Concepts also develop as they do because of the dynamics of competition and cooperation within the brain.

To see what I mean, consider how you might raise doubts about Darwin's theory of evolution. You could look for data showing that some species appeared much earlier than Darwin's theory would predict. Suppose you joined a team of paleontologists who found a regular progression of complexity among specimens unearthed in a dig. The higher the layer, the more complex the organism, and the lower the layer, the simpler the organism. In the midst of their digging, while already deep down and encountering nothing but the most primitive organisms, the paleontologists suddenly find, amidst the rock layers—no loose gravel or sand here—the remains of an *ape*. "What's this doing here?" they exclaim. They bring all the specimens to the lab to find out how old they are. Sure enough, the tiny invertebrates lived millions of years ago, and the deeper down the invertebrates were, the longer ago they lived. Much to everyone's surprise, however, the proto-ape lived right in the midst of the bygone times.

Finding an ape in the midst of millions-of-years-old invertebrates would upset the Darwinian applecart, for Darwin's theory describes *evolution*, not *revolution*. Finding ape remains in the midst of other, more primitive fossils would cast doubt on Darwin's theory.[10]

Why speak of too-soon apes? The reason is that, just as it would be surprising to discover an advanced species much too soon in evolution, it would be surprising to discover an advanced concept much too soon in learning. A superstar kid might be able to understand tensor calculus at an incredibly young age, but she would be unable to grasp tensor calculus before understanding numerators and denominators. A brilliant child engineer might be able to grasp the intricacies of integrated circuits, but she wouldn't be able to do so before learning Ohm's Law.[11] Concepts build on each other. They're learned in ways that make it impossible for more complex concepts to be formed before simpler ones are established. Educators know this and develop curricula accordingly. Parents know this, too, and teach their kids simple things before teaching them more complex things. Each of us knows this as well insofar as we choose to learn what we think we can handle so far.

A parallel exists, therefore, between the development of concepts and the development of species. Just as species can be placed in an evolutionary tree, so can concepts. When you were growing up, you didn't always know what dogs were, for example. When you were little, you may have called all furry animals "doggy." "Doggy, doggy!" you may have exclaimed while pointing at a beagle or a poodle. "Doggy, doggy!" you may have also called out while pointing at a cat or goat. You may have applied the "doggy" name to anything with four legs and fur. The doggy concept served you well at the time. Among other things, your calling too many animals "doggy" may have led your mommy or daddy to smile and nod and say things like "Yes, Nora, that's a doggy" or "Yes, Sarah, that's a doggy." My wife and I said those things to our daughters, Nora and Sarah, when they were little. We encouraged them to express themselves, even if the words they were using weren't exactly right.

Parents, in general, are more apt to reinforce cuteness than conceptual or grammatical accuracy.[12]

Developmental psychologists have traced the evolution of young children's concepts through a variety of techniques. One is preferential looking. Here, children are shown single pictures and then are shown two pictures at a time. One of the pictures in the pair belongs to the same category as the single picture shown earlier; the other does not. If a child appreciates what it means for a picture to be in a category, then he or she should look longer at the out-of-place picture than at the in-place picture.

This prediction has been supported so often enough that it has come to be used with a wide range of categories to discover children's classification schemes. With this method, it has been shown that over the course of development, children's concepts become more and more differentiated. Though young children see cats and dogs as being in the same category, as reflected in their early-age looking, older children see felines and canines as belonging to different categories.[13]

The other method for studying conceptual development uses questions and answers. Here, kids answer questions like "Is it silly to say that a pig can be sorry?" or "Is it silly that a rock can be an hour long?" Using this method, Frank Keil of Yale University inferred children's conceptual taxonomies. He did so by determining the descriptors children accepted for various categories.[14] If a child said a pig could be sorry and that a person could be sorry, Keil placed pigs and persons under the same "sorry" node. Continuing this exercise for children at different grades in school, Keil showed that children's conceptual taxonomies become more and more differentiated as they advance to higher grades.

What mechanism underlies this differentiation? Whatever mechanism it is, it must have the property that it doesn't allow concepts to leapfrog. The mechanism can't allow for the formation of a more advanced concept before its predecessors take hold. In addition, the mechanism must take time to work—as long, in fact, on average, as observed rates of concept formation. The rates at which concepts are formed occupy a range of values that must never be so high that 8-month-olds can do tensor calculus or design integrated circuits. In this sense, cognitive development, like species development, is evolutionary rather than revolutionary.

A hint about the neural mechanism that underlies concept development comes from the other end of development, when the neural system falls apart rather than comes together. In a syndrome known as *semantic dementia*, which is seen mainly but not exclusively in the elderly, there is a breakdown of concept knowledge. A key feature of semantic dementia is that the later a concept is acquired in early life, the earlier it's lost. Patients with semantic dementia forget what distinguishes dachshunds from beagles before they forget what distinguishes dogs from cats, and they forget what distinguishes dogs from cats before they forget what distinguishes mammals from birds.[15] This feature of semantic dementia suggests that the most basic concepts are welded into place more firmly than are the concepts that are less basic. This feature of concept learning is decidedly Darwinian in the sense that, over the course of evolution, adaptations that prove useful in a very wide range of circumstances—for example, wherever gravity exists—tend to be preserved.

The evolutionary nature of concept learning has been noticed by others. An influential developmental psychologist, Robert Siegler, of Carnegie Mellon University, advocated a Darwinian view of cognitive development. In the Preface (p. v) of his book on this subject, *Emerging Minds*, Siegler wrote:

> In both evolutionary and cognitive developmental contexts, adaptive change seems to require mechanisms for producing new variants (species or ideas), mechanisms that select among the varying forms available at any given time, and mechanisms that lead to the more successful forms becoming increasingly prevalent over time. This analogy leads to such assumptions as that children will generally think about any given phenomena in a variety of ways, rather than only having a single understanding; that they will choose adaptively among these alternative understandings; and that their thinking will change continuously and become increasingly adaptive over time. These assumptions prove to have large implications for the questions we ask about children's thinking, the methods we use to study it, and the mechanisms we propose to account for changes in it.[16]

Siegler was mainly concerned with higher-level cognition, but his proposal can also apply to lower-level cognition, to perception, to action, and, potentially, to all the cognitive functions afforded by the brain.

After Siegler advanced his theory, another book came out that propounded the selectionist view that Darwin's theory exemplified and that Siegler endorsed. This other book built on the neural network modeling approach that the book's second author (along with others) had pioneered nearly two decades earlier.[17] The specifics of the approach needn't be spelled out now. All that needs to be said at this juncture is that the model relies on neural or neural-style elements interconnected via excitatory and inhibitory links whose strengths change with experience. In the model, the earliest-learned and most often-used connections are strongest, whereas the latest-learned and least-often-used connections are weakest. This feature of the model makes it a good candidate for explaining the feature of semantic dementia referred to above—that the most basic concepts turn out to be the most secure.[18]

What makes this model especially exciting for understanding concept learning is that it can be used to simulate the formation of concept hierarchies. In addition, it can be sensitive to the ways the typicality of examples and the frequency of explicit propositions bollix the predictions of a strictly rule-based, tree-structure model. The same general neural-network architecture can also be used to model important features of visual perception, such as the word superiority effect (see Chapter 6), patterns of data for reaction times (see Chapter 5), and patterns of data for motor control (see Chapter 7).

Because the neural network approach is so powerful, you might wonder whether it already fills the bill as a general theory of cognitive psychology. In many ways, I think it does, though the model's emphasis is on neural mechanisms or, in particular, on neural mechanisms that exemplify parallel distributed processing, or PDP, as it is known among cognitive psychologists. The core concept of the PDP model lines up with the idea advanced by Darwin and other selectionists that there is no hidden overseer in the brain who determines what should be done, when, and by whom. Instead, as Darwin would have liked, all the elements of the system are always active to varying degrees, with the strengths of the connections between them, both excitatory and inhibitory, changing in ways that tend to promote greater adaptation to challenges that arise.[19]

Emotions, Sex, and Altered States of Consciousness

The way I introduced concept formation was to say it was a topic I had neglected, and then I devoted a section to concept formation. I did so for a couple of reasons. First, I wanted to redress the imbalance between my relatively heavy coverage of lower-level aspects of cognitive psychology compared to my relatively light coverage of higher-level aspects of cognition. This imbalance reflects my own interests, which are especially focused on human performance and the cognitive control of physical action.[20] Second, I couldn't resist the low-hanging fruit provided by research on concept formation. Because concept formation has been modeled in a way that allows concepts to be differentiated based on experience, I wanted to share that result because of its similarity to the branching structures of Darwin's "tree of life" (Figure 15).

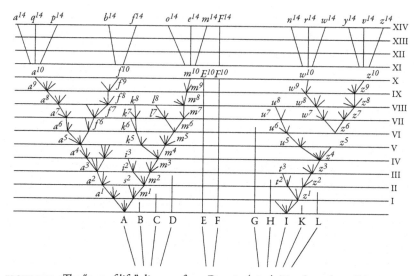

FIGURE 15. The "tree of life" diagram from Darwin (1859). Two branches of the tree are shown. The sole hypothesized origin is implied. It lies somewhere beneath the base of the picture.

The fact that the diversification patterns are similar for species and for concepts could, of course, be coincidental, but I think that's unlikely. What's more probable is that the same dynamic is at work in both domains. The notion that similar dynamics can be played out in different domains—in different scales of space and time and with different material substrates—is one of the core tenets of science. Scientists generally believe they're on the right track toward grasping core principles when they see the same principles playing out in different arenas.[21]

Darwin's dynamic applies to many other facets of cognition that I didn't yet cover in this book. Here's a brief overview of some of them. The overview is incomplete, though I can assure you no topic I omitted was left out because I thought the jungle principle couldn't accommodate it. I daresay every topic in cognitive psychology, when looked at from the standpoint of the jungle principle, can be understood with the principle.

Emotion wasn't covered very much here, though of course it's an immensely important topic. Likewise for affect and motivation, which include topics like hunger, thirst, aggression, addiction, and sex. Are those behaviors governed by processes that reflect inner Darwinism? I think so. Darwin himself analyzed the expression of emotion in terms of his own theory.[22]

Emotions play a pivotal role in experience, often accounting for why some memories survive and others don't. Emotionally charged events tend to be more resistant to forgetting than are emotionally neutral events. Frightening or life-threatening events activate the amygdala, a brain region that is strongly activated when emotions run high, and the amygdala plays an important role in memory consolidation.[23] This is just one indication of how emotion might be approached and understood from the perspective offered here.

Regarding sex, as I said in Chapter 2, I have deliberately shied away from sexualized Darwinism here; that is, I have avoided a Darwinism that emphasizes mating and creation of progeny within the brain. I did so not out of prudishness, but instead because of my uncertainty about what mating and reproduction could be like in the nervous system. Reproduction may be clear enough in that there could be replicas of memories, each a bit different from others. The notion that there are multiple memories of the same basic event is often raised in theories of cognitive psychology—especially in connection with so-called instance theories of memory, where the main idea is that each and every instance (or at least most or many) are stored.[24] Mating, on the other hand, may not apply, though one approach to concept formation relies on the mating analogy via genetic algorithms, as mentioned earlier. I have refrained from emphasizing this approach because I think it can distract from the broader selectionist perspective I have advocated. Neural mating in one form or another may occur, but I think the broader view put forth in this book is better advanced by remaining agnostic on this point.[25]

Altered states of consciousness also got short shrift in this volume, as they do in most books on cognitive psychology. Sleeping, dreaming, and otherworldly states shouldn't be a sideshow to the study of mental function, especially considering that, as regards sleep, we spend a third of our lives in that state. Are altered states, or the predisposition to fall into them, understandable from the perspective of the jungle principle? I'd be surprised if they weren't.[26]

There is one kind of altered state for which the jungle dynamic seems very clear: sensory deprivation. You might think that people floating in baths of warm water with their eyes closed and their ears plugged would enter a state of blissful tranquility. What actually happens is the opposite. These people hallucinate—hearing, seeing, and feeling things not there. Ghostly, self-invented stimuli come and go in an eerie glide. People deprived of sensory stimulation find the experience unsettling, to say the least. Unmoored from external reality, they feel themselves losing control and sometimes terrified. As a result, sensory deprivation is sometimes used for torture.[27]

What can be said about the effects of sensory deprivation from a theory that's all about the ruckus of everyday life? Sensory deprivation may unleash the metaphorical beasts within. Deprived of normal sensory input, they feud with one another, so to speak, in ways normally kept under wraps. When sensory input is severely limited, neural creatures freed from their normal duties strike out looking for new connections. Like kids with too much time on their hands, the result can be psychologically destabilizing.

Socializing

Social cognition was also omitted from this book despite its obvious importance in everyday life.[28] In recent years, there has been a surge of interest in this topic, with the most growth of interest occurring in the field of social neuroscience. An insight from social neuroscience has been that neuroscientific methods can be usefully applied to the study of social understanding.

One result from this field that I find particularly interesting is that an area of the brain becomes activated when people see other people. This area of the brain—the medial prefrontal cortex—is sensitive to other people as *social* beings. This brain site becomes activated when observers see people of reasonably high status but not when they see people of low status. A picture of a man wearing a suit and tie causes this brain area to light up, but a picture of the same man dressed as a vagrant does not.[29]

Does this sort of finding have anything useful to say about the inner jungle claim, and does the claim that it's a jungle in there help in any way to edify social neuroscience? If social appraisal is important, one would expect neural circuits to evolve accordingly. Socially useful neural niches would develop because humans rely on social interactions for their survival.

Consciousness and Qualities of Experience

Two other topics that deserve more discussion are consciousness and qualia. Consciousness is a topic that many people have written about and some have even said they've explained.[30] Defining consciousness is a challenge, but there has been no shortage of definitions. For example, the following definition appeared in a letter to *Scientific American*: "At its core, consciousness is a term we use to refer to our common human perception that we exist, are aware of ourselves, and are aware of our being part of the environment with which we are interacting."[31]

This is a perfectly fine, workaday definition, though if this statement is thought to explain what consciousness is, I confess I'd like to know more. I know that when I'm conscious, I'm thinking not just about what I'm doing, but also what I might be doing in other circumstances. Being told by various philosophers and psychologists that those experiences are what consciousness is tells me nothing I don't already know. Consciousness is clearly some emergent feature of neural activity, but saying that isn't an explanation, no matter how alluring the emergent-feature notion might be. For example, consciousness might be likened to murmuration, the ever-changing form of a flock of birds winging its way through the sky. Starlings best illustrate this kind of "swarm intelligence."[32] The form of the flock changes dramatically and can do so in an instant. The form is evident only from afar, however. It's an emergent feature of the birds flying together, and it's made possible by the fact that each bird responds to its local conditions.[33] No overseer is needed to shape the flock. The shape changes dynamically via self-organization.

Analogizing consciousness to murmuration makes for lovely images but hardly explains what the emergent feature of consciousness is, or what critically distinguishes consciousness from other emergent features of neural activity, like the factor—whatever it is—that distinguishes the brain activity of people who are conscious from the brain activity of people who aren't.[34]

Does the jungle principle explain consciousness? Frankly, I don't think so, or at least not in a way I'm aware of. Might it help explain it someday? I'd be delighted if it did, but this is just wishful thinking on my part.

Likewise for qualia, otherwise known as qualities of experience. Examples of qualia are the smell of a rose, the sight of a sunset, or the sound of a cello. These are experiences that are essentially impossible to put into words.

What accounts for the distinct aspects of experience? What makes a smell a smell, a sight a sight, a sound a sound? An early idea was that the nervous system has "specific nerve energies" for different sensory modalities. According to this hypothesis, nerve impulses from the nose, eye, or ear carry specific information about the modality they're conveying. Smell-related nerves have different signals than sight-related signals. Similarly, sound-related nerves have different signals than taste-related signals, and so on. That, anyway, was the hypothesis.

Johannes Müller, an eighteenth-century German physiologist who proposed this idea, noted that by pressing gently on his closed eye, he saw flashes.[35] Müller inferred from this observation that something about the nerve signals from his eye carried the quality of sight. It didn't matter, according to Müller, whether the energy that triggered the eye's neural signals was optical or mechanical. What mattered was that the source of the signals was the eye. By this way of thinking, something about nerve signals from the eye carries the quality of sight. Analogously, something about nerve signals from the ear carries the quality of sound, something about nerve signals from the skin carries the quality of touch, and so on.

Müller's inference was reasonable even if it failed to specify what the specific nerve energies might be or what about them signified the qualities they do. Later research called the specific-nerve notion into question, however. Edgar Adrian, a British physiologist who won the Nobel Prize in Physiology or Medicine in 1932 (sharing it with Charles Sherrington) found that nerve signals were the same throughout the nervous system. According to Adrian's research, nerve signals do *not* differ depending on which sensory pathway they're in. This meant that phenomenological differences between the senses arise from central rather than peripheral sources. What makes smells "smelly" or touches "touchy" depends on where sensory inputs land within the brain, not where the inputs launch in the periphery.

How can this idea be tested? An experiment by the American physiologist Roger Sperry lent support to the alternative "central-site" hypothesis—the idea that the place in the brain where inputs are registers determines experience. Sperry reasoned that if the source of experiential differences is where sensory inputs are registered in the brain, then altering where those sensory inputs arrive within the brain should alter the experiences they produce. Sperry worked with frogs, choosing them as subjects because the optic nerve of the frog's eye projects to the frog's opposite brain hemisphere. Thus, for a frog, the left eye's optic nerve projects to the right hemisphere and the right eye's optic nerve projects to the left hemisphere. This gave Sperry a logical opening to the problem of what matters more—where in the periphery sensory signals originate or where in the brain sensory signals go.

Sperry cut the optic nerves of a frog's two eyes and redirected the nerves to the same side of the brain as the eyes from which they projected. So following the surgery, the left eye's optic nerve projected to the left hemisphere, and vice versa (not the usual arrangement). The result was that the frogs carried out movements that were opposite to the ones they normally performed. If an object approached from the left, which normally caused the animal to move to the right, that same looming object now caused the frog to move to the left, toward the object, not away from it, and vice versa for an object approaching from the right. This outcome showed that it was where in the brain the sensory input was received that defined how the input was interpreted.[36]

What is it about the left hemisphere of the frog's brain that caused it to interpret input one way or another? All you need to say is that neural connections exist between the relevant brain sites and the sites responsible for producing leftward or rightward movements. If those connections are sufficiently strong, it doesn't matter whether the original activation comes from the left eye or right. Admittedly, it's a jump to say that if a frog's brain site causes one or another leg to move, the frog has different phenomenological experiences. You can't ask a frog what it's experiencing, or if you do, the conversation will be decidedly lopsided. Still, the frog's overt behavior gives a clue to the nature of its experience.

There is a finding that bears more directly on the nature of experience following neural transplantation. When neural transplantation occurs in people, albeit as a result of natural rather than laboratory experiments, people's experiences depend on where sensory inputs arrive in the brain, not where the sensory inputs originate in the periphery, just as Sperry concluded.

A relevant study was described earlier in this book. It concerned amputation. Recall from Chapter 3 that a man whose arm had been amputated nevertheless felt his fingers being touched when his face was palpated. The psychologist who discovered this—or at least made the finding public, as the amputee knew it all along—expected this result because of his knowledge of neural plasticity. Sensory signals from the face, the psychologist surmised, would infiltrate the finger region when no sensory signals came from the fingers themselves. With the finger inputs now dormant, they would be less able to fend off onslaughts from facial factions. The finger region of the brain, receiving inputs from a site whose true address in the periphery was unknown to the brain's finger region, sent signals to other centers that would translate the signals into finger feelings. Unlike Sperry's frogs, whose only means of communicating what was felt was by moving, the man with the amputated arm could say what he felt. What he said went along with the hypothesis that feeling was determined by where in the brain inputs were received, not by where the sensory signals originated on the body surface.

Based on these considerations, you can say that qualia depend on central rather than peripheral factors. Still, you're left with the mystery of how phenomenology and phenomenological differences arise in the first place. If you turn to one of the brightest lights in cognitive psychology to find an answer to this riddle, the result is a bit disappointing. Steven Pinker, the bright light to whom I refer, wrote the following sentence on this topic: "The problem is hard because no one knows what a solution might look like."[37]

Like Steven Pinker, I'm a member of the loosely knit team of cognitive psychologists who have no idea what the form of the solution might be to the problems of what consciousness is and, relatedly, what qualia are. It's not a fact I'm proud of. In the context of the jungle principle, I could suggest that different qualities are experienced because different kinds of inner agents are activated. But that's no explanation; it merely dresses up the problem.

A couple of remarks may prove useful, however. First, despite the fact that there are different qualities of perceptual experience, these forms of perceptual experience interact. Inter-sensory interactions are replete. For example, the place where you hear a puppet's voice is at the puppet, not at the ventriloquist.[38] How many flashes you see when a single prolonged light is shown depends on how many beeps sound when the light is presented.[39] And what you hear someone say when you watch him or her in a video depends on what his or her lips are doing. If the lips say one thing and the sound says something else, you hear a blend of the two.[40] Phenomena like these suggest that different forms of representation commune. Inputs from different sorts of receptors don't go off to their own separate worlds. Rather, they come together in ways that yield integrated experience.

The second potentially useful remark is that because qualia are emergent features of neural interactions, they can be likened, albeit loosely, to chemical phenomena. When chemicals mix, all sorts of unexpected things happen. The mixture can change color, it can form crystals, it can produce explosions, and so on. Characterizing the phenomena of chemical reactions is what chemists get paid to do. They're hired because the phenomena they uncover can have important applications. For example, finding that sulfur and rubber can jointly produce an extremely durable material capable of supporting automobiles can make for a Goodyear.[41]

The parallel to neurally based phenomena should be obvious, and indeed the parallel has been noticed by some influential cognitive psychologists. William Estes, a founder of mathematical psychology and a winner of the National Medal of Science in 1997, published an article in 1960 called "Learning Theory and the New 'Mental Chemistry.'"[42] John Anderson, a cognitive psychologist at Carnegie-Mellon University and the current editor of the journal *Psychological Review*, co-authored a book called *The Atomic Components of Thought*.[43] These two cognitive psychologists, like all the other cognitive psychologists I know, believe in *associations* among ideas.[44] If mental associations are like molecular bonds, then much as molecular bonds arranged in different ways can produce different emergent phenomena, so might mental links. What's not clear, though, is how to get from links to awareness. How the brain produces the mental equivalents of color changes, crystal formations, and explosions is as yet unknown. When we can explain such emergent phenomena, we psychologists will be able to say that, like the discoverer of hard rubber, we had a good year. For now, all we can say, or all I can say, on this matter is that I stand before you intellectually naked.

Evolutionary Psychology

Chances are you weren't tumescent while reading this book. If you were, it wasn't from the book itself. The word "tumescent" means "swollen or showing signs of swelling, usually as a result of a buildup of blood or water within body tissues."[45] When I suggest you weren't tumescent, I mean you probably didn't feel your genitals gorge with blood when you read this volume. Had this book been X-rated, the result might have been different.

Why do I bring up sex? Psychology has gotten very sexy lately, though, truth be told, it always has been. Freud said long ago that beneath the thin veneer of civilization, we harbor seething passions. To control those passions, he said, we have two levels of control—the ego and, on top of that, the superego.

Regardless of what drives you, it's likely that what you enjoy is consistent with the successful transmission of your genes. That, anyway, is the anthem of evolutionary psychology, a field I've not talked about much here, though it's always been in the background. I'll now bring it to the fore to compare and contrast it to the approach I've kept front and center.

Unlike cognitive psychologists, evolutionary psychologists often study very "juicy" subjects. For example, one group of evolutionary psychologists studied striptease dancers. The evolutionary psychologists found that the tips the strippers earned depended on when the performers danced relative to their menstrual cycles.[46] When the strippers were ovulating (when they were most fertile), the tips they got were large, but when the strippers were not ovulating, the tips they got were small. The dancers didn't stop flirting with the customers during their less fertile times. Teasing, after all, was their stock and trade. Instead, something about them—how lustrous their skin, how lilting their voice—caused customers to be more appreciative when the dancers happened to be physiologically primed for conception than when the dancers were less fecund.

A finding like this provides fuel for evolutionary psychologists, who take their cue, as do I, from Darwin. For evolutionary psychologists, the primary concern is the impact of the evolutionary past on present-day psychology. For me, by contrast, the primary concern is the impact of the *individual's* past on the organization of his or her mind in the here-and-now. For evolutionary psychologists, if strippers gyrate as gamely as they can but to less effect when they're infertile, that makes sense from an evolutionary perspective. Women who succeed in seducing men should, one would think, be more likely to produce offspring than women who are less successful. Similarly and shifting to a different domain, if you're spooked by snakes, that may be because it was adaptive for your ancestors to be scared of serpents.

Of special interest to evolutionary psychologists are features of current psychology that are mysterious until evolution is invoked. Getting bigger tips from customers at strip clubs at fertile times is just the sort of thing that turns on evolutionary psychologists. You probably wouldn't think of looking for this relation if you weren't tuned in to evolutionary psychology.

Evolutionary psychologists have uncovered many intriguing results besides the ones just mentioned. They've found, for example, that the ratio of waist diameter to hip diameter among Playboy models has remained relatively constant over many decades, the range of values being between .67 and .80. Supposedly, this range of ratios signals optimal fertility.[47]

Another finding from evolutionary psychology is that if married couples split up, they're more likely to do so after three or four years of marriage than earlier. Three to four years is when offspring are well enough along in their development that their chances of survival are relatively secure. A mom or, more likely, a dad is likelier to split once the stats tip in favor of offspring survival, or so goes the argument.[48]

Within cognitively oriented evolutionary psychology, some research suggests that memory may be specially tuned to what's most marked for survival. In this connection, consider a study by James Nairne and his colleagues at Purdue University.[49] They compared memory for words that were attended to in different ways by different groups of university students based on the instructions the participants were given. One group rated the words for their survival value. Their instructions were as follows:

> In this task, we would like you to imagine that you are stranded in the grasslands of a foreign land, without any basic survival materials. Over the next few months, you'll need to find steady supplies of food and water and protect yourself from predators. We are going to show you a list of words, and we would like you to rate how relevant each of these words would be for you in this survival situation. Some of the words may be relevant and others may not—it's up to you to decide.

The words were rated from 1 (totally irrelevant) to 5 (extremely relevant). Meanwhile, other students from the same population were randomly assigned to other groups and were asked to provide different sorts of ratings for the same words. One group rated how pleasant the words were. Another rated how easy it was to imagine the objects referred to by the words. Another group rated how well the words helped them recall personal experiences. Still another group generated words by unscrambling the initial letters and then gave the words' pleasantness ratings. A final group simply tried to remember the words. Behind this experimental design was the experimenters' expectation that rating the words for survival would make the words especially memorable. The expectation was borne out. Memory was better in the survival condition than in any other.

This result is impressive insofar as the other methods were known from prior research to be effective, at least as compared to testing recall on a purely incidental basis. No researcher had previously asked people to attend to words from the perspective of the words' survival value. Nor had anyone posited that rating words for survival would make the words more or even most memorable. That these manipulations boosted recall adds credence to the view that psychology reflects evolutionary pressures.

Given this last result and the other positive findings for evolutionary psychology—just a few of which have been mentioned above—is there anything not to like about the evo-psych approach? Consider the study just mentioned. Its finding is surprising. Who would have thought that focusing on the survival value of words would make the words stick so well? The finding is impressive insofar as it withstood a challenge from the authors themselves, who speculated that some other feature of the task might have actually accounted for the better memory for the survival-rated words—specifically, the fact that survival is a more coherent theme around which to organize words than were the other dimensions used in the study. A further test dispelled that alternative.[50]

You might still have a reservation, though. If survival is so important, why isn't everything *always* memorized as if life depends on it? If your brain evolved in ways that made you evolutionarily fit, then why should you need to be reminded to consider the survival value of information? You should *always* do so, for otherwise you'd be a dead duck.

Another way to frame this question is to ask how you would interpret a *failure* to find a difference between the rate-for-survival condition and the other conditions. What would it mean, in other words, if the study *didn't* show that words are most memorable when people are told to attend to the life-or-death importance of the words? That outcome could be taken to support the view that we are well prepared to remember whatever may bear on our chances for surviving in a dangerous world. Remembering what is pleasant or not is surely important for survival, as is remembering what can be imagined versus what cannot be, and other contrasts. Given these possibilities, you may wonder whether the results could have been interpreted as favoring evolutionary psychology no matter how they turned out.

This brings me to some other difficulties that people have had with evolutionary psychology. Those difficulties are of two general sorts. One is political. The other is scientific. The scientific concern is more germane to the main thesis here, but the political concern is worth mentioning along the way.

Politically, the problem some people have with evolutionary psychology is that they see it being used to justify or excuse practices that are ideologically ugly. The most ardent political critic of the evolutionary psychology approach is Natalie Angier, a popular-science writer whose best-known outlet is *The New York Times*. One of her *New York Times* articles was a scathing critique of the treatment of women by evolutionary psychologists.[51] Her arguments were replayed in a chapter of her book *The Canon* and in a chapter of another of her books, *Woman: An Intimate Geography*.[52] I admire Angier's writing and, in case it's not obvious to those who read Angier and have been reading me here, I emulate her style. Often, I recommend Angier's writing to my students to help them see how good writing can be. It happens, too, that I mainly agree with her politics. As she says, it can be a self-serving excuse to say that women have the station they do because of their biology. From this biological premise, maxims like "Boys will be boys," "Men need to have their way," "No means yes," and so on can become all-too-convenient slogans. "No to those slogans!" Natalie Angier insists, and I agree. Still, if evolutionary psychology has been misused by some with political or other agendas, that doesn't mean its core scientific claims are incorrect. Nazis used principles of chemistry to gas millions (including my father's parents), but that doesn't mean the principles of chemistry on which they relied must be rejected.

The concern with evolutionary psychology that's more germane to the theme of this book is scientific. It's a concern captured by two words: "Just so." Those words embody what's troubling to many people about evolutionary psychology—that much or at least some of it amounts to just-so stories.

Suppose you ask an evolutionary psychologist, "Why do heterosexual men like ripe breasts and succulent lips in women?" The evolutionary psychologist might reply, "Because those features signal the capacity to bear and sire children." "Fair enough," you might answer. "And why do we have the rules of grammar that we do in natural language?" "Uh, well," the evolutionary psychologist might stammer. "Somehow those rules, or their neural or cognitive concomitants, got selected for." "But why *those* rules?" you might continue. "Well, that's just the way it was," your evo-psych friend might say. If you persist, the evolutionary psychologist might stare at you in a menacing way, drawing on his or her knowledge that furrowed brows can make foes retreat. If reason won't win the argument, maybe an aggressive display will.

Having just-so stories can try people's patience. A few such stories are acceptable, especially if they're practical. No one, as far as I know, fully understands why aspirin works; it just does. It's a just-so story, which is good enough for the millions of people who take aspirin every day to relieve their aches and pains. Not knowing why some features of modern-day psychology evolved as they did, but claiming that without those features we'd not be here, doesn't buy you very much, at least if you're after a good predictive theory. This point was made in a blistering review of an evo-psych book[53] by Alison Gopnik of the University of California, Berkeley:

> [the] ... conclusions from all this research are that human childhood is the result of evolution and that genetics and culture interact—conclusions that are both surely obvious to everyone but creationists in the first place. This unsatisfying quality is common to much evolutionary psychology. Either the researchers make the empty general claim that behavior evolved or they draw substantive conclusions from this claim that simply don't follow. To say that a human behavior is adaptive or is the result of evolution tells us nothing about whether that behavior is innate or learned, universally triggered or culturally transmitted. This is because our particularly powerful ability to adapt through learning and culture, is, arguably, the most important human evolutionary advantage. For human beings, culture is our nature, and the drive to learn is our most important and fundamental instinct.[54]

Given such a complaint about the "outer jungle" theory of psychology, where does it leave the "inner jungle" theory offered here? Will the Alison Gopniks of the world be just as scathing in their condemnation of the inner-jungle idea? Will they, so to speak, "kill me off"? There are several reasons why they shouldn't, quite apart from the fact that I hope they won't.

First, the scale of time and space over which the inner-jungle principle is pursued is more restricted than the scale of time and space over which the outer-jungle theory (evolutionary psychology) is pursued. It's easier to trace the history of individuals than to trace the history of thousands of long-lost relatives stretching back millennia. You're on safer ground trying to say how a particular form of behavior or knowledge took hold in one person or in one animal than in an entire species.

Second, the inner-jungle principle isn't especially concerned with establishing whether a given trait or bit of knowledge is inborn or learned. Evolutionary psychologists tend to be nativists, looking for inherited proclivities. I too believe that there are built-in tendencies that, among other things, favor some concepts over others, notably in the domains of language, numbers, elementary physics, and basic social interaction. Evidence for these tendencies has been obtained through laboratory studies.[55] Anyone who still sanctions the idea that we are born as blank slates is out of touch with modern research.[56]

On the other hand, apropos of the just-so woe, the inner-jungle approach shares the fault that it doesn't make exact predictions. Absent from the theory are clear constraints for how much cooperation and competition can occur within the brain, over what scales of space and time they can occur, and so on. Some such constraints surely exist and may account for some of the critical constants of cognitive psychology, such as the number of meaningful elements that can be held in working memory: seven, plus or minus two.[57] As I suggested in Chapter 1, the number of meaningful elements or "chunks" may be something like the number of mobsters who can run rackets in a big city or, to make a friendlier analogy, the number of close personal friends you're likely to have. Via Facebook you might have hundreds or even thousands of "friends," but the number of people you're likely to be with at Thanksgiving or on your birthday or by you at your deathbed is likely to be closer to seven, plus or minus two. Which came first—the number of chunks that can be maintained in memory or the number of close friends you can have—is an interesting chicken-and-egg problem.

Just as I can't say why the number of chunks we hold in working memory is seven plus or minus two, I can't say why reaction times have the values they do, though as I argued in Chapter 5, it's significant that those times are as long as they are and not closer to the small values they potentially could be if you just counted synapses between receptors and effectors. The magical number seven, the lengths of reaction times, how long you can retain information, and other constants are all of a piece. All these values reflect the dynamics of competition and cooperation in the brain, I believe. A challenge for future research will be to explain why these numerical values are what they are. If the magical number were 70 rather than 7, would the rate of forgetting be much different than it is and would reaction times be much longer or shorter than they tend to be?

Transmission of Ideas

The jungle principle is all about the birth and death of ideas in individual minds, but if the principle is truly general, it should also apply to the birth and death of ideas transmitted between individuals. In recent years it has become clear, in fact, that ideas do survive, change, and die much as organisms do. Though ideas are abstract entities, they have lives and deaths of their own, commensurate with their existing in a competitive environment.

The notion that ideas are susceptible to natural selection was advanced by Richard Dawkins in his book *The Selfish Gene*.[58] In that volume, Dawkins argued that ideas and their conceptual kernels survive, mutate, and expire within and across individuals. He called these idea units *memes*. According to Dawkins, just as genes are passed on in various combinations from generation to generation, memes are passed on as well, either flourishing or dying based on their fits to the environment in which they're expressed.

I won't review Dawkins' arguments here or cover similar arguments offered by another influential author, Daniel Dennett, in his fine book, *Darwin's Dangerous Idea*.[59] Instead, I'll review two recent findings that illustrate the power of this approach. Neither finding was reported in Dawkins' book, or in Dennetts', for both of the findings came out after those books appeared.

The first finding concerned what's hot and what's not. I refer not to climate but to culture. It turns out that words and phrases appearing in print rise and fall like species in the wild. Take the term "1950." Before 1950, there weren't many in-print mentions of "1950," but as 1950 approached, its mention climbed. In the year of its name, "1950" was mentioned most, but afterward its mention dropped. By 1965, "1950" was mentioned about half as often as when it was mentioned the most.[60] Thus, the half-life of the word "1950" was about 15 years.

It turns out that the half-life of year names has gotten shorter over time. This led the authors of the study in which this finding was reported to conclude that "We are forgetting our past faster with each passing year." At the same time, the frequencies of year mentions have grown. In other words, years are mentioned more often now than they were 50 years ago or, assuredly, 1500 years ago.

What do these results imply about "inner jungleism"? They show that concepts in culture obey dynamics similar to concepts in people's minds. The evolution of ideas, whether represented by words appearing in print or by neural firing patterns of individual brains, can be studied profitably in selectionist terms. Being able to analyze data of seemingly different kinds in the same general terms is the hallmark of a good theory.

Evolution of Language

The last empirical finding I want to summarize in this book concerns the number of phonemes in different languages. A phoneme is a sound that differentiates words within a language. The sounds "r" and "l" are phonemes in English, so "right" and "light" are two distinct words for English listeners. But because "r" and "l" are not distinct phonemes in Japanese, "right" and "light" are not two distinct words for Japanese listeners. English listeners are likewise unable to hear some phonemic differences in other languages.

Some languages have few phonemes, but other languages have many. It turns out that the number of phonemes in a language is related to the number of speakers of that language. The smaller the number of speakers, the smaller the number of phonemes. This means that pockets of people in some locales may use phonemes that other groups of people in other places don't. In general, languages spoken in regions near one another tend to have more phonemes in common than languages spoken in regions more remote.

Given these facts, it should be possible to develop a tree of life for languages, similar to Darwin's tree of life for species. It should be possible, in other words, to draw a tree in which the languages of the world spring from one another, with a single proto-language at the root of the tree.

An article published in *Science* pursued this possibility and came up with a positive result. According to the article, there is a single source for human language, in Africa.[61] The evidence consisted of two main findings. First, it turned out that the place where phonemic diversity is greatest is Africa. The number of languages spoken on a *per capita* basis is higher in Africa than elsewhere. Second, phonemic diversity changes systematically as a function of physical distance from a region that, *a priori*, was unknown but, *a posteriori*, could be identified. That region turned out to be somewhere on the African continent. The exact location in African couldn't be pinpointed, but that's a detail not worth worrying about here.

Before this study was done, it wasn't obvious that Africa would be where phonemic diversity would be greatest. Nor was it obvious that a site in Africa, or anywhere for that matter, could claim to be the seat of language. The analysis I've just mentioned suggested that languages have a single origin, as do species.[62]

Does the successful modeling of language evolution in Darwinian terms imply that the best possible way of modeling cognition within individuals is

Darwinian? Not necessarily. Some other way might prove better. Still, the success of Darwin's approach in the domain of language, coupled with its success in culture and genetics, is uncanny. I doubt the same story could hold in so many domains by chance alone.

Theory Space

Because my aim in this book has been to advance a general theory of cognitive psychology, it's worth checking whether the jungle principle is the right kind of theory. To address this question, it may help to recognize that theories can be said to occupy an abstract two-dimensional space (Figure 16). One dimension of the space, along its abscissa or *x*-axis, is its number of assumptions or free parameters. The other dimension, along the ordinate or *y*-axis, is how well the theory predicts data or, in the parlance of statistics, accounts for the variance (variability) in the data. By "data" I don't just mean the data for which the theory was developed. Rather, I mean all the data that ultimately need explaining.[63]

It's useful to divide theory space into quadrants. One of the four quadrants, on the lower right, is a *bad* quadrant. This quadrant is bad because it has slews of free parameters and assumptions.

Two other quadrants are *mediocre*. In one, the upper right corner, the number of free parameters and assumptions approximates the number of points to be predicted. This region is mediocre because no serious investigator wants to offer a theory with as many distinct theory elements as data points to be explained.

The other mediocre quadrant, the lower left corner, has few free parameters or assumptions, but little variability is accounted for. Being in the lower left corner of the space is like being where you were when you started. At this

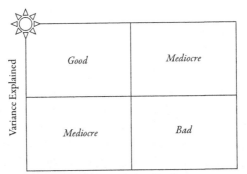

FIGURE 16. Theory space, with the holy grail shown in the top left corner.

early stage, you could make few assumptions because you had no idea what assumptions to make, and you could predict little or nothing.

Where you'd like to be is in the *good* quadrant, the upper left corner of the space. Here there are few assumptions or free parameters, and all or most of the variance is explained. The ideal point in the good quadrant is the top left corner. That point is the holy grail of science. It is where there are no assumptions or parameters but you explain everything.

Knowing where the good part of theory space is has led cognitive psychologists to limit the range of phenomena they've studied. They've limited their focus on the grounds that explaining all or most of the variance in a narrow range is at least suggestive of the possibility that the explanation is on the right track for explaining all the variance in the wider space.

Consider a hypothetical cognitive psychologist who spends his or her career studying how people judge whether one line is longer than the other. As it happens, I know of no such cognitive psychologist; the example is purely hypothetical.

By pursuing such a limited problem, the hypothetical investigator might be assured of developing a theory that occupies a relatively good part of a restricted theory space. He or she might investigate various facets of the problem: How does line-length discrimination depend on the colors of the lines, the thicknesses of the lines, where the lines are positioned in the visual field, how the lines are oriented, how long the lines can be inspected, whether the lines' positions are predictable, and so on. The researcher might be able to predict his or her data with reasonably high accuracy with a theory that is admirably simple. But would this be satisfying? Should a cognitive psychologist limit what s/he studies to increase the odds of yielding an outcome that only hints at where s/he would like to be in the larger theory space that we all care about ultimately?

Judging from the thousands of studies published in cognitive psychology journals, it's clear that many cognitive psychologists take this less-is-more approach.[64] Going to research conferences confirms this impression. This is where cognitive psychologists usually present their findings before submitting their manuscripts to research journals. Cognitive psychologists, like other researchers, want to have nice-looking data to show their peers.

A defense of this strategy is that you have to start somewhere. You might want to "explain everything," but that's hopeless. Better to begin with some manageable problem and make some headway with it.

The problem is that cognitive psychologists have been "starting somewhere" for years. Thousands of studies in cognitive psychology occupy the part of theory space where, while much of the variance within a narrow range is accounted for, very little variance is explained out of all the variance that ultimately needs explaining.

Studying things on a small scale is justified, of course, if the truths they expose are more broadly illuminating. Still, the number of cognitive psychologists who relate their focal questions to broader principles is small. Few investigators have the courage to offer grand, encompassing theories, or even to remark on the implications of their results for larger concerns. Their reticence is understandable given that espousing a grand theory or going beyond one's own results can put one at risk of occupying (or seeming to occupy) a mediocre or bad part of theory space. Why venture from a safe place if you don't have to?

Something interesting happens, however, if you look at the range of theories, models, and hypotheses that cognitive researchers report in research journals and at conferences. Their accounts tend to use similar terms and make similar assumptions. The particulars of the theoretical claims change a bit from study to study, but virtually all the claims rely on the same primitives: internal competition and cooperation among elements whose identities or strengths change over time. Virtually without exception, cognitive psychologists end up with an account that, in broad strokes, amounts to the claim that it's a jungle in there.

Realizing this, I managed to overcome the feeling of slight disappointment I had as I attended talks at conferences or as I read papers in academic journals, including the one I had the privilege of editing from 2000 to 2005, the *Journal of Experimental Psychology: Human Perception and Performance*.[65] Attending research conferences and reading published or as yet unpublished articles often gave me the feeling that, despite surface differences, most people were saying more or less the same thing—that inside the brain, there are components that cooperate or compete, and that out of these dynamics come the phenomena of cognition. I decided to write this book when I recognized this common view and came to believe that the commonness of the view is not so commonly appreciated.

Identifying commonalities is like boiling things down to basics. Have I boiled things down too much? If you boil vegetables too long, you can end up with mush. Have I taken cognitive psychology too far beyond the boiling point?

For some reading this book—students as well as professionals—the answer may be "Yes, the theory is too broad." If you prefer exact quantitative accounts of narrow data sets, you may not take kindly to the generalization offered here. Hopefully, though, even if you're in this camp, you may appreciate that my aim has been integrative. I've tried to present the material so it comes across as a coherent whole, not a hodgepodge of vaguely related findings.

There have been attempts at unification before, of course, including rallying cries meant to corral the findings of cognition. One such attempt was the proclamation that we go beyond the information given.[66] Another was the assertion that radical behaviorism was wrong. These are accepted statements now. If there is some other overarching theme for cognitive psychology, I don't know what it is.

If the theoretical framework presented here doesn't provide an exact quantitative account, it's worth asking whether such an account is actually the one you should always pursue. One way to approach this question is to return to theory space and ask how you would judge how good a theory is.

A first answer is to check which quadrant of theory space the theory occupies. Obviously, if it's in the bad quadrant it's bad. Similarly, if it's in a mediocre quadrant it's mediocre, and if it's in the good quadrant it's good. Beyond this, you can ask how far a theory is from the optimal point in theory space. The optimal spot—the holy grail of theory development—is the upper left corner, as mentioned earlier. That is where there are no assumptions and no free parameters, but all the variance is explained. The holy grail can't be obtained, of course, which is why it has the name it does. Still, like any holy grail, it's useful to imagine it as a goal to which you can aspire.

Even though the upper left corner of theory space is only a theoretical possibility, it's a useful anchor point for considering the quality of alternative theoretical accounts. All the points that are equally far from the upper left corner are equally good, at least in terms of their distance from the best locale.

Buying into this way of conceptualizing theory quality doesn't let you say which point equidistant from the upper left corner is best. A theory that accounts for a lot of variance and has many parameters is no better than a theory that accounts for less variance and has fewer parameters, at least if the two theories are equally far from the holy grail point and that distance is your metric of theory quality.

So which kind of theory should you prefer—a simple theory that accounts for less variance, or a more complex theory that accounts for more? One answer is "It's all a matter of taste." A better answer is "Be guided by experience." By the second quote I mean that it's better to favor a theory that has developed a good track record than one that's ad hoc.

No theory has gotten so consistently close to the upper left corner of theory space as Darwin's. This is what has made it so attractive to scholars in such a wide range of disciplines, including psychology, neuroscience, philosophy, and economics.[67,68]

Given the wide appeal and proven track record of Darwin's theory, it's a theory that's preferable to others whose locations in theory space may be just as far from the best point but whose track records are less secure. In that sense, Darwin's theory can be viewed as one that's as complete as you're likely to find if you hope to find an intellectually satisfying general theory.[69]

Has Darwin's theory measured up to its promise in cognitive psychology? I think so, especially because it accounts so naturally for so many cognitive phenomena. In addition, it has led to many useful lines of inquiry.[70]

Summing Up

Let me sum up with what I regard as the single most important statement of this entire book. It is that so many chapters ended with the observation that the most all-embracing theory for the material covered there was, in essence, Darwin's.

At the end of Chapter 3, on the brain, I concluded that the functional organization of the brain, and its dynamic reorganization based on experience, fit with the theory of natural selection, applied to the brain's constituents.[71]

At the end of Chapter 4, on attention, I observed that the most comprehensive theory of attention is, in effect, another statement of Darwin's theory, applied to a smaller scale of time and space than Darwin envisioned.

At the end of Chapter 5, on reaction time, I noted that the most promising general theory of the time to make elementary decisions is one that again basically claims there are internal elements cooperating or competing with one another. This model and others like it do a good job of capturing the essential features of reaction-time results. Such models are consistent with the selectionist framework I have advocated.

At the end of Chapter 6, on perception, I concluded that the jungle principle applies to perception and perceptual learning. I indicated there that the range of phenomena covered in the perception chapter, which mainly concerned the physiology and psychology of vision, all accord with the notion that neural ensembles tuned to particular features get selectively weakened or strengthened. Through the interactions of these elements, many aspects of perception, including some of its most curious manifestations, can be explained. The power of this explanation extends to other sensory modalities as well and to inter-sensory communication.

Chapter 7, on action, ended with a quote from a leading scientist in this field: "Coordination = Competition + Cooperation." The statement implies that the two forces at play in the nervous system, competition and cooperation, underlie the coordination of physical actions. Action, then, like perception, attention, and elementary decision-making, can be understood in terms of the same processes that provide the pushes and pulls that affect the chances of survival.

Chapter 8, on learning and memory, likewise ended with an homage to Darwin. I indicated in the close of that chapter that memories get strengthened or weakened based on their usefulness. From this simple idea, I could summarize a wide range of findings concerning learning and memory in Darwinian terms. At the end of Chapter 8, I provided a quote from a recent book on learning and memory that reflected the authors' belief that Darwin's scheme is the best one for understanding the data from this field.

Chapter 9, the chapter before this one, was concerned with problem-solving and creativity. That chapter ended with my observation that others before have noticed the usefulness of the analogy between Darwin's evolving species and individuals' evolving ideas. In both cases, evolution may lead to better fits. In the case of the fits of ideas to problems, aspects of the past and present may help or hinder steps that could prove useful for solving a problem, including recognizing that a problem exists and needs to be solved (as in the invention of Velcro). Darwin himself appreciated the connection between his theory of natural selection, as applied to the origin of species, and his theory as applied to the origin of ideas.

With all this support for Darwin's theory in cognitive psychology, I am led to declare, "How fortunate we are to be in receipt of Darwin's concept!" By applying Darwin's idea to cognitive psychology, we may be in a position to believe more seriously than we could before that a general theory of cognitive psychology is in reach. Such a theory has in fact been available to us in broad strokes for a long time—ever since Darwin conceived his idea. It's high time, I think, to pursue his insight in cognitive psychology, doing so more deliberately than we have before. It is that belief that impelled me to write this book.

Finally, if a Darwinian perspective will be adopted in cognitive psychology, we must accept the ruthlessness of the scrutiny to which it should be subjected, for that is the Darwinian way. The next challenge will be to hone the theory to see which variants of it should survive. It is in the nature of science to take this hard-headed, winnowing approach. I look forward to seeing how this process plays out, and I especially look forward to the possibility that you, whether you are a student or a seasoned professional, will feel inspired by what you have read here (or possibly irked by what you have read here!) to draw on the material to help advance the field of cognitive psychology and the other fields to which it's tied.

Notes

1   Daniel Kahneman (2011), the Nobel-prize winning cognitive psychologist (Nobel Prize in Economics, 2002), took a similar gambit in his recent book, *Thinking, Fast and Slow*. There he wrote, "...I describe mental life by the metaphor of two agents, called System 1 and System 2, which respectively produce fast and slow thinking. I speak of the features of intuitive and deliberate thought as if they were traits and dispositions of two creatures in your mind" [p. 13].

2   Lindsay and Norman (1977).

3   Selfridge (1959).

4   The article in which the Pandemonium model was introduced refers to demons, but it does not have cartoons. In the article itself, the author wrote that he "...was not going to apologize for a frequent use of anthropomorphic or biomorphic terminology." This quote appeared on p. 465 of the book where the Pandemonium paper was reprinted (Dodwell, 1970; see Selfridge, 1959).

5   Findings like those reviewed in this paragraph are typically reported by, and studied by, neuropsychologists (e.g., Banich, 2004).

6   Quiroga, Fried, and Koch (2013).

7   Mayr and Provine (1980).

8   For a recent discussion of the advantages of the population approach, see Nowak, Tarnita, and Wilson (2010). The Nobel laureate Gerald Edelman applied natural selection to neural organization in his book, *Neural Darwinism* (Edelman, 1987). The analysis to be presented here is inspired by Edelman's work, though the emphasis here is on psychology rather than neurophysiology.

9   James (1890).

10 I am replaying Thorndike's (1927) Law of Effect here, saying that the Law applies to neural ensembles even if it may not apply to entire organisms (cf. Chomsky, 1959). For a more current statement of the Law of Effect, see Blumberg and Wasserman (1995) and Wasserman and Blumberg (2010).

11 Miller (1956).

12 Recent studies suggest that preparing for physical actions interferes with working memory, which has been equated with consciousness (Spiegel et al., 2012; Weigelt

et al., 2009). It is possible that working memory is primarily or even exclusively an action launch pad or staging area. This exciting hypothesis was expressed to me by a young German researcher, Dr. Sabrina Trapp, in a series of emails. I want to give her credit for this provocative idea. Previously, it had been noted that action preparation is supported by working memory (Baddeley and Hitch, 1974; Logan, 1983; Rosenbaum, 1987), but Trapp's suggestion, which is not yet published as far as I know, is the strongest statement of the hypothesis that working memory is *for* acting.

13 Santamaria and Rosenbaum (2011).

14 Wegner (2002).

15 The popular science writer Malcolm Gladwell (2000) devoted a book to the emergence of fads, fashions, and trends.

16 A book about unconscious processes (Eagleman, 2011) also refers to *E pluribus unum* in this context.

CHAPTER 2

1 The proposal that minds are actually made up of many neural agents has been made before. A notable example is from a founder of artificial intelligence, Marvin Minsky (1988).

2 Erasmus Darwin was such a respected figure that he was invited to become Physician to King George III. He wrote a book called *Zoönomia* (1794) in which he anticipated the main idea of his grandson. Here is a relevant quote from a Wikipedia article about Erasmus Darwin, which I consulted on December 4, 2011: *Erasmus Darwin also anticipated natural selection in Zoönomia mainly when writing about the "three great objects of desire" for every organism: lust, hunger, and security.*

3 Moorehead (1969); Taylor (2008).

4 I have resisted referring to God as "He" or, for that matter, "She."

5 Darwin (1859). The other most influential book in the history of science was Isaac Newton's *Philosophiæ Naturalis Principia Mathematica*, which is Latin for *Mathematical Principles of Natural Philosophy*. That book was published in 1687.

6 Darwin, it turns out, wasn't the first to think of natural selection, as already indicated in connection with his grandfather, Erasmus Darwin. For a review of the intellectual forebears of Darwin's thinking, see Dennett (1995) and Richards (1987). The term "survival of the fittest" did not come from Darwin but from Herbert Spencer, as Darwin himself noted.

7 The phenomenon of hindsight bias was brought to the fore by Tversky and Kahneman (1974), two cognitive psychologists whose work will be discussed later in this book.

8 Sex requires cooperation as well as competition, of course, notwithstanding the despicable fact of rape. Cooperation, in general, is vital for survival, just as competition is (Nowak, 2012).

9 Hodges-Simeon, Gaulin, and Puts (2010).

10 To the best of my knowledge this hypothesis about human breasts has not been addressed in the scholarly literature, though the non-scholarly literature, both textual and photographic, provides ample proof of the sexual allure of breasts to members of our species.

11 My own research has focused on the planning of physical actions (Rosenbaum, 2010), building on landmark work by others—notably Lashley (1951); Miller, Galanter, and Pribram (1960); Norman (1981); Sternberg, Monsell, Knoll, and Wright (1978); and Turvey (1977).

12 Mathematical models of evolution are of particular interest here because they provide formal expressions that are abstract and therefore removed from particular physical or biological instantiations. If a mathematical model does a good job of explaining data concerning the origin of species, it may do a good job of explaining data concerning the origin of ideas. Influential mathematical-modeling work related to evolution has been done by Price (1970, 1971) and Maynard Smith (1982), among others. Price's contributions were summarized by Frank (1995).

13 For an extended and entertaining discussion of this topic, see Angier (2007). Other treatments are provided by Coyne (2009) and Pigliucci (2009).

14 See, for example, Futuyma (1998).

15 Ellis and van Creveld (1940).

16 Although Lorenz described this effect (e.g., Lorenz, 1981), I learned the following from a website, http://animalbehaviour.net/Imprinting.htm, which I consulted on December 5, 2011: "Although Lorenz was the first to record his observations in a scientific manner, the essence of imprinting had long been recognised. Indeed, Chinese peasants have for centuries capitalised on the tendency to imprint in making ducks more effective in the control of snails that otherwise damage rice crops. By imprinting ducklings onto a special stick, the peasants can not only take their brood out to the paddy fields as required but, by planting the stick sequentially in different parts of the plantation, they can ensure that molluscs in all areas can be subjected to predation." For more information about imprinting, click on http://www.apa.org/monitor/2011/12/imprinting.aspx or read the sources cited in this article, which are by Bateson (2003) and Hess (1958, 1973, 1985).

17 For printed words, see Morrison and Ellis (1995, 2000). For pictured objects, see Belke, Brysbaert, Meyer, and Ghyselinck (2005) and Carroll and White (1973).

18 Seminal research has been done on the basis for this effect by Kuhl et al. (1992).

19 Gould and Eldredge (1977).

20 Hoff (2009).

21 James (1890).

22 Evidence for niche opportunities was recently reported for a plant species in the Chihuahuan Desert of Mexico (Allington et al., 2013). I learned about this from a brief note in the Editor's Choice column of *Science* magazine (Hurtley and Yeston, 2012).

23 Schmidt and Lee (2011).

CHAPTER 3

1 The exact reference for this quote is unclear, even to Geoff Hinton himself, as he confirmed in an email he sent me on March 2, 2012, after I asked him what the source of this quotation was. In his email, he wrote, "I don't think I have ever published it. I just use it in talks."

2 For more on neurons and other features of the nervous system, see textbooks such as Kandel, Schwartz, and Jessel (2000).

3 For more information, see the Wikipedia article on "synaptic pruning."

4 Besides Wikipedia and references leading from it, see Bullock, Bennett, Johnston, Josephson, Marder, and Fields (2005).

5 Appreciating that there are excitatory and inhibitory interneuronal effects was one of the insights of Charles Sherrington, who, as mentioned earlier, won a Nobel Prize for his research.

6 This principle was introduced by Hebb (1949), though he did not use the actual phrase. According to the Wikipedia site devoted to Hebbian theory, http://en.wikipedia.org/wiki/Hebbian_theory#cite_note-1, which I consulted on February 7, 2013, "The mnemonic phrase is usually attributed to Carla Shatz at Stanford University." Wikipedia goes on to say that one place where the phrase is referenced is Doidge (2007, p. 427).

7 The effects of glucose availability on the brain's performance have been demonstrated in studies of ego depletion, a term that refers to reduced self-control following a very effortful task. Ego depletion is counteracted by drinking sweetened (glucose-laden) lemonade (Gailliot et al., 2007). A related, less uplifting result, but one that makes the same scientific point, is that judges in parole hearings are more likely to be lenient soon after meals, when their glucose levels are high, than long after meals, when their glucose levels are low (Danziger, Levov, and Avnaim-Pesso, 2011).

8 For a review, see Gallistel (1981).

9 See also Edelman (1987).

10 To learn the words "afferent" and "efferent," you can use the following mnemonic (memory-aiding) device: *A*fferent fibers carry signals *a*rriving *a*t the central nervous system. *E*fferent signals carry signals *e*xiting from the central nervous system.

11 There are many excellent textbooks about the nervous system. Examples are Gazzaniga, Ivry, and Mangun (2008); Kandel, Schwartz, and Jessell (2000); and Purves, Augustine, Fitzpatrick, and Hall (2011).

12 See Wikipedia's article on "cortical cooling."

13 The acronyms can be decoded as follows: EEG = electroencephalography; MEG = magneto-electroencephalography; ERP = event-related potentials; PET = positron-emission tomography; MRI = magnetic resonance imaging; fMRI = functional magnetic resonance imaging; DOI = diffusion optical imaging. You can begin to learn more about these techniques by reading the Wikipedia entry for Neuroimaging.

14 For a review, see Hubel and Wiesel (1979).

15 Neuroscience textbooks review these findings in much greater detail. See, for example, Gazzaniga, Ivry, and Mangun (2008) and Purves, Augustine, Fitzpatrick, and Hall (2011).

16 Doidge (2007) has a book about plasticity for the general public.

17 Merzenich et al. (1987).

18 To see these brain sites, look up "cerebral cortex" on Wikipedia.

19 Woolsey (1958).

20 Jenkins et al. (1990).

21 Sterr et al. (1999). For a review, see Neville and Sur (2009).

22 Weinstein (1968).

23 Elbert et al. (1995); Munte, Altenbuller, and Janke (2002); Sadato et al. (1998).

24 As further proof of the functional importance of this neural change, it has been shown that temporarily deactivating or scrambling neural signals in these transformed visual areas via transmagnetic stimulation adversely affects the Braille-reading ability of the volunteers in whom this is done. Once the transmagnetic stimulation is turned off, the ability to read Braille returns to its previously high level (Sadato et al., 1998). See also Bavelier and Hirshorn (2010).

25 Colapinto (2009).

26 This is an imaginary conversation. I've put words into the mouths of Ramachandran and the amputee for stylistic vividness. See Ramachandran and Blakeslee (1998).

27 Cytowic and Eagleton (2009); Marks (1975); Ramachandran and Hubbard (2001).

CHAPTER 4

1 Cherry (1958).

2 Broadbent (1958).

3 Gray and Wedderburn (1960). The fact that students in Broadbent's class disproved their teacher's theory encourages me to urge my students to think for themselves and challenge authority, including whatever (intellectual) authority I may have in the classroom.

4 A study with a similar conclusion was conducted by Treisman (1960). In her experiment, the word sequence presented to one ear was sensible up to a point and then turned nonsensical, while the word sequence to the other ear was nonsensical up to a point and then became sensible. A number of participants recalled what was meaningful by switching from one ear, or one message, to another.

5 I would have praised Oxford University even if this book weren't published by Oxford University Press.

6 Moray (1959).

7 Cherry (1958); Marlsen-Wilson (1973).

8 The instruction is given without the demonstration student's knowing it. A PowerPoint slide, shown out of the view of the shadower, indicates to the class what will happen.

9 James (1890), Chapter 11, pp. 403–404.

10 Rubin (1915).

11 More formal studies of spontaneous reversals with the Rubin figure, including studies with other figures, have been done by Attneave (1971) and by Kleinschmidt, Büchel, Zeki, and Frackowiak (1998). The latter authors explored the brain basis for spontaneous flips of reversible figures.

12 Necker (1832).

13 This account appeals to the concept of *embodied perception*, the notion that perception of the external environment is largely expressed in terms of what if affords for actions that can be carried out within it. The latter notion is often ascribed to Gibson (1979), who coined the word *affordance*, which means opportunity for action. Evidence for embodied perception has come from several sources, including the discovery of so-called mirror neurons, which are neurons that fire when one either observes someone carrying out an action or when one carries out that action oneself (Rizzolatti and Craighero, 2004).

14 Pashler (1993).

15 For earlier work on this phenomenon, which is known as the psychological refractory period, see Welford (1952).

16 Yarbus (1967).

17 Saccadic eye movements are eye jumps that occur when you visually scan pictures, text, and other static displays. A review of eye-movement control systems, written mainly for cognitive psychologists, can be found in Chapter 5 of my book (Rosenbaum, 2010) on human motor control.

18 Posner and Snyder (1975).

19 I don't know whether Posner used these exact words.

20 Cohen et al. (1994); Schall (2001).

21 Jonides and Mack (1984) considered this and other possibilities. A useful book about the importance of inhibition is Dagenbach and Carr (1994).

22 Posner and Cohen (1984); Klein (2000).

23 Wolfe (1934).

24 Tipper (1985).

25 Eriksen (1995).

26 Coles et al. (1985).

27 Stroop (1935); MacLeod (1991).

28 If, on theoretical grounds, you feel hesitant to say there is active inhibition, you can at least allow that it's harder for the needed response to reach the necessary activation when lots of activation is going to the response called for by the color name.

29 Reisberg, Baron, and Kemler (1980).

30 Logan (1988, 2002).

31 Schneider and Shiffrin (1977).

32 I'm putting words in the investigators' mouths here just for the sake of pedagogy.

33 I didn't use the terms late selection and early selection earlier in this chapter, but it's the distinction I was referring to when I discussed research bearing on the locus of attentional effects.

34 Cherry (1958).

35 Zatorre, Mondor, and Evans (1999).

36 Roelfsema, Lamme, and Spekrejse (1998).

37 O'Craven, Downing, and Kanwisher (1999).

38 Bredemeiser and Simon (2012); Duncan (1984); Neisser and Becklen (1975).

39 There is a great deal of evidence for the view that actions can be imagined. For a review, see Jeannerod (1995).

40 Sperling and Weichselgartner (1995).

41 Desimone and Duncan (1995).

42 Smith and Kosslyn (2007).

43 Moran and Desimone (1985).

44 An earlier, influential statement of this idea was offered by Kahneman (1973).

45 Desimone and Duncan (1995); Duncan, Humphreys, and Ward (1997).

46 To learn more about research on attention, see Anderson (2010), Johnson and Proctor (2003), Pashler (1998), and Smith and Kosslyn (2007).

CHAPTER 5

1 Donders (1969).

2 This isn't a real quote from Donders. I'm putting words in his mouth to convey his thinking as I imagine it.

3 Hick (1952); Hyman (1953).

4 Shannon and Weaver (1949).

5 Notice that with eight alternatives, the number of binary choices that's needed is three. Not accidentally, 8 equals 2 raised to the 3rd power. That power, the exponent of 3, relates to the number of S-R alternatives in a systematic way. The exponent to which 2 is raised is 1 for 2 alternatives ($2^1 = 2$), 2 for 4 alternatives ($2^2 = 4$), 3 for 8 alternatives ($2^3 = 8$), 4 for 16 alternatives ($2^4 = 16$), and so on.

6 Moles (1966).

7 Miller (1956). Although evidence for chunks comes from studies of recall, you can relate this evidence to RT research by considering how long it would take to memorize items that are easily chunked or not easily chunked. Material that is not easily chunked takes much longer to memorize than material that is.

8 Kornblum (1969).

9 Experimental psychologists have long known that more frequent S-R alternatives have shorter choice RTs than less frequent S-R alternatives. This intuitive phenomenon, called the *frequency effect*, is one of the most robust phenomena in experimental psychology. See, for example, Frekeriksen and Kroll (1976) and Balota and Spieler (1999).

10   Sternberg (1966). This paper was cited 2,252 times, according to Google Scholar on February 7, 2012.

11   Occam's razor is named for a medieval English friar, William of Occam, whose (conceptual) razor, it is said, shaves off unnecessary assumptions.

12   Townsend (1974, 1990).

13   For modeling along these lines, see Townsend (1974, 1990).

14   In his 1966 paper, Sternberg did consider a parallel search model, but not one in which the search items, or their neural representatives, interact in such a way that they drain one another.

15   Fitts and Seeger (1953).

16   Proctor and Vu (2006).

17   Simon and Ruddell (1967); Simon (1990).

18   Yamaguchi and Proctor (2012).

19   The Simon effect isn't manifested only in connection with *spatial* relations between stimuli and responses. It is also manifested in connection with attitudes. This has been shown in a famous implicit association test (Greenwald, McGhee, and Schwartz, 1998) in which people who claim not to be biased against dark-skinned individuals may take longer to confirm that "pleasant" characterizes a dark-skinned person than a light-skinned person. Skin color is irrelevant to the choice, but it intrudes, revealing an implicit association.

20   For a review of the literature on RT distributions, see Luce (1986).

21   de Jong, Coles, Logan, and Gratton (1990); Logan and Cowan (1984); Osman, Kornblum, and Meyer (1986).

22   I was first alerted to the fact that RTs are puzzlingly long by Emilio Bizzi, head of MIT's Department of Cognitive and Brain Science at the time, in a seminar of his that I audited while I was on sabbatical at MIT in 1985. He briefly mused on the fact that RTs are much longer than one might expect considering the speed of nerve conduction.

23   The speeds range from 24.6 to 38.4 meters per second, as shown by the great German physiologist, Hermann von Helmholtz, and as reported in a Wikipedia article about Helmholtz.

24   Latash (2008).

25   Meyer and Schvaneveldt (1971). There are many other kinds of priming related to language. A critical feature of priming is that it reflects opportunism. Virtually any potential source of priming—for instance, meaning, syntax, or episodic associations—contribute. Some authors have pushed this perspective, including MacDonald, Pearlmutter, and Seidenberg (1994) and MacWhinney and Bates (1989), who described their account of the relevant effects as the *competition* model.

26   Tipper (1985).

27   Stroop (1935).

28   Kiesel et al. (2010).

29   For reviews of work on task switching, see Monsell (2003) and Kiesel et al. (2010).

30 One anti-inhibition paper was by Mahon et al. (2007). For a response, see Starreveld, La Heij, and Verdonschot (2013).

31 Miller and Ulrich (2003).

32 Another illustration of a racehorse model is an influential model of visual word recognition known as the two-route model. According to this model, defended by Coltheart, Curtis, Atkins, and Haller (1993), there are two routes to recognizing a word. One is based on whether the visual appearance of the letter arrangement looks familiar. The other is based on whether the way the word sounds to one's "inner ear" is familiar.

33 Duncan and Desimone (1995).

34 Usher and McClelland (2001).

35 Another overarching view of RT that dovetails with the jungle view and, in broad terms, is consistent as well with the model of Usher and McClelland (2001) has been offered by Michael Spivey (2007). Another leading RT theorist is Roger Ratcliff, whose general model can be thought of in similar terms (e.g., Ratcliff, Van Zandt, and McKoon, 1999).

CHAPTER 6

1 Ratliff and Hartline (1959).

2 For more information about Mach bands, see Eagleman (2001).

3 For more information about the neural basis of the grid illusion, see Eagleman (2001).

4 For a discussion of this topic, see Schiller and Carvey (2005).

5 Hurvich and Jameson (1957). The Wikipedia article on "opponent process" provides a lot of useful information and leads on this topic.

6 The Wikipedia article on color vision is very useful. A good textbook on this and other topics in perception is by Mather (2006).

7 The Wikipedia article on "color blindness" provides a lot of useful information and leads to this topic. Also see Mather (2006).

8 For a video of the waterfall aftereffect, search for "The Waterfall Effect" on YouTube.

9 Huk, Rees, and Heeger (2001).

10 Videos can be found on YouTube using the search phrase "spiral aftereffect."

11 These interpretations, or ones that can be expressed more precisely, have been confirmed through physiological recordings (Barlow and Hill, 1963).

12 Once again, Wikipedia is a good place to learn more. Use "Helmholtz" as the search term.

13 More information about Ames and pictures of the Ames room can be found on the web. Videos showing the Ames room are available via YouTube.

14 Binocular rivalry is reviewed in Wikipedia, or see Blake (2001).

15 Some influential scholars who have endorsed the inferential approach to perception are Gregory (1973), Hochberg (1981), and Rock (1983).

16 Consistent with this interpretation, if instead of holding up your extended thumb, which is a relatively narrow object, you hold up an object that is significantly wider than your thumb, you won't be able to find your blind spot. For more information, look up "blind spot (vision)" in Wikipedia.

17 For research on the proofreader's error, see Healy (1981). I should add that to the best of my knowledge, Healy (1981) did not address the hypothesis that proofreaders are more proficient when they return to text than when they first deal with that same text. I am reporting my own impression that this is the case, echoing anecdotes from friends and colleagues that it is for them as well.

18 Warren (1970).

19 I offer this particular example because of a photo I saw in the sport pages of my local newspaper. A baseball player had blown a big bubblegum bubble that covered most of his face. I had no trouble recognizing that a face was behind the bubble. The thought did occur to me that I might have had a bit more trouble recognizing that a face was behind the bubble if it had been an executive dressed in a jacket and tie.

20 Lindsay and Norman (1977).

21 Reicher (1969); Wheeler (1970).

22 This model was introduced by McClelland and Rumelhart (1981) and Rumelhart and McClelland (1982). When it was introduced, it was widely acclaimed as a major step in the understanding of perception and mental function more generally. The model instantiated a general approach to cognition called *parallel distributed processing* (McClelland, Rumelhart, and the PDP Research Group, 1986; Rumelhart, McClelland, and the PDP Research Group, 1986). The picture of information processing it offered was more chaotic than the neat and tidy model of perception that prevailed in the 1960s and 1970s, where perception was depicted as a series of information processing stages, each waiting (respectfully, one might say) for output from the stage before.

23 Pirates, or at least pirates of yore, wore a patch over one eye not just to cover injuries sustained in sword fights but also to enter the dark hulls of captured ships. The patched eye was dark-adapted, so yanking the patch off the eye let the pirate, who may have just been out in the sun, plunder the dark innards of the invaded ship.

24 For reviews, see Hubel and Wiesel (1979) and Barlow (1982).

25 Weisstein (1973).

26 Neisser (1964).

27 Treisman (1986).

28 Hubel and Wiesel (1963).

29 Similar logic is used to treat patients who have reduced use of a limb due to stroke or other brain damage. If such a patient has trouble moving one arm, the treatment may involve binding the other, more mobile arm (Gordon, 2011; Taub and Uswatt, 2006).

30 Critical periods were discussed in Chapter 2 in connection with the founder effect in evolutionary biology.

31 Barry (2009).

32 Also see Bavelier, Levi, Ri, Dan, and Hensch (2010) and Sinha (2013).

33 Hirsch and Spinelli (1970, 1971).

34 Fahle and Edelman (1993).

35 Weiss, Edelman, and Fahle (1993).

CHAPTER 7

1 Cohen and Rosenbaum (2004).

2 Rosenbaum, Marchak, Barnes, Vaughan, Slotta, and Jorgensen (1990).

3 For a review, see Rosenbaum, Chapman, Weigelt, Weiss, and van der Wel (2012).

4 Lashley (1951).

5 Freud (1901/1971).

6 Garrett (1975).

7 Many examples of action slips like this have been documented, and a taxonomy of action slips has been developed (Norman, 1981). Another example of a common action slip that illustrates the tendency of actions with common features to substitute for one another comes from touch typing. If you touch-type, you may often make the mistake of typing "k" instead of "d" or "s" instead of (the letter) "l." These letter pairs are typed with the same finger in the middle row of the QWERTY typewriter. The letters "k" and "d" are both typed with the middle finger. The letters "s" and "l" are both typed with the ring finger. The fact that "s" and "l" are often confused, and the fact that "d" and "k" are often confused, suggests that homologous fingers on the two hands tend to compete, with the outcome of the competition being erroneous (see Rosenbaum, 2010, Chapter 9). These mistakes may be likened to illusory conjunctions in vision, as discussed in the "Features" section of Chapter 6. Of course, the larger point is that, fundamentally, the same dynamic is playing out.

8 Dell (1986).

9 Aglioti, Cesari, Romani, and Urgesi (2008).

10 Rabbitt (1978).

11 Gehring, Goss, Coles, Meyer, and Donchin (1993).

12 Beilock, Carr, MacMahon, and Starkes (2002)

13 Beilock and her coworkers reached a similar conclusion in another experiment. They asked soccer players to dribble a soccer ball through a slalom course. While doing the dribbling, the players engaged in the same kinds of attention-demanding tasks as did the golfers. In one condition, the soccer players attended to extraneous stimuli that diverted attention from their dribbling. In the other condition, they directed attention to the step-by-step nature of their foot movements. The soccer players, like the golfers, did worse when they focused on the *main* task than when they focused on the extraneous task.

14 Georgopoulos, Caminiti, Kalaska, and Massey (1983); Georgopoulos, Schwartz, and Kettner (1986).

15 Erickson (1984); Chaisanguanthum and Lisberger (2011).

16   For those with a mathematical bent, note that this outcome is a direct consequence of vector summation.

17   All the neurons in the nervous system can be said to contribute to every arm movement and, for that matter, to every kind of movement all the time. The weights assigned to the neurons' activations simply become vanishingly small when the neurons' preferences are remotely related to the task at hand. Hence, no divisions are needed among sectors of the nervous system to account for the specificity of movement or, for that matter, the specificity of any behavior, thought, or emotion. Thus, you can say that all neurons contribute to all behavior all the time, just to varying degrees. The generality of the population coding scheme has been demonstrated in perception as well as action (Erickson, 1984). Population coding has been used in brain-computer interfaces to help paralyzed individuals transmit their intentions to robots (Veeliste, Perel, Spalding, Whitford, and Schwartz, 2008). An episode of *60 Minutes* was devoted to this. The episode was called "Breakthrough: Robotic Limbs Moved by the Mind." It aired December 30, 2012, and can be watched on the web via http://www.cbsnews.com/video/watch/?id=50137987n.

18   Forssberg, Grillner, and Rossignol (1975, 1977).

19   Abbs, Gracco, and Cole (1984).

20   If you try to touch your index finger and thumb of the same hand, a tug on your thumb by a device like the one used in the lip-lowering experiment just described causes your index finger to race more forcefully in the thumb direction. However, that same tug has little or no effect on the index finger if you are *not* engaged in a pinching task (Abbs, Gracco, and Cole, 1984).

21   Aruin and Latash (1995).

22   This model was introduced by Rosenbaum (2010).

23   Saying that learning works by trial and error is a weak criterion for a Darwinian process, but as I said earlier in this book, I am using Darwinism here in weak form, synonymously with *selectionism*—that is, referring to the idea that fitter solutions tend to survive while less fit solutions tend not to survive. A claim that would adhere more closely to Darwin's claim would insist on a single origin for learning, some primitive perception-action relation that provides a seed for others. The reflex has been thought by some to be that relation.

24   Goldfield, Kay, and Warren (1993).

25   Goldfied, Kay, and Warren (1993) showed that, with experience, babies in Jolly Jumpers become less variable in their bounce periods but better able to achieve large jumps.

26   Adolph, Vereijken, and Denny (1998).

27   The maturation perspective was the prevailing view of motor development before Adolph and others (Thelen, 1995) came along. A chief proponent of the maturation view was McGraw (1943).

28   Others have made similar arguments about the ad hoc, opportunistic nature of motor development (Thelen, Kelso, and Fogel, 1987; Thelen, 1995).

29 Sutton and Barto (1998).

30 These examples are mentioned because they are all backed up by research. For summaries, see Rosenbaum (2010) and Schmidt and Lee (2011).

31 Baddeley and Longman (1978).

32 Skinner (1957).

33 Chomsky (1959).

34 Brown (1973).

35 Elman, Karmiloff-Smith, Bates, Johnson, Parisi, and Plunkett (1996).

36 Pinker (1994).

37 Of course, as an advocate of a Darwinian perspective, I certainly am not opposed to the idea that genes play a role in shaping form and function.

38 Bayes' Rule can be expressed in terms of four terms: the probability, p(S), that a source of data is present; the probability, p(D), of the data; the probability, p(D|S), of the data given the source; and the probability, p(D|S), of the source given the data. Bayes' Rule can be written as $\dfrac{p(S\,|\,D)}{p(S)} = \dfrac{p(D\,|\,S)}{p(D)}$. The two terms on the left often go by two special terms. The denominator, p(S), is often called the *prior*, which is short for the prior odds of the source. The numerator, p(S|D), is often called the *posterior*, which is short for the posterior or after-the-fact odds of the source given the data. An entire book has been written about the history and applications of Bayes' Rule (McGrayne, 2011).

39 Körding and Wolpert (2004).

40 Tenenbaum, Kemp, Griffiths, and Goodman (2011).

41 For more information, look up "Bayesian network" in Wikipedia.

42 Bandura, Ross, and Ross (1961).

43 For a study of trial-and-error learning of walking, see Adolph et al. (2012).

44 Volkmann, Riggs, and Moore (1980).

45 Matin (1974); Volkmann (1976).

46 Blakemore, Wolpert, and Frith (1998).

47 Lötze (1852); James (1890).

48 Shin, Proctor, and Capaldi (2010).

49 Greenwald (1970).

50 Franz, Zelaznik, Swinnen, and Walter (2001); Mechsner, Kerzel, Knoblich, and Prinz (2001); Rosenbaum, Dawson, and Challis (2006).

51 Rizzolatti and Craighero (2004).

52 Gallese and Goldman (1998).

53 Calvo-Merino, Glaser, Grezes, Passingham, and Haggard (2005).

54 Gentner, Grudin, and Conway (1980); Flanders and Soechting (1992); McLeod and Hume (1994).

55 Estes (1972). Other models that assign behaviors to serial order beg the question of how those positions are identified. Likewise for models that assign behaviors

to left-right positions in a hierarchical tree, such as a model I proposed along with others who deserve none of the blame (Rosenbaum, Kenny, and Derr, 1983).

56 The inhibitory model of behavior ordering has another component that allows behaviors to be expressed: Whenever a behavior is produced, it inhibits itself. This causes the just-performed behavior to stop inhibiting its successors. Note that this idea might be applied, on a somewhat larger scale, to explain why sustained practice has no greater benefit than less sustained practice, as discussed earlier in this chapter in connection with the general advantage of spaced over massed practice.

57 For an extended discussion of this topic, see Chapter 3 of my book about human motor control (Rosenbaum, 2010).

58 Rumelhart and Norman (1982).

59 Baylis, Tipper, and Houghton (1997); McKinstry, Dale, and Spivey (2008); Song and Nakayama (2009); Welsh and Elliott (2004).

60 Fowler (2007).

61 Rosenbaum, Loukopoulos, Meulenbroek, Vaughan, and Engelbrecht (1995); Rosenbaum, Meulenbroek, Vaughan, and Jansen (2001).

62 Holst (1950).

63 Holst (1939).

CHAPTER 8

1 You can see the cartoon by looking for "Mr. Total Recall" on the Internet, or by going directly to http://www.condenaststore.com/-sp/Mr-Total-Recall-New-Yorker-Cartoon-Prints_i8478505_.htm.

2 Learning that something made you sick can occur after just one exposure (Garcia, Kimeldorf, and Koeling, 1955; Gustavson, Garcia, Hankins, and Rusiniak, 1974).

3 MacLeod (1998); Wegner (1994). Insights into the neural basis of intentional forgetting have been provided by Rizio and Dennis (2012).

4 There is a long tradition of explaining, or trying to explain, learning and memory in terms conducive to natural selection. My aim in this chapter is to review the literature in those terms for pedagogic purposes.

5 I refer to Avenue du Docteur Penfield.

6 The brain lacks pain receptors—a curious fact considering that the brain is the organ that transforms neural impulses from pain receptors in the body (so-called *nocioceptors*) into the experience of pain.

7 Penfield and Rasmussen (1950).

8 Loftus and Loftus (1980).

9 Bahrick, Bahrick, and Witlinger (1975).

10 In this fictional example of the elderly lady, she first has a sense of familiarity and then, via cuing, manages to recollect. Recollection can sometimes occur without a prior sense of familiarity (Bowles et al., 2007), a result that attests to the multifaceted nature of memory.

11 Brown (1991).

12 Bower (1967).

13 Graf and Schacter (1985).

14 This is called the mere exposure effect (Zajonc, 1968).

15 Yet another way that implicit memory has been demonstrated is in learning sequences of keypress responses. As shown by Willingham, Nissen, and Bullemer (1989), people performing in serial reaction-time tasks, where they press keys in response to lights, can get faster and faster on repeated sequences even if they have no conscious awareness of the sequence repetition.

16 Bahrick (1984); Bahrick and Phelps (1987).

17 The reference to hidden neural niches here is meant to call to mind the reference to niche opportunities in Chapter 2. See the section in that chapter called "Some More from Evolutionary Biology."

18 Savings was first used by the late-nineteenth and early-twentieth-century German psychologist, Hermann Ebbinghaus. The method is often described in textbooks. Articles that cover it in some depth are by Nelson (1985) and Roediger (1990).

19 There is a lot of anecdotal evidence that people returning to skills they haven't practiced for years can relearn the skills quickly. The best known example is returning to bicycle riding, for which there is the well-known saying, "You never forget how to ride a bike." Schmidt and Lee (2011) offered a personal anecdote about returning to skiing after many years away from the slopes. A related principle from memory research is Ribot's (1882) Law of Retrograde Amnesia: *Older memories are less prone to disruption than are younger memories.* For a discussion of Ribot's Law and a related law of memory, Jost's (1897) Law of Forgetting, see Wixted (2004). According to Jost's Law, older memories decay less rapidly than younger memories do. Wixted argued that data collected in relation to Ribot's Law and Jost's Law fit with the view that "New memories degrade (but do not necessarily overwrite) previously formed memories, more so for recently formed memories than for ones formed longer ago" [p. 878]. It will be important to sort out when degrading or overwriting occurs. The classical argument is that overwriting occurs only for memories that have not yet been "consolidated." In jungle terms, consolidation would mean gaining a secure foothold, where the probability of extinction falls below some (low) value.

20 In his book about seminal experiments in science, *The Ten Most Beautiful Experiments*, Johnson (2008) devotes a chapter to Pavlov.

21 Pavlov (1928).

22 Another remark about extinction pertains to a striking similarity between patterns of extinction in the wild and patterns of learning in the brain. According to a Wikipedia article entitled "Extinction," which I consulted on March 4, 2012, "…99.9% of all species that have ever existed are now extinct." On the other hand, "A typical species becomes extinct within 10 million years of its first appearance." Obviously, any species that takes millions of years to become extinct was robust for a long time. An analogy can be made to signals entering the brain. The vast majority

of such signals never take hold, or if they do, they do so for only a very brief time. On the other hand, a few signals (or experiences, more broadly) do manage to take hold and manage to linger for a very long time through the process of consolidation (McGaugh, 2000).

23 Kamin (1969).

24 Rescorla and Wagner (1972).

25 To the best of my knowledge, Pavlov never did the flower/no-flower study. I offer it just as a vivid and fanciful way of describing blocking. Forming strange visual images in one's mind can help memory (Hunt and Worthen, 2006).

26 Kamin (1969) did not use a flower as the added stimulus in his pioneering study.

27 A related phenomenon in conditioning is latent inhibition. This is a tendency to take longer to learn a stimulus that is relevant to conditioning if it was previously irrelevant (Lubow and Gerwitz, 1995).

28 Rescorla and Wagner (1972).

29 Crossman (1959).

30 Seibel (1963).

31 Kolers (1976).

32 Neves and Anderson (1981).

33 Ohlsson (1992).

34 The curve relating speed of performance to amount of practice was initially thought to be described by a power function of the form $y = ax^{-b}$, where a and b are real numbers whose values shape y, the dependent variable, over the course of changes in x, the independent variable (typically time or the number of practice or study trials). This relation was proposed by Crossman (1959) and was explained in terms of chunking by Newell and Rosenbloom (1981). Later, others realized that the data may be better described in terms of a different function, a negative exponential function rather than a power function (Heathcote, Brown, and Mewhort, 2000; Speelman and Kirsner, 2005). A negative exponential function has the general form $y = ae^{-bx}$, where a and b are real numbers, e is the base of the natural logarithms (i.e., the value whose derivative equals itself), x is the independent variable (often time), and y is the dependent variable. The question of which function better describes learning, a power function or a negative exponential, is more than just a technical issue. As emphasized by Heathcote, Brown, and Mewhort, "an exponential function implies a constant learning rate relative to the amount left to be learned. By contrast, the power function implies a learning process in which some mechanism is slowing down the rate of learning" [p. 186]. Heathcote, Brown, and Mewhort demonstrated that a negative exponential better describes speeding with practice than does a power function. This fits with the suggestion that a similar dynamic may underlie the change of performance speed with practice as well as the strengthening of conditioned responses with practice. A constant learning rate is assumed by Rescorla and Wagner (1972).

35 Accuracy of responding tends to improve with practice at a diminishing rate. An example is the accuracy of aiming for a target while viewing the target through a displacing prism (Redding and Wallace, 1997).

36 Reitman (1974).

37 Jenkins and Dallenbach (1924).

38 I am not the first psychologist to intone interference as a powerful shaper of memory. The most influential endorser of this view was McGeoch (1932). I should clarify, however, that I am using the term "interference" here in a broad sense, intending it to be synonymous with "competition." For me in this chapter and all through this book, it doesn't matter if inner enclaves vie for some resource or inhibit one another directly. For a discussion of this difference, see Raaijmakers and Jakab (2013).

39 Memory interference for recent verbal material can be induced by adding an extraneous syllable that is supposed to be ignored (Morton, Crowder, and Prussin, 1971).

40 To name just one other study at this juncture, Kroll, Michael, and Sankaranarayanan (1998) showed that people could learn words in a foreign language more easily if the words were paired with upside-down pictures than if the words were paired with rightside-up pictures. The researchers hypothesized, in effect, that foreign-language words would benefit from "less bullying" by native-language words when the native-language words took longer to arouse, as could be achieved with inverted as opposed to normally oriented pictures. The results fit with this hypothesis.

41 Light and Carter-Sobell (1970).

42 Tulving and Thomson (1973).

43 Godden and Baddeley (1975).

44 Another phenomenon that makes this point clear is *retrieval induced forgetting* (Anderson and Spellman, 1995). Here, participants study paired associates such as "fruit-orange," "fruit-plum," "drink-wine," and "drink-brandy." The participants are given many opportunities to recall the response to one of the stimuli when that stimulus is presented with a partial cue, as in "fruit-or…," "fruit-or…," "fruit-or…," allowing for repeated retrievals of "orange." After getting many such trials and no (or very few) trials with the other "fruit" item, participants have a great deal of trouble recalling "fruit-plum." Anderson and Spellman hypothesized that the source of retrieval-induced forgetting is inhibition of the seldom-retrieved response. Support for this view was provided by Román, Soriano, Gómez-Ariz, and Bajo (2009).

45 My source for this is the Wikipedia entry on the "cranial nerve."

46 I thank Sarah Kroll-Rosenbaum (personal communication, March 4, 2012) for sharing this mnemonic with me for publication in this book.

47 Bower (1970).

48 Bransford, Franks, Morris, and Stein (1977).

49 Roediger and McDermott (1995). The analogous phenomenon also occurs for recall (Deese, 1957).

50 For a review of Loftus's work, see Loftus (1991).

51 Loftus, Miller, and Burns (1978).

52 This interesting result wasn't a reflection of the uninteresting possibility that par-
    ticipants didn't happen to pay attention to the sign at first. When no leading ques-
    tions were given, participants recognized the sign that was actually shown with
    high (~90%) accuracy.

53 For readers unfamiliar with the ethical standards that must be adhered to in exper-
    imental psychology, be assured that though deception is sometimes used in this
    field, as in the study just referred to, investigators must get approval from their
    institutional review boards to deceive research participants. The deception must be
    critical to the issue being studied, it must do no harm, whatever costs it incur must
    be outweighed by the benefits of the research, and it must be divulged to partici-
    pants afterward.

54 Neisser (1967).

55 Martin (2012).

56 Loftus and Palmer (1974).

57 Anderson and Schooler (2000).

58 Also see Benjamin (2011).

CHAPTER 9

 1 Poincaré (1929, p. 388).

 2 One of the many appearances of this ad was in *Science* on May 6, 2011, page 643.

 3 For a cognitive psychologist's discussion of crossword puzzles, see Nickerson (2011).

 4 The solution is to turn one of the 3-link segments into connectors for the other
    3-link chains. Thus, each of the links in that to-be-disassembled segment is opened,
    costing 3×2 cents = 6 cents, and then each of the opened links is closed around two
    ends of the remaining 3-link segments, costing 3×3 cents = 9 cents.

 5 Silveira (1971), reported in Anderson (2010).

 6 Luchins (1942).

 7 Bilalic, McLeod, and Gobet (2010).

 8 Maier (1931).

 9 For a picture, look up "Maier 1931 two string problem" in Google Images.

10 Cho and Proctor (2011).

11 Thomas and Lleras (2009).

12 Duncker (1945).

13 Tversky and Kahneman (1974). Only Kahneman received the Nobel Prize (in
    Economics) because of Tversky's untimely death at age 59, six years before the Prize
    was awarded. The Nobel Prize is not awarded posthumously.

14 I learned about this from an editorial titled "The Unexamined Society," by
    David Brooks of the New York Times (July 7, 2011). http://www.nytimes.
    com/2011/07/08/opinion/08brooks.html?_r=1

15 For an image and further discussion, look up "Thinking outside the box" in Wikipedia.

16 When people are explicitly told that they can go outside the box, they are more likely to solve the problem than if they are not, as shown by Weisberg and Alba (1981). In deference to Weisberg and Alba, it should be noted that these authors argued that concepts like functional fixedness and insight are less useful for the analysis of problem-solving than many have said. I mean neither to show them right nor wrong, owing to the more broad-brush style of this presentation.

17 Bower (2012) or http://www.sciencenews.org/view/generic/id/338406/title/Vodka_delivers_shot_of_creativity. Relatedly, mind-wandering while performing a cognitively undemanding task also promotes creativity (Baird et al., 2012).

18 Gick and Holyoak (1980).

19 I got this information by looking up "Velcro" in Wikipedia.

20 The invention of the rotary lawn mower is another interesting example. As reported by Greenbaum and Rubinstein on March 18, 2012, in *The New York Times Magazine* column, *Who Made That?*, "Before a British inventor named Edwin Beard Budding conceived of the mower, the cropped lawn was the province of the landed gentry, who employed teams of men to trim grass with scythes. But lawn care was far from Budding's mind when he invented the push mower. His original brief was to solve a mechanical problem for a clothing mill regarding the production of guardsmen's uniforms. Budding was asked to come up with a way to 'cut all the tufts and bobbly bits off the nap of the cloth,' writes Brian Radam in 'Lawn Mowers and Grasscutters: A Complete Guide.' Budding soon realized the device had other applications. In 1830, he filed a patent for a machine that, when pushed and pulled, would cause a cylindrical blade to rotate over a stationary shear, cutting grass and collecting the clippings. The mower may have put the scythe men out of work, but it enabled the English fashion for grass carpets."

21 Limb and Braun (2008).

22 Campbell (1960). You can learn more about this man's life and career by looking up Donald T. Campbell in Wikipedia. The opening section of this website says: "He coined the term 'evolutionary epistemology' and developed a selectionist theory of human creativity."

23 For reviews, see Simonton (1999, 2003).

24 Holland (1975); Mitchell (1996).

25 Boden (2004).

26 Simonton (1999). Also see Simonton (2003).

27 Richards (1987).

CHAPTER 10

1 Sometimes in my classes I go on for quite some time with unabashed attempts at inspiration, offering another saying I have hit upon: "I aspire to inspire." I reveal to

the students that I grew up in a tiny row house in a very tough neighborhood in Philadelphia, that I had to jump through all the same hoops that they've had to, and that if I could succeed to whatever point I had, they could too. I say the same to you now, dear reader.

2   In case you don't understand the reference, and you might not depending on the country where you were raised, I refer to a short tale by Hans Christian Andersen, "The Emperor's New Clothes." Here, tailors hired to make a new suit for a king present him with an invisible suit that, they say, is visible only to discerning viewers. The king, too embarrassed to admit that he sees nothing, parades down the street wearing his new invisible vestments. The fawning crowd applauds the king's costume, hiding their true observations, until a young child, oblivious to how he is supposed to behave, blurts out "But he's not wearing anything!" The jig is up at that point, and we are reminded by Hans Christian Andersen not take authority on faith alone.

3   Collins and Quillian (1969).

4   Conrad (1972).

5   Rosch (1973).

6   Rosch (1975).

7   Rosch (1977).

8   Armstrong, Gleitman, and Gleitman (1983).

9   Smith, Patalano, and Jonides (1998).

10 I have drawn upon a well-known argument in evolutionary biology called the "Precambrian rabbit." Rabbits didn't exist in the Cambrian period. During that time, the most advanced creatures were arthropods and chordates. So rabbits certainly should not have existed in the Precambrian era, according to Darwin's evolutionary theory. See Angier (2007).

11 Quoting from an article in Wikipedia on Ohm's Law, "Ohm's law states that the current through a conductor between two points is directly proportional to the potential difference across the two points."

12 Pinker (1994).

13 Mandler (2001).

14 Keil (1979, 1981).

15 Warrington (1975).

16 Siegler (1996).

17 Rogers and McClelland (2004); Rumelhart, McClelland, and the PDP Research Group (1986).

18 Also see the discussion of Ribot's Law and Jost's Law in Chapter 8.

19 The PDP approach owes much to the thinking of Donald Hebb (1949), originator of the idea that neurons that fire together wire together. Hebb himself did not coin this catchy phrase. Instead, it has been attributed to Carla Shatz of Stanford University, according to a Wikipedia article entitled "Hebbian theory."

20 Rosenbaum et al. (2009).

21 It might be that concept diversification differs from species diversification in that species evolved from a single proto-species whereas concepts evolve, within individuals, not from a single proto-concept but instead from some *set* of proto-concepts, pertaining, for example, to aspects of physical interactions among objects (Spelke, 1994), number (Dehaene, 1997), or other knowledge domains. Conversely, it is possible that there is, indeed, some single as-yet-unidentified proto-concept, some single "great idea" at the root of all ideas within individuals. Discovering such a single conceptual origin would be enormously exciting.

22 Darwin (1872/1965).

23 Maren (1999).

24 Landauer (1975); Logan (1988, 2002).

25 The classic reference to genetic algorithms is Holland (1975).

26 At least one author (Blechner, 2001) has suggested that dreaming might amount to creating random thoughts, some of which may be retained and prove useful.

27 See the Wikipedia article entitled "Torture."

28 For example, the discussion of problem-solving in Chapter 9 focused exclusively on lone-wolf problem-solvers. Many problems are solved through collaborative efforts (Johnson, 2010), though sometimes two heads are not better than one (Koriat, 2012).

29 Fiske (2011), reviewed by Tracy (2012).

30 Dennett (1992).

31 Hayes-Roth (2010).

32 I encourage you to look up "murmuration" on YouTube. The videos are astonishing.

33 For a wonderful article on the dynamics of starling flight formations, see Hayes (2010).

34 When people wake from anesthesia, primitive parts of the brain, such as the brainstem, come online before more advanced parts of the brain do, such as the neocortex (Gorman, 2012).

35 See the Wikipedia article entitled "Law of specific nerve energies."

36 Sperry (1945).

37 Pinker (2007).

38 Alais and Burr (2004).

39 Eagleman (2011).

40 McGurk and MacDonald (1976).

41 I refer to Charles Goodyear, who found a way to make rubber tough enough for tires; hence the Goodyear Tire and Rubber Company.

42 Estes (1960).

43 Anderson and Lebiere (1998).

44 Associationism is traceable to Plato and Aristotle, and finds modern form in connectionism (Rumelhart, McClelland, and the PDP Research Group (1986)). For a recent treatment, see Mandler (2011).

45 I obtained this quote by clicking on Microsoft Word's Look-Up function.

46 Miller, Tybur, and Jordan (2007).

47 Singh (1993).

48 Fisher (1994).

49 Nairne, Pandeirada, and Thompson (2008).

50 Also see Wilson, Darling, and Sykes (2011).

51 Angier (1999a).

52 Angier (199b, 2007).

53 Konner (2010).

54 Gopnik (2010, p. 321).

55 Arguably, the leading researcher in this domain is Elizabeth Spelke, who was pro-
filed in *The New Yorker* (Talbot, 2006). Spelke's lab webpage is http://www.wjh.
harvard.edu/~lds/index.html?spelke.html

56 Pinker (2002).

57 Miller (1956). Also see Simon (1974) and Cowan (2001).

58 Dawkins (1989).

59 Dennett (1995).

60 Michel et al. (2011).

61 Atkinson (2011).

62 The study of language origin reviewed here has had its critics. To see commentaries
on it as well as responses to those commentaries, go to http://www.sciencemag.
org/content/332/6027/346.full?sid=abfe3b52-c1b8-4751-8ca7-4550fa35fe74.

63 I introduced this way of representing theory space elsewhere (Rosenbaum, 2010).

64 I am no exception. I have studied such narrowly focused topics as where people
grasp handles of toilet plungers depending on where they plan to move the plungers (Cohen and Rosenbaum, 2004) or whether people choose to walk along the left
or right side of a table to pick up a bucket (Rosenbaum, Brach, and Semenov, 2011;
Rosenbaum, 2012). My colleagues and I studied these things to get at larger truths.

65 I was responsible for the 2000–2005 volumes. I served for the maximum term
of six years allowed by the organization that publishes JEP: HPP, the American
Psychological Association.

66 Bruner (1973).

67 That the germ of the idea I've laid out here has in fact been with us for a long time
is conveyed in a passage of a book by a colleague of mine at Penn State, Bill Ray
(2013). Describing a lecture given by William James to the Harvard Natural History
Society, Ray wrote, "James…suggests that evolution occurs within individuals as
much as it occurs between individuals and their environment. The implication is
that our internal physiological processes and our current set of thoughts, feelings,
and actions serve as an environment for natural selection in terms of spontaneously
arising internal impulses" [pp. 65–66].

68 Neuroscientists who have embraced Darwin's theory include Calvin (1987) and
Edelman (1987). Psychologists who have embraced Darwin's theory include Boakes
(1984), Campbell (1960), Pinker and Bloom (1990), Simonton (1999), Skinner

(1957), and Thorndike (1927). A philosopher who has advocated the Darwinian perspective is Dennett (1995). An economist who has embraced the Darwinian perspective is Harford (2011), whose book on the application of Darwin's theory to economics was reviewed by Rankin (2011).

69 An author who recognized the applicability of Darwin's theory to a wide range of disciplines was Price (1971, 1995), whose contribution was reintroduced to the public by Frank (1995).

70 Theory fecundity is sometimes used as a measure of theory utility, particularly when theory provability is in question (Clarke and Primo, 2012; Nozick, 1981). I should add that it is, in principle, difficult to generate highly specific predictions from the present theoretical perspective because adaptations are, by their nature, haphazard: What sticks is what just happens to work. The result is a "kluge" (Marcus, 2008), not a system whose every detail can be predicted from "first principles."

71 While I was in the final stages of completing this book, an article appeared in *Science* on "Multisensory Control of Hippocampal Spatiotemporal Selectivity" (Varassard et al., 2013). The question was: How does the hippocampus, a brain region with cells that fire differentially to where one is in a familiar environment, incorporate the range of sensory cues that inform spatial navigation? The last sentence of the abstract included this statement: "These results reveal cooperative and competitive interactions between sensory cues for control over hippocampal spatiotemporal selectivity…" [p. 1342].

References

Abbs, J. H., Gracco, V. L., & Cole, K. J. (1984). Control of multimovement coordination: Sensorimotor mechanisms in speech motor programming. *Journal of Motor Behavior, 16*, 195–231.

Adolph, K. E., Cole, W. G., Komati, M., Garciaguirre, J. S., Badaly, D., Lingeman, J. M., Gladys, L. Y., & Sotsky, R. B. (2012). How do you learn to walk? Thousands of steps and dozens of falls per day. *Psychological Science, 23*, 1387–1394.

Adolph, K. E., Vereijken, B., Denny, M. A. (1998). Learning to crawl. *Child Development, 69*, 1299–1312.

Aglioti, S. M., Cesari, P., Romani, M., & Urgesi, C. (2008). Action anticipation and motor resonance in elite basketball players. *Nature Neuroscience, 11*, 1109–1116.

Alais, D., & Burr, D. (2004). The ventriloquist effect results from near-optimal bimodal integration. *Current Biology, 14*, 257–262.

Allington, G. R., Koons, D. N., Ernest, S. K., Shutzenhofer, M. R., & Valone, T. J. (2013). Niche opportunities and invasion dynamics in a desert annual community. *Ecology Letters, 16*, 158–166.

Anderson, J. R., & Schooler, L. J. (2000). The adaptive nature of memory. In E. Tulving & F. I. Craik (Eds.), *The Oxford handbook of memory* (pp. 557–570). New York, NY: Oxford University Press.

Anderson, J. R. (2010). *Cognitive psychology and its implications* (7th ed.). New York: Worth Publishers.

Anderson, J. R., & Lebiere, C. (1998). *The atomic components of thought.* Mahwah, NJ: Erlbaum.Anderson, M. C., & Spellman, B. A. (1995). On the status of inhibitory mechanisms in cognition: Memory retrieval as a model case. *Psychological Review, 102*, 68–100.

Angier, N. (February 21, 1999a). Men, women, sex and Darwin. *The New York Times Magazine*, p. 48.

Angier, N. (1999b). *Woman: An intimate geography.* New York, NY: Houghton Mifflin.

Angier, N. (2007). *The canon: A whirligig tour of the beautiful basics of science.* New York, NY: Houghton Mifflin.

Armstrong, S. L., Gleitman, L. R., & Gleitman, H. (1983). What some concepts might not be. *Cognition, 13*, 263–268.

Aruin, A. S., & Latash, M. L. (1995). Directional specificity of postural muscles in feed-forward postural reactions during fast voluntary arm movements. *Experimental Brain Research, 103*, 323–332.

Atkinson, Q. (2011). Phonemic diversity supports a serial founder effect model of language expansion from Africa. *Science, 332*, 346–349.

Attneave, F. (1971). Multistability in perception. *Scientific American, 225*, 62–71.

Baddeley, A. D., & Hitch, G. (1974). Working memory. In G. H. Bower (Ed.), *Psychology of Learning and Motivation* (Vol. 8, pp. 47–89). New York, NY: Academic Press.

Baddeley, A. D., & Longman, D. J. A. (1978). The influence of length and frequency of training session on the rate of learning to type. *Ergonomics, 21*, 627–635.

Bahrick, H. P., & Phelps, E. (1987). Retention of Spanish vocabulary over 8 years. *Journal of Experimental Psychology: Learning, Memory, and Cognition, 13*, 344–349.

Bahrick, H. P. (1984). Semantic memory content in permastore: Fifty years of memory for Spanish learning in school. *Journal of Experimental Psychology: General, 113*, 1–29.

Bahrick, H. P., Bahrick, P. O., & Wittlinger, R. P. (1975). Fifty years of memory for names and faces: A cross-sectional approach. *Journal of Experimental Psychology: General, 104*, 54–75.

Baird, B., Smallwood, J., Mrazek, M. D., Kam, J. W., Franklin, M. S., & Schooler, J. W. (Oct. 1, 2012). Inspired by distraction: Mind wandering facilitates creative incubation. *Psychological Science, 23*(10), 1117–1122. doi: 10.1177/0956797612446024.

Balota, D. A., & Spieler, D. H. (1999). Word frequency, repetition, and lexicality effects in word recognition tasks: Beyond measures of central tendency. *Journal of Experimental Psychology: General, 128*, 32–55.

Bandura, A., Ross, D., & Ross, S. A. (1961). Transmission of aggression through imitation of aggressive models. *Journal of Abnormal and Social Psychology, 63*, 575–582.

Banich, M. T. (2004). *Cognitive neuroscience and neuropsychology* (2nd ed.). Boston, MA: Houghton Mifflin.

Barlow, H. B. (1982). David Hubel and Torsten Wiesel: Their contributions towards understanding the primary visual cortex. *Trends in the Neurosciences, 5*, 145–152.

Barlow, H. B., & Hill, R. M. (1963). Evidence for a physiological explanation of the waterfall illusion. *Nature, 200*, 1345–1347.

Barry, S. (2009). *Fixing my gaze: A scientist's journey into seeing in three dimensions.* New York, NY: Basic Books.

Bateson, P. (2003). The promise of behavioural biology. *Animal Behaviour, 65*, 11–17.

Bavelier, D., & Hirshorn, E. A. (2010). I see where you're hearing: How cross-modal plasticity may exploit homologous brain structures. *Nature Neuroscience, 13*, 1309–1311.

Bavelier, D., Levi, D. M., Li, R. W., Dan, Y., & Hensch, T. K. (2010). Removing brakes on adult brain plasticity: From molecular to behavioral interventions. *Journal of Neuroscience, 30*, 14964–14971.

Baylis, G. C., Tipper, S. P., & Houghton, G. (1997). Externally cued and internally generated selection: Differences in distractor analysis and inhibition. *Journal of Experimental Psychology: Human Perception & Performance, 23*, 1617–1630.

Beilock, S. L. (2010). *Choke: What the secrets of the brain reveal about getting it right when you have to.* New York, NY: Simon & Schuster, Free Press.

Beilock, S. L., Carr, T. H., MacMahon, C., & Starkes, J. L. (2002). When paying attention becomes counterproductive: Impact of divided versus skill-focused attention on novice and experienced performance of sensorimotor skills. *Journal of Experimental Psychology: Applied, 8*, 6–16.

Belke, E., Brysbaert, M., Meyer, A. S., & Ghyselinck, M. (2005). Age of acquisition effects in picture naming: Evidence for a lexical-semantic competition hypothesis. *Cognition, 96*, B45–B54.

Benjamin, A. (2011). *Successful remembering and successful forgetting: A festschrift in honor of Robert A. Bjork.* New York, NY: Psychology Press.

Bilalic, M., McLeod, P., & Gobet, F. (2010). The mechanism of the Einstellung (set) effect: A pervasive source of cognitive bias. *Current Directions in Psychological Science, 19*, 111–115.

Blake, R. (2001). A primer on binocular rivalry, including current controversies. *Brain and Mind, 2*, 5–38.

Blakemore, S. J., Wolpert, D. M., & Frith, C. D. (1998). Central cancellation of self-produced tickle sensation. *Nature Neuroscience, 1*, 635–640.

Blechner, M. (2001). *The dream frontier.* Hillsdale, NJ: The Analytic Press.

Blumberg, M. S., & Wasserman, E. A. (1995). Animal mind and the argument from design. *American Psychologist, 50*, 133–144.

Boakes, R. (1984). *From Darwin to behaviorism.* New York, NY: Cambridge University Press.

Boden, M. (2004). *The creative mind: Myths and mechanisms* (2nd ed.). London, England/New York, NY: Routledge.

Bower, B. (March 24, 2012). Vodka delivers shot of creativity: A boozy glow may trigger problem-solving insights. *Science News, 181*, 12.

Bower, G. H. (1967). A multi-component theory of the memory trace. In K. W. Spence & J. T. Spence (Eds.), *The psychology of learning and motivation* (Vol. 1, pp. 229–325). New York, NY: Academic Press.

Bower, G. H. (1970). Analysis of a mnemonic device: Modern psychology uncovers the powerful components of an ancient system for improving memory. *American Scientist, 58*, 496–508.

Bowles, B., Crupi, C., Mirsattari, S. M., Pigott, S. E., Parrent, A. G., Pruessner, J. C., Yonelinas, A. P., & Köhler, S. (2007). Impaired familiarity with preserved recollection after anterior temporal-lobe resection that spares the hippocampus. *Proceedings of the National Academy of Sciences, 104*, 16382–16387.

Bransford, J. D., Franks, J. J., Morris, C. D., & Stein, B. S. (1977). Some general constraints on learning and memory research. In L. S. Cermak & F. I. M. Craik (Eds.), *Levels of processing in human memory* (pp. 331–354). Hillsdale, NJ: Erlbaum.

Bredemeiser, K., & Simons, D. J. (2012). Working memory and inattentional blindness. *Psychonomic Bulletin & Review, 19,* 239–244.

Broadbent, D. (1958). *Perception and communication.* London, England: Pergamon Press.

Brown, A. S. (1991). The tip of the tongue phenomenon. *Psychological Bulletin, 109,* 204–223.

Brown, R. (1973). *A first language.* Cambridge, MA: Harvard University Press.

Bruner, J. S. (1973). *Beyond the information given: Studies in the psychology of knowing.* New York, NY: W. W. Norton.

Bullock, T. H., Bennett, M. V. L., Johnston, D., Josephson, R., Marder, E., Fields, R. D. (2005). The neuron doctrine, redux. *Science, 310,* 791–793.

Calvin, W. H. (November 5, 1987). The brain as a Darwin machine. *Nature, 330,* 33–34.

Calvo-Merino, B., Glaser, D. E., Grezes, J., Passingham, R. E., & Haggard, P. (2005). Action observation and acquired motor skills: An fMRI study with expert dancers. *Cerebral Cortex, 15,* 1243–1249.

Campbell, D. T. (1960). Blind variation and selective retention in creative thought as in other knowledge processes. *Psychological Review, 67,* 380–400.

Carroll, J. B., & White, N. (1973). Word frequency and age of acquisition as determiners of picture-naming latency. *Quarterly Journal of Experimental Psychology, 25,* 85–95.

Chaisanguanthum, K. S., & Lisberger, S. G. (2011). A neurally efficient implementation of sensory population decoding. *Journal of Neuroscience, 31,* 4868–4877.

Cherry, E. C. (1958). Some experiments on the recognition of speech with one and two ears. *Journal of the acoustical society of America, 25,* 975–979.

Cho, D., & Proctor, R. W. (2011). Correspondence effects for objects with opposing left and right protrusions. *Journal of Experimental Psychology: Human Perception And Performance, 37,* 737–749. doi: 10.1037/a0021934

Chomsky, N. (1959). A review of B. F. Skinner's verbal behavior. *Language, 35,* 26–58.

Clarke, K. A., & Primo, D. M. (April 1, 2012). Overcoming 'physics envy.' *The New York Times Sunday Review Section,* p. 9.

Cohen, J. D., Romero, R. D., Servan-Schreiber, D., & Farah, M. J. (1994). Mechanisms of spatial attention: The relation of macrostructure to microstructure in parietal neglect. *Journal of Cognitive Neuroscience, 6,* 377–387.

Cohen, R. G., & Rosenbaum, D. A. (2004). Where objects are grasped reveals how grasps are planned: Generation and recall of motor plans. *Experimental Brain Research, 157,* 486–495.

Colapinto, J. (2009). Brain games: The Marco Polo of neuroscience. *The New Yorker,* May 11, pp. 76–87.

Coles, M. G. H., Gratton, G., Bashore, T. R., Eriksen, C. W., & Donchin, E. (1985). A psychophysiological investigation of the continuous flow model of human information processing. *Journal of Experimental Psychology: Human Perception and Performance, 11,* 529–553.

Collins, A. M., & Quillian, M. R. (1969). Retrieval time from semantic memory. *Journal of Verbal Learning and Verbal Behavior, 8,* 240–247.

Coltheart, M., Curtis, B., Atkins, P., & Haller, M. (1993). Models of reading aloud: Dual-route and parallel-distributed-processing approaches. *Psychological Review, 100*, 589–608.

Conrad, C. (1972). Cognitive economy in semantic memory. *Journal of Experimental Psychology, 92*, 149–154.

Cowan, N. (2001). The magical number 4 in short-term memory: A reconsideration of mental storage capacity. *Behavioral and Brain Sciences, 24*, 87–114.

Coyne, J. A. (2009). *Why evolution is true.* New York, NY: Viking.

Crossman, E. R. F. W. (1959). A theory of the acquisition of speed skill. *Ergonomics, 2*, 153–166.

Cytowic, R. E., & Eagleman, D. M. (2009). *Wednesday is indigo blue: Discovering the brain of synesthesia.* Cambridge, MA: MIT Press.

Dagenbach, D., & Carr, T. H., Eds. (1994). *Inhibitory processes in attention, memory, and language.* San Diego, CA: Academic Press.

Danziger, S., Levav, J., & Avnaim-Pesso, L. (2011). Extraneous factors in judicial decisions. *Proceedings of the National Academy of Sciences, 108*, 6889–6892.

Darwin, C. (1859). *On the origin of species by means of natural selection.* London, England: Murray.

Darwin, C. R. (1872/1965). *The expression of the emotions in man and animals.* Chicago, IL: University of Chicago Press. (Original work published in 1872).

Darwin, E. (1794). *Zoönomia, or the laws of organic life.* London, England: J. Johnson.

Dawkins, R. (1989). *The selfish gene.* Oxford, England: Oxford University Press.

Dehaene, S. (1997). *The number sense: How the mind creates mathematics.* New York, NY: Oxford University Press.

de Jong, R., Coles, M. G., Logan, G. D., & Gratton, G. (1990). In search of the point of no return: The control of response processes. *Journal of Experimental Psychology: Human Perception and Performance, 16*, 164–182.

Deese, J. (1957). On the prediction of occurrence of particular verbal intrusions in immediate recall. *Journal of Experimental Psychology, 58*, 17–22.

Dell, G. S. (1986). A spreading activation theory of retrieval in sentence production. *Psychological Review, 93*, 283–321.

Dennett, D. C. (1992). *Consciousness explained.* New York, NY: Little, Brown and Co.

Dennett, D. C. (1995). *Darwin's dangerous idea: Evolution and the meanings of life.* New York, NY: Simon & Schuster.

Desimone, R., & Duncan, J. (1995). Neural mechanisms of selective attention. *Annual Review of Neuroscience, 18*, 193–222.

Doidge, N. (2007). *The brain that changes itself.* New York, NY: Viking.

Donders, F.C. (1969). Speed of mental processes. *Acta Psychologica, 30*, 412–431. (Original work published in Dutch in 1868).

Duncan, J. (1984). Selective attention and the organization of visual information. *Journal of Experimental Psychology: General, 113*, 501–517.

Duncan, J., Humphreys, G. W., & Ward, R. (1997). Competitive brain activity in visual attention. *Current Opinion in Neurobiology, 7*, 255–261.

Duncker, K. (1945). On problem solving. *Psychological Monographs, 58*(5), i–113.

Eagleman, D. M. (2001). Visual illusions and neurobiology. *Nature Reviews Neuroscience, 2,* 920–926.

Eagleman, D. M. (2011). *Incognito—The secret lives of the brain.* New York, NY: Pantheon.

Edelman, G. M. (1987). *Neural Darwinism.* New York, NY: Basic Books.

Elbert, T., Pantev, C., Weinbruch, C., Rockstroh, B., & Taub, E. (1995). Increased cortical representation of the fingers of the left hand. *Science, 270,* 305–307.

Ellis, R. W. B., & van Creveld, S. (1940). A syndrome characterized by ectodermal dysplasia, polydactyly, chondro-dysplasia and congenital morbus cordis: Report of three cases. *Archives of Disease in Childhood, 15,* 65–84.

Elman, J., Karmiloff-Smith, A., Bates, E., Johnson, M., Parisi, D., & Plunkett, K. (1996). *Rethinking innateness: A connectionist perspective on development.* Cambridge, MA: MIT Press.

Erickson, R. P. (1984). On the neural bases of behavior. *American Scientist, 72,* 233–241.

Eriksen, C. W. (1995). The flankers task and response competition: A useful tool for investigating a variety of cognitive probems. *Visual Cognition, 2,* 101–118.

Estes, W. K. (1960). Learning theory and the new "mental chemistry." *Psychological Review, 67,* 207–223.

Estes, W. K. (1972). An associative basis for coding and organization in memory. In A. W. Melton & E. Martin (Eds.), *Coding processes in human memory* (pp. 161–190). Washington, DC: Winston.

Fahle, M., & Edelman, S. (1993). Long-term learning in Vernier acuity: Effects of stimulus orientation, range and of feedback. *Vision Research, 33,* 397–412.

Faye, C. (December 2011). Lessons from bird brains. *Monitor on Psychology, 42,* 30.

Fisher, H. E. (1994). *Anatomy of love: The natural history of love, mating, and why we stray.* New York, NY: Random House.

Fiske, S. L. (2011). *Envy up, scorn down: How status divides us.* New York, NY: Russell Sage Foundation.

Fitts, P. M., & Seeger, C. M. (1953). S-R compatibility: Spatial characteristics of stimulus and response codes. *Journal of Experimental Psychology, 46,* 199–210.

Flanders, M., & Soechting, J. F. (1992). Kinematics of typing: Parallel control of the two hands. *Journal of Neurophysiology, 67,* 1264–1274.

Forssberg, H., Grillner, S., & Rossignol, S. (1975). Phase dependent reflex reversal during walking in chronic spinal cats. *Brain Research, 55,* 247–304.

Forssberg, H., Grillner, S., & Rossignol, S. (1977). Phasic gain control of reflexes from the dorsum of the paw during spinal locomotion. *Brain Research, 132,* 121–139.

Fowler, C. A. (2007). Speech production. In M. G. Gaskell (Ed.), *The Oxford handbook of psycholinguistics* (pp. 489–502). New York, NY: Oxford University Press.

Frank, S. A. (1995). George Price's contributions to evolutionary genetics. *Journal of Theoretical Biology, 175,* 373–388.

Franz, E. A., Zelaznik, H. N., Swinnen, S., & Walter, C. (2001) Spatial conceptual influences on the coordination of bimanual actions: When a dual task becomes a single task. *Journal of Motor Behavior, 33,* 103–112.

Frederiksen, J. R., & Kroll, J. F. (1976). Spelling and sound: Approaches to the internal lexicon. *Journal of Experimental Psychology: Human Perception and Performance, 2*, 361–379.

Freud, S. (1901/1971). *The psychopathology of everyday life.* Translated by A. Tyson. New York, NY: Norton.

Futuyma, D. J. (1998). *Evolutionary biology* (3rd ed.). Sunderland, MA: Sinauer Associates.

Gailliot, M. T., Baumeister, R. F., DeWall, C. N., Maner, J. K., Plant, E. A., Tice, D. M., Brewer, L. E., & Schmeichel, B. J. (2007). Self-control relies on glucose as a limited energy source: Willpower is more than a metaphor. *Journal of Personality and Social Psychology, 92*, 325–336.

Gallese, V., & Goldman, A. (1998). Mirror neurons and the simulation theory of mind-reading. *Trends in Cognitive Sciences, 2*, 493–501.

Gallistel, C. R. (1981). Bell, Magendie, and the proposals to restrict the use of animals in neurobehavioral research. *American Psychologist, 36*, 357–360.

Garcia, J., Kimeldorf, D., & Koeling, R. (1955). Conditioned aversion to saccharin resulting from exposure to gamma radiation. *Science, 122*, 157–158.

Garrett, M. F. (1975). The analysis of sentence production. In G. H. Bower (Ed.), *Psychology of learning and motivation* (Vol. 9, pp. 133–177). New York, NY: Academic Press.

Gazzaniga, M. S., Ivry, R. B., & Mangun, G. R. (2008). *Cognitive neuroscience, the biology of the mind* (3rd ed.). New York, NY: Norton & Co.

Gehring, W. J., Goss, B., Coles, M. G., Meyer, D. E., & Donchin, E. (1993). A neural system for error detection and compensation. *Psychological Science, 4*, 385–390.

Gentner, D. R., Grudin, J., & Conway, E. (1980). *Finger movements in transcription typing.* La Jolla, CA: University of California, San Diego, Center for Human Information Processing (Technical Report 8001).

Georgopoulos, A. P., Caminiti, R., Kalaska, J. F., & Massey, J. T. (1983). Spatial coding of movement: A hypothesis concerning the coding of movement direction by motor cortical populations. *Experimental Brain Research Supplement, 7*, 327–336.

Georgopoulos, A. P., Schwartz, A. B., & Kettner, R. E. (1986). Neuronal population coding of movement direction. *Science, 233*, 1416–1419.

Gibson, J. J. (1979). *The ecological approach to visual perception.* Boston, MA: Houghton-Mifflin.

Gick, M. L., & Holyoak, K. J. (1980). Analogical problem solving. *Cognitive Psychology, 12*, 306–355.

Gladwell, M. (2000). *The tipping point: How little things can make a big difference.* New York, NY: Little Brown and Company.

Godden, D. R., & Baddeley, A. D. (1975). Context-dependent memory in two natural environments: On land and underwater. *British Journal of Psychology, 66*, 325–331.

Goldfield, E. C., Kay, B. A., & Warren, W. H. (1993). Infant bouncing: The assembly and tuning of action systems. *Child Development, 64*, 1128–1142.

Gopnik, A. (2010). Our evolving view of childhood. *Science, 330,* 321–322.

Gordon, A. M. (2011). To constrain or not to constrain, and other stories of intensive upper extremity training for children with unilateral cerebral palsy. *Developmental Medicine and Child Neurology, 53,* 56–61.

Gorman, J. (2012). Awake or knocked out? The line gets blurrier. *The New York Times,* April 17, D3.

Gould, S. J., & Eldredge, N. (1977). Punctuated equilibria: The tempo and mode of evolution reconsidered. *Paleobiology, 3,* 115–151.

Graf, P., & Schacter, D. L. (1985). Implicit and explicit memory for new associations in normal and amnesic subjects. *Journal of Experimental Psychology: Learning, Memory, and Cognition, 11,* 501–518.

Gray, J. A., & Wedderburn, A. A. (1960). Grouping strategies with simultaneous stimuli. *Quarterly Journal of Experimental Psychology, 12,* 180–184.

Greenbaum, H., & Rubinstein, D. (March 16, 2012). Who made that lawn mower? *The New York Times Magazine,* p. 22.

Greenwald, A. G. (1970). Sensory feedback mechanisms in performance control: With special reference to the ideomotor mechanism. *Psychological Review, 77,* 73–99.

Greenwald, A. G., McGhee, D. E., & Schwartz, J. L. K. (1998). Measuring individual differences in implicit cognition: The implicit association test. *Journal of Personality and Social Psychology, 74,* 1464–1480.

Gregory, R. L. (1973). *Eye and brain* (2nd ed.). New York, NY: McGraw-Hill.

Gustavson, C. R., Garcia, J., Hankins, W. G., & Rusiniak, K. W. (1974). Coyote predation control by aversive conditioning. *Science, 184,* 581–583.

Harford, T. (2011). *Adapt: Why success always starts with failure.* New York, NY: Farrar, Straus and Giroux.

Hayes, B. (2010). Flights of fancy. *American Scientist, 99,* 10–14.

Hayes-Roth, B. (October 2011). Conscious efforts. *Scientific American,* 8–10.

Healy, A. F. (1981). The effects of visual similarity on proofreading for misspellings. *Memory & Cognition, 9,* 453–460.

Heathcote, A., Brown, S., & Mewhort, D. J. K. (2000). The power law repealed: The case for an exponential law of practice. *Psychonomic Bulletin and Review, 7,* 185–207.

Hebb, D. O. (1949). *The organization of behavior: A neuropsychological theory.* New York, NY: John Wiley.

Hess, E.H. (1958). Imprinting in animals. *Scientific American, 198,* 81–90.

Hess, E.H. (1973). *Imprinting: Early experience and the developmental psychobiology of attachment.* New York, NY: Van Nostrand Reinhold Company.

Hess, E. H. (1985). The wild goose chase. In D. A. Dewsbury (Ed.), *Leaders in the study of animal behavior: Autobiographical perspectives* (pp. 183–191). Cranberry, NJ: Associated University Presses.

Hick, W. E. (1952). On the rate of gain of information. *Quarterly Journal of Experimental Psychology, 4,* 11–26.

Hirsch, H. V. B., & Spinelli, D. N. (1970). Visual experience modifies distribution of horizontally and vertically oriented receptive fields in cats. *Science, 168,* 869–871.

Hirsch, H. V. B., & Spinelli, D. N. (1971). Modification of the distribution of receptive field orientation in in cats by selective visual exposure during development. *Experimental Brain Research, 13,* 509–527.

Hochberg, J. (1981). On cognition in perception: Perceptual coupling and unconscious inference. *Cognition, 10,* 127–134.

Hodges-Simeon, C. R., Gaulin, S. J. C., & Puts, D. A. (2010). Voice correlates of mating success in men: Examining "contests" vs. "mate choice" modes of sexual selection. *Archives of Sexual Behavior, 40,* 551–557.

Hoff, E. (2009). *Language development* (4th ed.). Belmont, CA: Wadsworth.

Holland, J. H. (1975). *Adaptation in natural and artificial systems.* Ann Arbor, MI: University of Michigan Press.

Holst, E. von (1939). Die relative Koordination als Phänomenon und als Methode zentral-nervöse Funktionsanalyze. *Erg. Physiol., 42,* 228–306. [English translation in Holst, E. von. (1973). Relative coordination as a phenomenon and as a method of analysis of central nervous functions. In *The behavioural physiology of animal and man: The collected papers of Erich von Holst* (Vol. 1) [R. Martin, Translator]. London, England: Methuen.

Holst, E. von, & Mittelstaedt, H. (1950). Das Reafferenzprinzip. Wechselwirkungen zwischen Zentralnervensystem und Peripherie. *Naturwissenschaften, 37,* 464–476. (English translation in Holst, E. von (1973). *The reafference principle. The behavioral physiology of animals and man: The collected papers of Erich von Holst* (Vol. 1) [R. Martin, Translator] (pp. 139–173). London, England: Methuen.

Hubel, D. H., & Wiesel, T. N. (1963). Receptive fields of cells in striate cortex of very young, visually inexperienced kittens. *Journal of Neurophysiology, 26,* 994–1002.

Hubel, D. H., & Wiesel, T. N. (1979). Brain mechanisms of vision. *Scientific American, 241,* 150–162.

Huk, A., Ress, D., & Heeger, D. (2001). Neuronal basis of the motion aftereffect reconsidered. *Neuron, 32,* 161–172.

Hunt, R. R., & Worthen, J. B. (2006). *Distinctiveness and memory.* New York, NY: Oxford University Press.

Hurtley, S., & Yeston, J. (2012, December 7). Desert invaders. *Science, 338,* 1264.

Hurvich, L. M., & Jameson, D. (1957). An opponent-process theory of color vision. *Psychological Review, 64,* 384–404.

Hyman, R. (1953). Stimulus information as a determinant of reaction time. *Journal of Experimental Psychology, 45,* 188–196.

James, W. (1890). *The principles of psychology.* New York, NY: Henry Holt and Co.

Jeannerod, M. (1995). Mental imagery in the motor context. *Neuropsychologia Special Issue: The neuropsychology of mental imagery, 33,* 1419–1432.

Jenkins, J. G., & Dallenbach, K. M. (1924). Obliviscence during sleep and waking. *American Journal of Psychology, 35,* 605–612.

Jenkins, W. M., Merzenich, M. M., Ochs, M. T., Allard, T., & Giuc-Robles, E. (1990). Functional reorganization of primary somatosensory cortex in adult owl monkeys after behaviorally controlled tactile stimulation. *Journal of Neurophysiology, 63,* 82–104.

Johnson, A., & Proctor, R. W. (2003). *Attention: Theory and practice.* Los Angeles, CA: Sage.

Blumberg, M. S., & Wasserman, E. A. (1995). Animal mind and the argument from design. *American Psychologist, 50,* 133–144.

Johnson, G. (2008). *The ten most beautiful experiments.* New York, NY: Alfred A. Knopf.

Johnson, S. (2010). *Where good ideas come from: The natural history of innovation.* New York, NY: Riverhead Books.

Jonides, J., & Mack, R. (1984). On the cost and benefit of cost and benefit. *Psychological Bulletin, 96,* 29–44.

Jost, A. (1897). Die Assoziationsfestigkeit in ihrer Abha¨ngigkeit von der Verteilung der Wiederholungen [The strength of associations in their dependence on the distribution of repetitions]. *Zeitschrift fur Psychologie und Physiologie der Sinnesorgane, 16,* 436–472.

Kahneman, D. (1973). *Attention and effort.* Englewood Cliffs, NJ: Prentice-Hall.

Kahneman, D. (2011). *Thinking, fast and slow.* New York, NY: Farrar, Straus and Giroux.

Kamin, L. J. (1969). Predictability, surprise, attention and conditioning. In B. A. Campbell & R. M. Church (Eds.), *Punishment and aversive behavior* (pp. 279–96). New York, NY: Appleton-Century-Crofts.

Kandel, E. R., Schwartz, J. H., & Jessell, T. M. (Eds.) (2000). *Principles of neural science* (4th ed.). New York, NY: McGraw Hill.

Keil, F. C. (1979). *Semantic and conceptual development: An ontological perspective.* Cambridge, MA: Harvard University.

Keil, F. C. (1981). Constraints on knowledge and cognitive development. *Psychological Review, 88,* 197–227.

Kiesel, A., Stenhauser, M., Wendt, M., Falkenstein, M., Jost, K., Philipp, A., & Koch, I. (2010). Control and interference in task switching—A review. *Psychological Bulletin, 136,* 849–874.

Klein, R. M. (2000). Inhibition of return. *Trends in Cognitive Sciences, 4,* 138–147.

Kleinschmidt, A., Büchel, C., Zeki, S., & Frackowiak, R. S. J. (1998). Human brain activity during spontaneously reversing perception of ambiguous figures. *Proceedings of the Royal Society of London. Series B: Biological Sciences, 265*(1413), 2427–2433.

Kolers, P. A. (1976). Reading a year later. *Journal of Experimental Psychology: Human Learning and Memory, 2,* 554–565.

Konner, M. (2010). *The evolution of childhood: Relationships, emotion, mind.* Cambridge, MA: Harvard University Press.

Körding, K. P., & Wolpert, D. M. (2004). Bayesian integration in sensorimotor learning. *Nature, 437,* 244–247.

Koriat, A. (2012). When are two heads better than one and why? *Science, 336,* 360–362.

Kornblum, S. (1969). Sequential determinants of information processing in serial and discrete choice reaction time. *Psychological Review, 76*, 113–131.

Kroll, J. F., Michael, E., & Sankaranarayanan, A. (1998). A model of bilingual representation and its implications for second language acquisition. In A. F. Healy & L. E. Bourne (Eds.), *Foreign language learning: Psycholinguistic experiments on training and retention* (pp. 365–395). Mahwah, NJ: Erlbaum.

Kuhl, P., Williams, K. A., Lacerda, F., Stevens, K. N., & Lindblom, B. (1992). Linguistic experience alters phonetic perception in infants by 6 months of age. *Science, 255*, 606–608.

Landauer, T. K. (1975). Memory without organization: Properties of a model with random storage and undirected retrieval. *Cognitive Psychology, 7*, 495–531.

Lashley, K. S. (1951). The problem of serial order in behavior. In L. A. Jeffress (Ed.), *Cerebral mechanisms in behavior* (pp. 112–131). New York, NY: Wiley.

Latash, M. L. (2008). *Neurophysiolgical basis of movement* (2nd ed.). Champaign, IL: Human Kinetics.

Light, L., & Carter-Sobell, L. (1970). Effects of changed semantic context on recognition memory. *Journal of Verbal Learning and Verbal Behavior, 9*, 1–11.

Limb, C. J., & Braun, A. R. (2008). Neural substrates of spontaneous musical performance: An fMRI study of jazz improvisation. *PLoS ONE, 3*(2), e1679.

Lindsay, P. H., & Norman, D. A. (1977). *Human information processing: An introduction to psychology* (2nd ed.). New York, NY: Academic Press.

Loftus, E. F., & Palmer, J. C. (1974). Reconstruction of automobile destruction: An example of the interaction between language and memory. *Journal of Verbal Learning and Verbal Behavior, 13*, 585–589.

Loftus, E. F. (1991). The glitter of everyday memory…and the gold. *American Psychologist, 46*, 16–18.

Loftus, E. R., & Loftus, G. R. (1980). On the permanence of stored information in the human brain. *American Psychologist, 35*, 409–420.

Logan, G. D. (1983). Time, information, and the various spans in typewriting. In W. E. Cooper (Ed.), *Cognitive aspects of skilled typewriting* (pp. 197–224). New York, NY: Springer-Verlag.

Logan, G. D. (1988). Toward an instance theory of automatization. *Psychological Review, 95*, 492–527.

Logan, G. D. (2002). An instance theory of attention and memory. *Psychological Review, 109*, 376–400.

Logan, G. D., & Cowan, W. B. (1984). On the ability to inhibit thought and action: A theory of an act of control. *Psychological Review, 91*, 295–327.

Lorenz, K. (1981). *The foundations of ethology*. New York, NY: Springer-Verlag.

Lötze, R. H. (1852). *Medicinische Psychologie oder Physiologie der Seele*. Leipzig: Weidmann'sche Buchhandlung.

Lubow, R. E., & Gewirtz, J. C. (1995). Latent inhibition in humans: Data, theory, and implications for schizophrenia. *Psychological Bulletin, 117*, 87–103.

Luce, R. D. (1986). *Response times: Their role in inferring elementary mental organiza-tion.* New York, NY: Oxford University Press.

Luchins, A. S. (1942). Mechanization in problem solving. *Psychological Monographs, 54* (Whole No. 248).

MacDonald, M. C., Pearlmutter, N. J., & Seidenberg, M. S. (1994). The lexical nature of syntactic ambiguity resolution. *Psychological Review, 101,* 676–703.

MacLeod, C. M. (1991). Half a century of research on the Stroop effect: An integrative review. *Psychological Bulletin, 109,* 163–203.

MacLeod, C. M. (1998). Directed forgetting. In J. Golding & C. M. MacLeod (Eds.), *Intentional forgetting: Interdisciplinary approaches* (pp. 1–58). Mahwah, NJ: Erlbaum.

MacWhinney, B., & Bates, E. (1989). *The cross-linguistic study of sentence processing.* Cambridge, England: Cambridge University Press.

Mahon, B. Z., Costa, A., Peterson, R., Vargas, K. A., & Caramazza, A. (2007). Lexical selection is not by competition: A reinterpretation of semantic interfer-ence and facilitation effects in the picture-word interference paradigm. *Journal of Experimental Psychology: Learning, Memory and Cognition, 33,* 503–535.

Maier, N. R. (1931). Reasoning in humans. II. The solution of a problem and its appear-ance in consciousness. *Journal of Comparative Psychology, 12,* 181–194.

Mandler, G. (2011). From association to organization. *Current Directions in Psychological Science, 20,* 232–23.

Mandler, J. (2001). On the foundations of the semantic system. In E. M. Forde & G. Jumphreys (Eds.), *Category specificity in mind and brain* (pp. 315–374). East Sussex, U.K.: Psychology Press.

Marcus, G. (2008). *Kluge: The haphazard construction of the human mind.* Boston, MA: Houghton Mifflin.

Maren, S. (1999). Long-term potentiation in the amygdala: A mechanism for emotional learning and memory. *Trends in Neuroscience, 22,* 561–567.

Marks, L. E. (1975). On colored-hearing synesthesia: Cross-modal translations of sen-sory dimensions. *Psychological Bulletin, 82,* 303–331.

Marlsen-Wilson, W. (1973). Linguistic structure and speech shadowing at very short latencies. *Nature, 244,* 522–523.

Martin, D. (February 25, 2012). Ulric Neisser Is Dead at 83; Reshaped Study of the Mind. *New York Times* obituary. http://www.nytimes.com/2012/02/26/us/ulric-neisser-who-reshaped-thinking-on-the-mind-dies-at-83.html?page wanted=all

Mather, G. (2006). *Foundations of perception.* Sussex, England: Psychology Press.

Matin, E. (1974). Saccadic suppression. *Psychological Bulletin, 81,* 899–918.

Maynard Smith, G. (1982). *Evolution and the theory of games.* Cambridge, England: Cambridge University Press.

Mayr, E., & Provine, E. B. (Eds). (1980). *The evolutionary synthesis.* Cambridge, MA: Harvard University Press.

McClelland, J. L., & Rumelhart, D. E. (1981). An interactive activation model of context effects in letter perception: Part 1: An account of basic findings. *Psychological Review, 88*, 375–407.

McClelland, J. L., Rumelhart, D. E., & the PDP Research Group. (1986). *Parallel distributed processing.* Volume 2: *Psychological and biological models.* Cambridge, MA: MIT Press.

McGaugh, J. L. (2000). Memory—A century of consolidation. *Science, 287*, 248–251.

McGeoch, J. A. (1932). Forgetting and the law of disuse. *Psychological Review, 39*, 352–370.

McGraw, M. B. (1943). *Neuro-muscular maturation of the infant.* New York, NY: Columbia University Press.

McGrayne, S. B. (2011). *The theory that would not die: How Bayes' Rule cracked the enigma code, hunted down Russian submarines and emerged triumphant from two centuries of controversy.* New Haven, CT: Yale University Press.

McGurk, H., & MacDonald, J. (1976). Hearing lips and seeing voices. *Nature, 264*, 746–748.

McKinstry, C., Dale, R., & Spivey, M. J. (2008). Action dynamics reveal parallel competition in decision making. *Psychological Science, 19*, 22–24.

McLeod, P., & Hume, M. (1994). Overlapping mental operations in serial performance with preview: Typing. A reply to Pashler. *Quarterly Journal of Experimental Psychology, 47A*, 193–199.

Mechsner, F., Kerzel, D., Knoblich, G., & Prinz, W. (2001). Perceptual basis of bimanual coordination. *Nature, 414*, 69–73.

Merzenich, M. M., Nelson, R. J., Kaas, J. H., Stryker, M. P., Zook, J. M., Cynader, M. S., & Schoppmann, A. (1987). Variability in hand surface representations in areas 3b and 1 in adult owl and squirrel monkeys. *Journal of Comparative Neurology, 258*, 281–296.

Meyer, D. E., & Schvaneveldt, R. W. (1971). Facilitation in recognizing pairs of words: Evidence of a dependence between retrieval operations. *Journal of Experimental Psychology, 90*, 227–234.

Michel, J. B., Shen, Y. K., Aiden, A. P., Veres, A., Gray, M. K., The Google Books Team, Pickett, J. P., Hoiberg, D., Clancy, D., Norvig, P., Orwant, J., Pinker, S., Nowak, M. A., & Lieberman Aiden, E. (2011). Quantitative analysis of culture using millions of digitized books. *Science, 331*, 176–182.

Miller, G. A. (1956). The magical number seven, plus or minus two: Some limits on our capacity for processing information. *Psychological Review, 63*, 81–97.

Miller, G. A., Galanter, E., & Pribram, K. H. (1960). *Plans and the structure of behavior.* New York, NY: Holt, Rinehart, & Winston.

Miller, G., Tybur, J. M., & Jordan, B. D. (2007). Ovulatory cycle effects on tip earnings by lap dancers: Economic evidence for human estrus? *Evolution and Human Behavior, 28*, 375–381.

Miller, J. O., & Ulrich, R. (2003). Simple reaction time and statistical facilitation: A parallel grains model. *Cognitive Psychology, 46*, 101–151.

Minsky, M. (1988). *The society of mind.* New York, NY: Simon & Schuster.

Mitchell, M. (1996). *An introduction to genetic algorithms.* Cambridge, MA: MIT Press.

Moles, A. A. (1966). *Information theory and esthetic perception.* Urbana, IL: University of Illinois Press.

Monsell, S. (2003). Task switching. *Trends in Cognitive Sciences, 7,* 134–140.

Moorehead, A. (1969). *Darwin and the Beagle.* New York, NY: Harper & Row.

Moran, J., & Desimone, R. (1985). Selective attention gates visual processing in the extrastriate cortex. *Science, 229,* 782–784.

Moray, N. (1959). Attention in dichotic listening: Affective cues and the influence of instructions. *Quarterly Journal of Experimental Psychology, 11,* 58–60.

Morrison, C. M., & Ellis, A. W. (1995). Roles of word frequency and age of acquisition in word naming and lexical decision. *Journal of Experimental Psychology: Learning, Memory, and Cognition, 21,* 116–133.

Morrison, C. M., & Ellis, A. W. (2000). Real age of acquisition effects in word naming and lexical decision. *British Journal of Psychology, 91,* 167–180.

Morton, J., Crowder, R. G., & Prussin, H. A. (1971). Experiments with the stimulus suffix effect. *Journal of Experimental Psychology, 91,* 169–190.

Munte, T. F., Altenbuller, E., & Janke, I. (2002). The musician's brain as a model of neuroplasticity. *Nature Reviews Neuroscience, 3,* 473–478.

Nairne, J. S., Pandeirada, J. N., & Thompson, S. R. (2008). Adaptive memory: The comparative value of survival processing. *Psychological Science, 19,* 176–180.

Necker, L. A. (1832). Observations on some remarkable optical phaenomena seen in Switzerland, and on an optical phaenomenon which occurs on viewing a figure of a crystal or geometrical solid. *London and Edinburgh Philosophical Magazine and Journal of Science, 1,* 329–337.

Neisser, U. (1964). Visual search. *Scientific American, 17,* 94–100.

Neisser, U. (1967). *Cognitive psychology.* New York, NY: Appleton-Century-Crofts.

Neisser, U., & Becklen, R. (1975). Selective looking: Attending to visually specified events. *Cognitive Psychology, 7,* 480–494.

Nelson, T. O. (1985). Ebbinghaus's contribution to the measurement of retention: Savings during relearning. *Journal of Experimental Psychology: Learning, Memory, and Cognition, 11,* 472–479.

Neves, D. M., & Anderson, J. R. (1981). Knowledge compilation: Mechanisms for the automatization of cognitive skills. In J. R. Anderson (Ed.), *Cognitive skills and their acquisition* (pp. 57–84). Hillsdale, NJ: Erlbaum.

Neville, H., & Sur, M. (2009). Neuroplasticity. In M. Gazzaniga (Ed.), *The cognitive neurosciences IV* (pp. 89–90). Cambridge, MA: MIT Press.

Newell, A. M., & Rosenbloom, P. S. (1981). Mechanisms of skill acquisition and the law of practice. In J. R. Anderson (Ed.), *Cognitive skills and their acquisition* (pp. 1–55). Hillsdale, NJ: Erlbaum.

Nickerson, R. S. (2011). Five down, Absquatulated: Crossword puzzle clues to how the mind works. *Psychonomic Bulletin & Review, 18,* 217–241.

Norman, D. A. (1981). Categorization of action slips. *Psychological Review, 88,* 1–15.

Nowak, M. A. (2012). Why we help. *Scientific American, 307,* 1, 34–39.

Nowak, M. A., Tarnita, C. E., & Wilson, E. O. (2010). The evolution of eusociality. *Nature, 466,* 1057–1062.

Nozick, R. (1981). *Philosophical explanations.* Cambridge, MA: Harvard University Press.

O'Craven, K. M., Downing, P., & Kanwisher, N. (1999). fMRI evidence for objects as the units of attentional selection. *Nature, 401,* 584–587.

Ohlsson, S. (1992). The learning curve for writing books: Evidence from Professor Asimov. *Psychological Science, 3,* 380–383.

Osman, A., Kornblum, S., & Meyer, D. E. (1986). The point of no return in choice reaction time: Controlled and ballistic stages of response preparation. *Journal of Experimental Psychology: Human Perception and Performance, 12,* 243–258.

Pashler, H. (1993). Doing two things at the same time. *American Scientist, 81,* 48–55.

Pashler, H. (1998). *The psychology of attention.* Cambridge, MA: MIT Press.

Pavlov, I. P. (1928). *Lectures on conditioned reflexes.* New York, NY: International Publishers.

Penfield, W., & Rasmssen, T. (1950). *The cerebral cortex of man: A clinical study of localization of function.* New York, NY: MacMillan.

Pigliucci, M. (2009). The overwhelming evidence. *Science, 323,* 716.

Pinker, S., & Bloom, P. (1990). Natural language and natural selection. *Behavioral and Brain Sciences 13,* 707–784.

Pinker, S. (1994). *The language instinct: How the mind creates language.* New York, NY: Harper Collins.

Pinker, S. (2002). *The blank slate: The modern denial of human nature.* New York, NY: Viking.

Pinker, S. (January 19, 2007). *The mystery of consciousness.* http://www.time.com/time/printout/0,8816,1580394,00.html

Poincaré, H. (1929). *The foundations of science.* New York, NY: Science House.

Posner, M. I., & Cohen, Y. (1984). Components of visual orienting. In H. Bouma & D. Bouwhuis (Eds.), *Attention and performance X* (pp. 531–556). Hillsdale, NJ: Erlbaum.

Posner, M. I., & Snyder, C. R. (1975). Facilitation and inhibition in the processing of signals. In P. M. A. Rabbitt & S. Dornic (Eds.), *Attention and performance V* (pp. 669–682). London, England: Academic Press.

Price, G. R. (1971). Selection and covariance. *Nature, 227,* 520–521.

Price, G. R. (1995). The nature of selection. *Journal of Theoretical Biology, 175,* 389–396.

Proctor, R. W., & Vu, K.-P. L. (2006). *Stimulus-response compatibility principles: Data, theory, and application.* Boca Raton, FL: CRC Press.

Purves, D., Augustine, G. J., Fitzpatrick, D., & Hall, W. C. (2011). *Neuroscience* (5th ed.). Sunderland, MA: Sinauer Associates.

Quiroga, R. Q., Fried, I., & Koch, C. (2013). Brain cells for grandmother. *Scientific American, 308*(2), 30–35.

Rabbitt, P. M. A. (1978). Detection of errors by skilled typists. *Ergonomics, 21,* 945–958.

Raaijmakers, J. G. W., & Jakab, E. (2013). Is forgetting caused by inhibition? *Current Directions in Psychological Science, 22,* 205–209.

Ramachandran, V. S., & Blakeslee, S. (1998). *Phantoms in the brain.* New York, NY: William Morrow and Company.

Ramachandran, V. S., & Hubbard, E. M. (2001). Psychophysical investigations into the neural basis of synaesthesia. *Proceedings of the Royal Society of London, 268,* 973–983.

Rankin, D. J. (2011). Economics: A Darwinian approach. *Science, 333,* 526.

Ratcliff, R., Van Zandt, T., & McKoon, G. (1999). Connectionist and diffusion models of reaction time. *Psychological Review, 106,* 261–300.

Ratliff, F., & Hartline, H. K. (1959). The response of limulus optic nerve fibers to patterns of illumination on the receptor mosaic. *Journal of General Physiology, 42,* 1241–1255.

Ray, W. J. (2013). *Evolutionary psychology—Neuroscience perspectives concerning human behavior and experience.* Los Angeles, CA: Sage.

Redding, G. M., & Wallace, B. (1997). *Adaptive spatial alignment.* Mahwah, NJ: Erlbaum.

Reicher, G. M. (1969). Perceptual recognition as a function of meaningfulness of stimulus material. *Journal of Experimental Psychology, 81,* 275–280.

Reisberg, D., Baron, J., & Kemler, D. G. (1980). Overcoming Stroop interference: The effects of practice on distractor potency. *Journal of Experimental Psychology: Human Perception and Performance, 6,* 140–150.

Reitman, J. S. (1974). Without surreptitious rehearsal, information in short-term memory decays. *Journal of Verbal Learning and Verbal Behavior, 13,* 365–377.

Rescorla, R. A., & Wagner, A. R. (1972). A theory of Pavlovian conditioning: Variations in the effectiveness of reinforcement and nonreinforcement. In A. H. Black & W. F. Prokasy (Eds.), *Classical conditioning II: Current research and theory* (pp. 64–99). New York, NY: Appleton-Century-Crofts.

Ribot, T. (1882). *Diseases of the memory: An essay in the positive psychology.* New York, NY: Appleton and Company.

Richards, R. J. (1987). *Darwin and the emergence of evolutionary theories of mind and behavior.* Chicago, IL: University of Chicago Press.

Rizio, A. A., & Dennis, N. A. (2012). The neural correlates of cognitive control: Successful remembering and intentional forgetting. *Journal of Cognitive Neuroscience, 25*(2), 297–312.

Rizzolatti, G., & Craighero, L. (2004). The mirror-neuron system. *Annual Review of Neuroscience, 27,* 169–192.

Rock, I. (1983). *The logic of perception.* Cambridge, MA: MIT Press.

Roediger, H. L., & McDermott, K. B. (1995). Creating false memories. Creating false memories: Remembering words not presented in lists. *Journal of Experimental Psychology: Learning, Memory, and Cognition, 21,* 803–814.

Roediger, H. L. (1990). Implicit memory: Retention without remembering. *American Psychologist, 45,* 1043–1056.

Roelfsema, P. R., Lamme, V. A. F., & Spekrejse, H. (1998). Object-based attention in the primary visual cortex of the macaque monkey. *Nature, 395*, 376–381.

Rogers, T., & McClelland, J. (2004). *Semantic cognition: A parallel distributed processing approach*. Cambridge, MA: MIT Press.

Román, P., Soriano, M. F., Gómez-Ariz, C. J., & Bajo, M. T. (2009). Retrieval-induced forgetting and executive control. *Psychological Science, 20*, 1053–1058.

Rosch, E. (1973). On the internal structure of perceptual and semantic categories. In T. Moore (Ed.), *Cognitive development and the acquisition of language* (pp. 111–114). New York, NY: Academic Press.

Rosch, E. (1975). Cognitive representation of semantic categories. *Journal of Experimental Psychology: General, 104*, 192–223.

Rosch, E. (1977). Human categorization. In N. Warren (Ed.), *Advances in cross-cultural psychology* (Vol. 1, pp. 1–72). London, England: Academic Press.

Rosenbaum, D. A. (1987). Successive approximations to a model of human motor programming. *Psychology of Learning and Motivation, 21*, 153–182.

Rosenbaum, D. A. (2010). *Human motor control* (2nd ed.). San Diego, CA: Academic Press/Elsevier.

Rosenbaum, D. A. (2012). The tiger on your tail: Choosing between temporally extended behaviors. *Psychological Science, 23*, 855–860.

Rosenbaum, D. A., Brach, M., & Semenov, A. (2011). Behavioral ecology meets motor behavior: Choosing between walking and reaching paths. *Journal of Motor Behavior, 43*, 131–136.

Rosenbaum, D. A., Chapman, K. M., Weigelt, M., Weiss, D. J., & van der Wel, R. (2012). Cognition, action, and object manipulation. *Psychological Bulletin, 138*, 924–946.

Rosenbaum, D. A., Dawson, A. M., & Challis, J. H. (2006). Haptic tracking permits bimanual independence. *Journal of Experimental Psychology: Human Perception and Performance, 32*, 1266–1275.

Rosenbaum, D. A., Kenny, S., & Derr, M. A. (1983). Hierarchical control of rapid movement sequences. *Journal of Experimental Psychology: Human Perception and Performance, 9*, 86–102.

Rosenbaum, D. A., Loukopoulos, L. D., Meulenbroek, R. G. M., Vaughan, J., & Engelbrecht, S. E. (1995). Planning reaches by evaluating stored postures. *Psychological Review, 102*, 28–67.

Rosenbaum, D. A., Marchak, F., Barnes, H. J., Vaughan, J., Slotta, J., & Jorgensen, M. (1990). Constraints for action selection: Overhand versus underhand grips. In M. Jeannerod (Ed.), *Attention and performance XIII: Motor representation and control* (pp. 321–342). Hillsdale, NJ: Erlbaum.

Rosenbaum, D. A., Meulenbroek, R. G., Vaughan, J., & Jansen, C. (2001). Posture-based motion planning: Applications to grasping. *Psychological Review, 108*, 709–734.

Rosenbaum, D. A., Vaughan, J., Meulenbroek, R. G. J., Jax, S., & Cohen, R. (2009). Smart moves: The psychology of everyday perceptual-motor acts. In E. Morsella,

J. A. Bargh, & P. M. Gollwitzer (Eds.), *Oxford handbook of human action* (pp. 121–135). New York, NY: Oxford University Press.

Rubin, E. (1915). *Synsoplevede Figurer*. Kobenhavn: Gyldendalske Boghandel.

Rumelhart, D. E., & McClelland, J. L. (1982). An interactive activation model of context effects in letter perception: II. The contextual enhancement effect and some tests and extensions of the model. *Psychological Review, 89*, 60–94.

Rumelhart, D. E., McClelland, J. L., & the PDP Research Group. (1986). *Parallel distributed processing: Explorations in the microstructure of cognition*. Vol. 1: Foundations. Cambridge, MA: MIT Press.

Rumelhart, D. E., & Norman, D. A. (1982). Simulating a skilled typist: A study of skilled cognitive-motor performance. *Cognitive Science, 6*, 1–36.

Sadato, N., Pascual-Leone, A., Grafman, J., Deiber, M. P., Ibanez, V., & Hallett, M. (1998). Neural networks for Braille reading by the blind. *Brain, 121*, 1213–1229.

Santamaria, J. P., & Rosenbaum, D. A. (2011). Etiquette and effort: Holding doors for others. *Psychological Science, 22*, 584–588.

Schall, J. D. (2001). Neural basis of deciding, choosing and acting. *Nature Reviews Neuroscience, 2*, 33–42.

Schiller, P. H., & Carvey, C. E. (2005). The Hermann grid illusion revisited. *Perception, 34*, 1375–1397.

Schmidt, R. A., & Lee, T. D. (2011). *Motor control and learning: A behavioral emphasis* (5th ed.). Champaign, IL: Human Kinetics.

Schneider, W., & Shiffrin, R. M. (1977). Controlled and automatic human information processing: I. Detection, search, and attention. *Psychological Review, 84*, 1–66.

Seibel, R. (1963). Discrimination time for a 1,023-alternative task. *Journal of Experimental Psychology, 66*, 215–255.

Selfridge, O. G. (1959). Pandemonium: A paradigm for learning. In D. V. Blake & A. M. Uttley (Eds.), *Proceedings of the Symposium on Mechanization of Thought Processes* (pp. 511–527). London, England: Her Majesty's Stationary Office. [Reprinted in P. C. Dodwell (Ed.). (1970). *Perceptual learning and adaptation*. Middlesex, England: Penguin.]

Shannon, C., & Weaver, W. (1949). *The mathematical theory of communication*. Urbana, IL: Univeristy of Illinois Press.

Shin Y. K., Proctor R. W., & Capaldi, E. J. (2010). A review of contemporary ideomotor theory. *Psychological Bulletin, 136*, 943–974.

Siegler, R. S. (1996). *Emerging minds: The process of change in children's thinking*. New York, NY: Oxford University Press.

Silveira, J. M. (1971). *Incubation: The effect of timing and length on problem solution and quality of problem processing*. Unpublished doctoral thesis. University of Oregon, Eugene, Oregon.

Simon, J. R. (1990). The effect of an irrelevant directional cue on human information processing. In R. W. Proctor & T. G. Reeve (Eds.), *Stimulus-response compatibility: An integrated perspective* (pp. 31–86). Amsterdam, Netherlands: North-Holland.

Simon, J. R., & Rudell, A. P. (1967). Auditory S-R compatibility: The effect of an irrelevant cue on information processing. *Journal of Applied Psychology, 51,* 300–304.

Simon, H. A. (1974). How big is a chunk? *Science, 813,* 482–488.

Simonton, D. (1999). *Origins of genius: Darwinian perspectives on creativity.* New York: NY: Oxford University Press.

Simonton, D. (2003). Scientific creativity as constrained stochastic behavior. *Psychological Bulletin, 129,* 475–494.

Sinha, P. (July 2013). Once blind and now they see. *Scientific American,* 49–55.

Singh, D. (1993). Adaptive significance of female physical attractiveness: Role of waist-to-hip ratio. *Journal of Personality and Social Psychology, 65,* 293–307.

Skinner, B. F. (1957). *Verbal behavior.* Englewood Cliffs, NJ: Prentice-Hall.

Smith, E. E., & Kosslyn, S. M. (2007). *Cognitive psychology.* Upper Saddle River, NJ: Pearson Prentice Hall.

Smith, E. E., Patalano, A., & Jonides, J. (1998). Alternative strategies of categorization. *Cognition, 65,* 167–196.

Song, J.-Y., & Nakayama, K. (2009). Hidden cognitive states revealed in choice reaching tasks. *Trends in Cognitive Science, 13,* 360–366.

Speelman, C. P., & Kirsner, K. (2005). *Beyond the learning curve: The construction of mind.* Oxford, England: Oxford University Press.

Spelke, E. (1994). Initial knowledge: Six suggestions. *Cognition, 50,* 431–445.

Sperling, G., & Weichselgartner, E. (1995). Episodic theory of the dynamics of spatial attention. *Psychological Review, 102,* 503–532.

Sperry, R. W. (1945). Restoration of vision after crossing of optic nerves and after transplantation of eye. *Journal of Neurophysiology, 8,* 15–28.

Spiegel, M. A., Koester, D., Weigelt, M., & Schack, T. (2012). The costs of changing an intended action: Movement planning, but not execution, interferes with verbal working memory. *Neuroscience Letters, 509,* 82–86.

Spivey, M. (2007). *The continuity of mind.* New York, NY: Oxford University Press.

Starreveld, P. A., La Heij, W., & Verdonschot, R. (2013). Time course analysis of the effects of distractor frequency and categorical relatedness in picture naming: An evaluation of the response exclusion account. *Language and Cognitive Processes, 28*(5), 633–654.

Sternberg, S. (1966). High-speed scanning in human memory. *Science, 153,* 652–654.

Sternberg, S., Monsell, S., Knoll, R. L., & Wright, C. E. (1978). The latency and duration of rapid movement sequences: Comparisons of speech and typewriting. In G. E. Stelmach (Ed.), *Information processing in motor control and learning* (pp. 117–152). New York, NY: Academic Press.

Sterr, A., Teder-Salejarvi, W., Frank Rosler, A., Hillyard, S. A., Neville, H. J., & Roder, B. (1999). Improved auditory spatial tuning in blind humans. *Nature, 400,* 162–166.

Stroop, J. R. (1935). Studies of interference in serial verbal reactions. *Journal of Experimental Psychology, 18,* 643–662.

Sutton, R. S., & Barto, A. G. (1998). *Reinforcement: An introduction.* Cambridge, MA: MIT Press.

Talbot, M. (2006). The baby lab. *The New Yorker*, September 4, p. 90. http://www. newyorker.com/archive/2006/09/04/060904fa_fact_talbot

Taub, E., & Uswatt, G. (2006). Constraint induced movement therapy: Answers and questions after two decades of research. *NeuroRehabilitation, 21*, 93–95.

Taylor, J. (2008). The voyage of the Beagle: Darwin's extraordinary adventure aboard FitzRoy's famous survey ship. London, England: Conway.

Tenenbaum, J. B., Kemp, C., Griffiths, T. L., & Goodman, N. D. (2011). How to grow a mind: Statistics, structure, and abstraction. *Science, 331*, 1279–1285.

Thelen, E. (1995). Motor development: A new synthesis. *American Psychologist, 50*, 79–95.

Thomas, L. E., & Llleras, A. (2009). Swinging into thought: Directed movement guides insight in problem solving. *Psychonomic Bulletin & Review, 16*, 719–723.

Thorndike, E. L. (1927). The law of effect. *American Journal of Psychology, 39*, 212–222.

Tipper, S. P. (1985). The negative priming effect: Inhibitory priming by ignored objects. *Quarterly Journal of Experimental Psychology Section A, 37*, 571–590.

Townsend, J. T. (1974). Issues and models concerning the processing of a finite number of inputs. In B. H. Kantowitz (Ed.), *Human information processing: Tutorials in performance and cognition* (pp. 133–168). Hillsdale, NJ: Erlbaum.

Townsend, J. T. (1990). Serial vs. parallel processing: Sometimes they look like Tweedledum and Tweedledee but they can (and should) be distinguished. *Psychological Science, 1*, 46–54.

Tracy, J. L. (2012). Emotions of inequality. *Science, 333*, 289–290.

Treisman, A. M. (1960). Verbal cues, language, and meaning in selective attention. *Quarterly Journal of Experimental Psychology, 12*, 242–248.

Treisman, A. M. (1986). Features and objects in visual processing. *Scientific American, 255*, 114–125.

Tulving, E., & Thomson, D. M. (1973). Encoding specificity and retrieval processes in episodic memory. *Psychological Review, 80*, 352–373.

Turvey, M. T. (1977). Preliminaries to a theory of action with reference to vision. In R. Shaw & J. Bransford (Eds.), *Perceiving, acting, and knowing* (pp. 211–265). Hillsdale, NJ: Erlbaum.

Tversky, A., & Kahneman, D. (1974). Judgment under uncertainty: Heuristics and biases. *Science, 185*, 1124–1131.

Usher, M., & McClelland, J. L. (2001). On the time course of perceptual choice: The leaky competing accumulator model. *Psychological Review, 108*, 550–592.

Varassard, P., Kees, A., Willer, B., Ho, D., Aharoni, D., Cushman, J., Aghajan, Z. M., & Mehta, M. R. (2013). Multisensory control of hippocampal spatiotemporal selectivity. *Science, 340*, 1342–1346.

Veeliste, M., Perel, S., Spalding, M. C., Whitford, A. S., & Schwartz, A. B. (2008). Cortical control of a prosthetic arm for self-feeding. *Nature, 453*, 1098–1101. Received 14 November 2007; Accepted 4 April 2008 (2008). doi:10.1038/nature06996

Volkmann, F. C. (1976). Saccadic suppression: A brief review. In R. A. Monty & J. W. Senders (Eds.), *Eye movements and psychological processes* (pp. 73–84). Hillsdale, NJ: Erlbaum.

Volkmann, F. C., Riggs, L. A., & Moore, R. K. (1980). Eyeblinks and visual suppression. *Science, 207*, 900–902.

Warren, R. M. (1970). Restoration of missing speech sounds. *Science, 167*, 392–393.

Warrington, E. K. (1975). Selective impairment of semantic memory. *Quarterly Journal of Experimental Psychology, 27*, 635–657.

Wasserman, E. A., & Blumberg, M. S. (2010). Designing minds. *American Scientist, 98*, 183–185.

Wegner, D. M. (1994). Ironic processes of mental control. *Psychological Review, 101*, 34–52.

Wegner, D. M. (2002). *The illusion of conscious will*. Cambridge, MA: MIT Press.

Weigelt, W., Rosenbaum, D. A., Huelshorst, S., & Schack, T. (2009). Moving and memorizing: Motor planning modulates the recency effect in serial and free recall. *Acta Psychologica, 132*, 68–79.

Weinstein, S. (1968). Intensive and extensive aspects of tactile sensitivity as a function of body part, sex, and laterality. In D. R. Kenshalo (Ed.), *The skin senses* (pp. 195–222). Springfield, IL: Charles C. Thomas.

Weisberg, R. W., & Alba, J. W. (1981). An examination of the alleged role of "fixation" in the solution of several "insight" problems. *Journal of Experimental Psychology: General, 110*, 169–192.

Weiss, Y., Edelman, S., & Fahle, M. (1993). Models of perceptual learning in Vernier hyperacuity. *Neural Computation, 5*, 695–718.

Weisstein, N. (1973). Beyond the yellow Volkswagen detector and the grandmother cell: A general strategy for the exploration of operations in human pattern recognition. In R. L. Solso (Ed.), *Contemporary issues in cognitive psychology: The Loyola Symposium* (pp. 17–51). New York, NY: Halsted Press, A Division of John Wiley & Sons.

Welford, A. T. (1952). The "psychological refractory period" and the timing of high speed performance—A review and a theory. *British Journal of Psychology, 43*, 2–19.

Welsh, T. N., & Elliott, D. (2004). Movement trajectories in the presence of a distracting stimulus: Evidence for a response activation model of selective reaching, *Quarterly Journal of Experimental Psychology, 57*, 1031–1057.

Wheeler, D. D. (1970). Processes in word recognition. *Cognitive Psychology, 1*, 59–85.

Willingham, D. B., Nissen, M. J., & Bullemer, P. (1989). On the development of procedural knowledge. *Journal of Experimental Psychology: Learning, Memory, and Cognition, 15*, 1047–1060.

Wilson, S., Darling, S., & Sykes, J. (2011). Adaptive memory: Fitness relevant stimuli show a memory advantage in a game of pelmanism. *Psychonomic Bulletin & Review, 18*, 781–786.

Wixted, J. T. (2004). On common ground: Jost's (1897) Law of Forgetting and Ribot's (1881) Law of Retrograde Amnesia. *Psychological Review, 111,* 864–879.

Wolfe, T. (1934). *You can't go home again.* New York, NY: Harper & Row.

Woolsey, C. N. (1958). Organization of somatic sensory and motor areas of the cerebral cortex. In H. F. Harlow & C. N. Woolsey (Eds.), *Biological and biochemical bases of behavior* (pp. 63–81). Madison, WI: University of Wisconsin Press.

Yamaguchi, M., & Proctor, R. W. (2012). Multidimensional vector model of stimulus–response compatibility. *Psychological Review, 119,* 272–304.

Yarbus, A. L. (1967). *Eye movements and vision.* New York, NY: Plenum.

Zajonc, R. B. (1968). Attitudinal effects of mere exposure. *Journal of Personality and Social Psychology, 9,* 1–27.

Zatorre, R. J., Mondor, T. A., & Evans, A. C. (1999). Auditory attention to space and frequency activates similar cerebral systems. *Neuroimage, 10,* 544–554.

Index

Note: Page numbers followed by the letter "f" indicate material found in figures; page numbers followed by the letter "n" indicate material found in notes.